Judea under Greek and Roman Rule

ESSENTIALS OF BIBLICAL STUDIES

JUDEA UNDER GREEK AND ROMAN RULE
David A. deSilva

THE PSALMS
Keith Bodner

EARLY JEWISH WRITINGS AND NEW TESTAMENT INTERPRETATION
C.D. Elledge

AN INVITATION TO BIBLICAL POETRY
Elaine T. James

AN INTRODUCTION TO THE GOSPELS AND ACTS
Alicia D. Myers

ANCIENT ISRAEL'S NEIGHBORS
Brian R. Doak

SIN IN THE NEW TESTAMENT
Jeffrey Siker

WOMEN IN THE NEW TESTAMENT WORLD
Susan E. Helyn

THE HISTORY OF BRONZE AND IRON AGE ISRAEL
Victor H. Matthews

READING HEBREW BIBLE NARRATIVES
J. Andrew Dearman

NEW TESTAMENT CHRISTIANITY IN THE ROMAN WORLD
Harry O. Maier

Judea under Greek and Roman Rule

DAVID A. DESILVA

Trustees' Distinguished Professor of New Testament and Greek
Ashland Theological Seminary

OXFORD
UNIVERSITY PRESS

OXFORD
UNIVERSITY PRESS

Oxford University Press is a department of the University of Oxford. It furthers
the University's objective of excellence in research, scholarship, and education
by publishing worldwide. Oxford is a registered trade mark of Oxford University
Press in the UK and certain other countries.

Published in the United States of America by Oxford University Press
198 Madison Avenue, New York, NY 10016, United States of America.

CIP data is on file at the Library of Congress

ISBN 978-0-19-026325-6 (pbk.)
ISBN 978-0-19-026324-9 (hbk.)

DOI: 10.1093/oso/9780190263249.001.0001

Printed by Integrated Books International, United States of America
Hardback printed by Bridgeport National Bindery, Inc., United States of America

To Eric and Dvorah Eisen
and their growing family

Contents

Introduction

This book provides a reconstruction of the history of Judea from 334 BCE, when Alexander's eastward conquests brought Judea into the Greek empire, through 135 CE, when Hadrian refounded Jerusalem as Aelia Capitolina and banished Jews from the city limits—a formative period both for early Judaism and the Christian movement. As the title suggests, but as the realities demonstrate to an extent that may surprise the reader, international politics are determinative for developments within Judea throughout this period. The story of Judea and its surrounding regions is deeply embedded in, and properly told only in the context of, the larger story of the activities and interests of the Seleucid, Ptolemaic, Roman, and Parthian empires. To tell this story, therefore, we must also give attention to the following:

- The eastward and southward expansion of Alexander's short-lived empire
- The ongoing strife between two of the successor kingdoms to Alexander's empire—the Seleucid empire in Syria and Babylon and the Ptolemaic empire in Egypt—over the narrow strip of land between them that included Judea and its environs
- The endless series of pretenders to the Seleucid throne and the civil wars that weakened the empire to such an extent that Judea was able to assert its independence for a brief period
- The growing empire of the Roman Republic that exercised significant pressure upon the Seleucid and Ptolemaic empires from the early second century BCE onward, finally swallowing up both and determining how Judea would be governed, leading eventually to two catastrophic, unsuccessful revolts

Judea under Greek and Roman Rule. David A. deSilva, Oxford University Press.
© Oxford University Press 2024. DOI: 10.1093/oso/9780190263249.003.0001

It is important to acknowledge at the outset that all historical narrative inevitably involves the historian's imagination. As one of the most erudite historians of Judea during this period has put it:

> Historians cannot discover the past, since it is no longer there to be found; they *construct* (aspects of) it hypothetically as a way of explaining the artifacts that have survived from the past.[1]

The artifacts available for this endeavor vary significantly from century to century or episode to episode. There are literary artifacts, chiefly the works of ancient historians, whether Greek or Roman historians (such as Polybius, Diodorus Siculus, Livy, Tacitus, Suetonius, Arrian, Appian, and Dio Cassius) or Jewish historians (such as the authors of 1 and 2 Maccabees, Philo, and, above all, Flavius Josephus).[2] Each author provides an indispensable window into this history, but each does so for his own purposes in telling that part of the story that is of concern to him, and thus the glass is inevitably tinted or distorted. There are literary works the purpose behind which was not to write history but which, nevertheless, provide important perspectives on or supplements to history (like the *Psalms of Solomon*, several texts from the collection known as the Dead Sea Scrolls, the New Testament writings, and *4 Ezra*). There are nonliterary works that are nevertheless "texts," such as inscriptions, the legends and images on coins, contracts, letters, and decrees. And there is the archaeological record, uncovering remains of the lived spaces where the story unfolded. This volume represents one attempt to review and evaluate the testimony of these various artifacts and, on this basis, offer a plausible reconstruction of the events, conditions, interests, and agendas that played themselves out on the stage of Judea and its surrounding territories during this period.

Nomenclature is important. How should we refer to the territories that once constituted Solomon's or Herod's kingdom? The term "Israel," a fitting designation in the monarchical period, is no longer

---

[1] Mason 2014:155.

[2] On Josephus as a source for historical reconstruction, see especially Cohen 1979, Rajak 2002, Mason 2009, and Atkinson 2016.

a geographic designation during the Greek and Roman periods, though it still occurs as an ideological one. For example, the author of 1 Maccabees uses "Israel" to refer to all the God-fearing, covenant-maintaining people living within the occupied territory of Judea. It is also anachronistic to refer to these combined territories as "Palestine" before the reign of the emperor Hadrian and the failure of the Second Jewish Revolt. Thus, this book will more cumbersomely but precisely refer to the specific regions of Idumea, Judea, Galilee, and Perea as appropriate. There is the additional problem that a city named Samaria and a region typically called Samaria both play important roles in this story. For the sake of clarity, "Samaria" will be used to refer to the city and the less common "Samaritis" to refer to the region.

Finally, every subject touched upon in this book invites and, indeed, merits further investigation. It is hoped that the notes and the bibliography will provide helpful starting points for these explorations.

1

Living with Giants

From Alexander to Antiochus III

The story of Judea under Greek rule unfolds against the backdrop of
Alexander's rapid conquest of the territories joined under Persian domination, the splintering of Alexander's empire into rival kingdoms, and
the eventual disintegration of the two kingdoms bordering Judea—the
Ptolemaic empire in Egypt and the Seleucid empire in Syria—on account of internal rivalries. The fortunes of Judea and its neighboring,
historically Israelite territories during this period were bound up with,
and directly affected by, this larger regional story. Literary sources for
that larger story are rich, including Arrian's *Anabasis*, Appian's *Roman
History* (especially book 11 on the Syrian Wars), Livy's *History of Rome*,
Diodorus of Sicily's *Bibliotheca Historica*, and Polybius's *History*.
Josephus (*Antiquities* 12–14) provides material from a Judean perspective as well, though it is difficult to discern the historical through
the legendary, the accurate from the fabricated, particularly in his
treatment of events prior to about 167 BCE. Nonliterary records such
as the Zenon papyri, combined with archaeological and numismatic
finds, help both to anchor and to thicken the historical data, while literary works like Daniel, 1 Enoch, and Ben Sira reveal how particular
participants in the unfolding story interpreted their experiences.

Alexander the Great

For two and a half centuries—since the Babylonian conquest of
597 BCE—Judea had looked east to its imperial overlords. Samaritis
and Galilee had looked in this direction for their masters considerably longer, namely since the Assyrian conquest of 722 BCE. The axis
of power in their world was about to change dramatically. In the years

Judea under Greek and Roman Rule. David A. deSilva, Oxford University Press.
© Oxford University Press 2024. DOI: 10.1093/oso/9780190263249.003.0002

334–331 BCE, Alexander the Great and his armies swept eastward from Greece and Macedonia through Asia Minor, driving back the Persian forces of Darius III. Alexander then moved southward through Syria and the Palestinian coastlands with a view to securing Egypt (which had itself been incorporated into the Persian empire under Cambyses II in 525 BCE) before continuing his eastward campaign into the Persian heartland. He appears to have pursued the most direct path toward his objective, staying in the coastal plains of Palestine. Berytus and Sidon readily agreed to terms and came over to Alexander's side (Arrian, *Anabasis* 2.15.6); Tyre famously resisted, resulting in a siege that lasted for nine months in 332 BCE (Arrian, *Anabasis* 2.15.7–2.24.6).

Other local leaders were comfortable swimming with rather than against the tide. Sanballat, the governor of Samaritis, volunteered his support by bringing eight thousand troops to assist Alexander at the siege of Tyre. Josephus regards this action to have prompted Alexander to authorize, by way of reward, the construction of a temple on Mt. Gerizim (*Ant.* 11.321–24), though notable archaeologists suggest that the temple's construction predated Alexander by a century.[1] Alexander continued to push south after successfully taking Tyre. Gaza also resisted, falling to Alexander after a siege of two months (Arrian, *Anabasis* 2.26.1–2.27.7). Events at Tyre and Gaza show that the Persian rulers had inspired considerable loyalty in some of their territories and that a change to Greek domination was not welcomed by all. At this point, Arrian relates that "most of what is called Palestinian Syria had already come over to him" (Arrian, *Anabasis* 2.25.4).

Josephus spins a clearly legendary tale about Alexander's visit to Jerusalem at this time (*Ant.* 11.325–339).[2] According to him, Alexander

---

[1] Magen 2009; Dušek 2020:7–8; Grabbe 2020:51. The question of the Samaritans' origins and ethnicity is highly contested. As worshipers of the God of Israel, the Samaritans themselves claimed to be descendants of the northern tribes of Israel, faithful to the Law of Moses (which they possessed in a distinctive textual tradition), worshiping God at a site that had been divinely sanctioned long before Jerusalem was settled by Jews. Judeans denied them this genealogical continuity, claiming the Samaritans to be the descendants of Gentiles resettled in the region after the Assyrian invasion of the Northern Kingdom and deportation (some portion of) its population, who incorporated the worship of the God of Israel alongside their own in order to enjoy his protection in his land (see, e.g., 2 Kings 17:22–34—the "canonical," but perhaps still highly partisan and biased, account of their origins).

[2] See, for example, Tcherikover 1959:42–45; Momigliano 1979.

had requested assistance for his siege of Tyre from all the local leaders in the region, but the high priest in Jerusalem respectfully declined on the ground that he could not violate his sacred oath not to take up arms against Darius. Alexander completes his sieges of Tyre and Gaza and then is said to have marched inland toward Jerusalem. The high priest went out in full priestly regalia accompanied by many others in white, meeting Alexander on Mt. Scopus. Alexander, upon seeing the high priest, prostrated himself before him—or, rather, as he would later explain, before the name of God emblazoned upon the priest's headdress. Alexander reveals to his general Parmenion, shocked that Alexander would bow to a local chief after so many rulers had bowed to him, that he had seen this man years before in a dream, urging Alexander to pursue his ambitions eastward in full confidence of success. Alexander offers sacrifice to the God of Israel at his temple and is shown the scroll of Daniel, "in which he had declared that one of the Greeks would destroy the empire of the Persians" (Josephus, *Ant.* 11.329–337; see especially Dan 8:1–8a, 20–21).

While the story has little to commend itself as contributing to our historical knowledge of the period, it speaks eloquently to the theological concerns of its originators, namely to discover ways by which to affirm their local God's sovereignty over the transfer of world empires, within which Judea was but one small trophy. The explicit reference to Daniel 8 is particularly telling in this regard (especially since it was likely written as "prophecy after the fact" in the second century BCE). It is more likely that Jerusalem simply sent word of its acquiescence along with the other cities of "what is called Palestinian Syria" that "had already come over to him" (Arrian, *Anabasis* 2.25.4)—and that did not end up besieged, as were Tyre and Gaza. Only those who resisted received special—and most unwanted—attention on this march southward. In Arrian's account, Alexander was wholly occupied with the coastal cities en route to Egypt, with no mention of activity inland (*Anabasis* 2.15.6–2.27.7). The legend suggests, however, a memory of Judea's peaceful acceptance of Greco-Macedonian rule (even if its leaders took a passive stance rather than supporting either side in the battle for empire).

Egypt submitted peaceably to Alexander in 331 BCE. With Sanballat dead, however, the city of Samaria revolted against Alexander while he was occupied in Egypt, going so far as to capture and burn Alexander's appointed governor alive (Quintus Curtius, 4.8.9–11). Alexander (or perhaps his general Parmenion) retaliated harshly and destroyed the city. The discovery of the skeletons of about two hundred Samarian men, women, and children who sought refuge in some caves in the Wadi ed-Daliyeh, about fourteen kilometers [eight miles] north of Jericho, bears corroborating testimony to the thoroughness of Alexander's reprisals.[3] Alexander rebuilt the city of Samaria in Hellenistic fashion to serve as a Macedonian military colony, giving the city and its hinterlands to his veterans.[4] As a consequence, the settlement at Shechem, in the vicinity of Mt. Gerizim, grew in both size and importance for the indigenous worshipers of the God of Israel.

A key element of Alexander's plan for empire-building involved the founding of Greek cities (mostly involving the refounding of existing cities after the Greek pattern) in Egypt (Alexandria), along the coastal plain (Strato's Tower, Ptolemais), and at the major urban centers of Syria (for example, Damascus)—as he would continue to do as he pressed eastward into Babylonia, Persia, and Bactria. It is probably too naïve to assume that Alexander's motivation was the spread of Greek civilization throughout the known world. Rather, these cities would serve primarily as a means of establishing centers of control and mechanisms of ongoing extraction of resources from the newly won territories for the benefit of the empire's heartland and for the maintenance of armies for the defense of these territories and the continued conquest of new ones through a permanent presence of administrators, garrisons, and veterans, as well as opening up spaces for growing economic exchange.[5] This would inevitably also lead to cultural exchange, the learning of the language of the conquerors, the desire to imitate the conquerors and assimilate to the conquerors so as to stake out a claim to honor and status on the conqueror's map of honor and status, since the native map was, as a whole, now secondary and inferior. But these

---

[3] Dušek 2020; Lapp and Lapp 1974. The largest group of names attested in these documents are Yahwistic (i.e., names including the element *yhw-*, *yh-*, or *-yhw* as in Yehoshua or Eliyahu), suggesting the cultural and religious continuity between Samaritans and the ancient Israelites (Dušek 2020:7).

[4] Tcherikover 1959:47–48; Purvis 1989:600–601; Atkinson 2016:72.

[5] Perdue and Carter 2015:139–140, 144.

were more *effects* than *purposes*. Judea appears not to have been a priority for such investments.

Alexander died in Babylon in 323 BCE at the age of thirty-two or thirty-three, leaving his empire with no viable long-term heirs.[6] Initial attempts to hold the empire together as a single unit under one sovereign soon failed. His principal generals (the *Diadochoi* or "Successors") fought one another in a series of wars that would stretch out for decades as each sought to establish himself in some part of Alexander's empire and to vie with the others for a larger share of the same.[7] Judea changed hands several times during these wars, though, fortunately for the majority of the people, the battles and sieges tended to focus on the coastal plain rather than the interior. Daniel clearly refers to these struggles of succession, though his scheme of a four-way division of Alexander's empire as the outcome (Dan 8:8, 21–22; 11:3–4) is better understood figuratively, as already suggested by the image of "the four winds of heaven" (8:8; 11:4), rather than as a precise historical claim, as if Daniel has four particular "winners" in mind.[8]

Ptolemy established himself in Egypt (holding the island of Cyprus as well) as Ptolemy I Soter (322–285 BCE), the first "king of the South" in Daniel's cryptic narrative of the period (see Dan 11:5, 8) and founder of the Ptolemaic dynasty. In the early decades of the struggles for succession, Ptolemy and Antigonus Monophthalmos (the "One-Eyed")— probably the most formidable of the generals and the least inclined to share Alexander's empire with his peers—competed for possession of the territorial bridge known as Coele-Syria (which included Idumaea, Judea, Samaritis, and Galilee), which passed back and forth between these giants several times in the years between 320 and 302 BCE.

Seleucus, a capable officer who had served under Ptolemy, secured Babylon and Syria by 312 BCE with Ptolemy's assistance (Dan 11:5), eventually establishing himself as Seleucus I Nicator (312–280 BCE), founder of the Seleucid dynasty. Antigonus Monophthalmos held the largest block of Alexander's former empire, including Greece, Asia

---

[6] His elder half-brother, Philip Arrhidaeus, was murdered in 317 BCE; his adolescent son (by Roxane of Bactria) in 309 BCE.

[7] On these wars through the Battle of Ipsus (323–303 BCE), see especially Diodorus Siculus, *Bibl. Hist.* 18.1–21.5.

[8] Gallagher 2022.

Minor, Syria, Palestine, and parts of Mesopotamia. Seleucus joined forces with two other generals, Cassander and Lysimachus, against Antigonus, finally defeating him at the Battle of Ipsos in 301 BCE and dividing his territory between them (though his heirs would eventually found a dynasty in Macedonia). Even though the settlement that followed the battle was intended to establish the boundaries of these successors' empires, in reality it merely served as a fresh starting point for the massive game of Risk® that would continue among all of the successor kingdoms until Rome, late to the game, swept all their pieces off the board over the course of the second and first centuries BCE.

The settlement awarded the territories along the eastern Mediterranean coast as far south as Gaza to Seleucus I, along with Syria and his territories in Babylonia (Polybius, *Hist.* 5.67). There was a problem, however. While Seleucus, Lysimachus, and Cassander were engaging Antigonus, Ptolemy I seized the opportunity to invade and reestablish control over Coele-Syria, which Antigonus was no longer in any position to defend. Ptolemy was clearly interested in dominating maritime trade in the eastern Mediterranean, and holding the cities and ports of the coastal plains was essential to this interest. During this invasion, Ptolemy is said to have made a direct assault upon Jerusalem (*Ag. Ap.* 1.22 §§209–212; *Ant.* 12.1.1 §§5–6). After securing it, he deported thousands of the inhabitants to Egypt, some to serve in his military, an arena in which expatriate Judeans would retain an influential place in the centuries to come (Appian, *Syr.* 8.50; *Let. Aris.* 12–14; Josephus, *Ag. Ap.* 1.209–211). Others may have been deported as slaves, likely as part of the booty to which Ptolemy's soldiers laid claim for their efforts (reportedly later freed by his son, Ptolemy II Philadelphus).

Ptolemy I was not inclined to relinquish this spear-won extension of his kingdom just because of some settlement in which he had had no voice. Seleucus, who essentially owed his place at the game board to Ptolemy—his former commander who supported his rise from subordinate officer to a peer among the "Successors"—was not inclined to press his claim against his former patron.[9] Seleucus's own successors, however, would always consider this territory to be rightly theirs, and

9 Tcherikover 1959:53; Grabbe 1992:204.

a series of wars would be waged between the Ptolemaic and Seleucid empires contending, in part at least, for control of Coele-Syria. Daniel's summary of the history of the descendants of Ptolemy and Seleucus as an alternation between uneasy truces and attempts to conquer some part of each other's territory for themselves is quite apt (Dan 2:41–43; 11:11–30). In retrospect, it is perhaps not surprising that Judean authors were attracted to the obscure story of the angels who mated with human females, producing a race of giants (Gen 6:1–4)—nor that they came to speak of these giants as wreaking havoc throughout the world, devouring its produce insatiably and afflicting its inhabitants with violence (as in 1 Enoch 6–7).[10]

Ptolemaic Rule

During the Persian period, Judah (Yehud) was under the dual authority of a native high priest and a Persian-appointed governor. At some point the Judean high priest emerged as the primary figure responsible *for* the administration of Judah and responsible *to* the imperial power for the same, particularly for the extraction of the required tribute and taxes on its behalf. It seems reasonable to connect this transition with the transition to Greek rule under Alexander and his first successors in this region. The high priest was assisted in some fashion by an advisory council of elders, likely drawn from the landed elite, both priestly and lay. This body is variously called a "senate" (*gerousia*) or a "council" (*synedrion*, from which is ultimately derived the term "Sanhedrin").[11] Priests, along with village leaders (*komarchai*), continued to be responsible for providing judicial arbitration throughout the region, as in the Persian period.[12]

The Ptolemies administered Judea and its surrounding regions without serious contest throughout most of the third century. They displayed a broad tolerance for local governance and religious practice as long as the resources continued to flow toward Egypt in their

---

[10] Nickelsburg 2001:170; deSilva 2012a:104–105.
[11] Grabbe 1992:191; Tcherikover 1959:59.
[12] Hecataeus of Abdera, according to Diodorus 40.3.5; Grabbe 2008:201–202.

requisite quantities. The Ptolemies were interested in the territories of Coele-Syria and Phoenicia, in the first instance, for the resources they could extract through tribute, taxation in various forms, and agricultural produce. Documentary evidence for conditions in Judea and its environs during the Ptolemaic period is admittedly sparse. One important collection of documents, however, emerges among the papyrus archives of a high-ranking financial officer under Ptolemy II Philadelphus named Zenon. Zenon appears to have served directly under Apollonius, the chief finance minister for the empire. He made a tour of Coele-Syria in 259 BCE on Apollonius's behalf and about forty papyri out of his immense archive pertain to this trip. The documents in his archive provide windows into the ongoing extraction of produce and coin from the territories of historic Israel.

The interior regions, including Judea, Samaritis, and Galilee, hosted a largely agrarian economy focused on the staple products of grain, olive oil, and wine.[13] These were important exports for Egypt, which lacked olive trees entirely, grew inferior grapes, and whose native grain took longer to ripen. Exporting grain and olive oil to Egypt was a royal monopoly and closely supervised. Of first importance was the produce of "royal lands" claimed by the crown. These royal lands included the fertile Jezreel Valley, large swaths of Galilee and the Golan, and at some point came to include the oases of Jericho and En Gedi, which were particularly valuable for their crops of balsam and dates. These lands might have already been in the hands of the state during the Persian period, and they would continue to be passed on as such to the Seleucids, the Hasmoneans, Herod, and finally the Romans. These lands were populated by villages of peasants who worked the land on behalf of the imperial power, to whom they would give the lion's share of the produce, while also maintaining livestock sufficient for their families' needs. Galilee appears otherwise to have been treated largely as the hinterlands of Ptolemais and Tyre during the Hellenistic period, the fertile land to be farmed on behalf of, and for the profit of, these urban centers. Twelve hundred stone field towers in

---

[13] See, further, the excellent description of the geography/topography and the agricultural potential of each region eventually incorporated into Herod's kingdom in Richardson 1996:131–145.

the fields of Samaritis, interpreted as shelters for agricultural workers and possibly also for storage of produce at harvest time, attest to the agricultural productivity of that region.[14] A subsistence agricultural economy would remain the norm for the majority of the population throughout Judea, Samaritis, and Galilee in the third century BCE and largely throughout the Greek and Roman periods. Human trafficking is also strongly attested in the Zenon papyri, with slaves (particularly women and children) destined for domestic service or sexual exploitation also constituting a significant export from the region of Syria to Egypt, where a profit could be realized. Reducing a freeborn person to slavery remained illegal, where enforceable.[15]

Care appears to have been taken to calculate the maximum wealth that could be extracted before negatively impacting the economies that supported this maximum (at which point tribute and taxation would become counter-productive). The annual tribute for Judea appears to have been set at twenty talents in the early Ptolemaic period. The increase in tribute to three hundred talents by the time Antiochus IV steps onto the stage in 175 BCE suggests a corresponding increase in the general prosperity of the population throughout the third and early part of the second century. In addition, the Ptolemies levied a head tax on individuals, taxes on livestock and slaves, taxes on imports and exports, and taxes in kind on the land's produce. The Zenon papyri give evidence once again of the importance of the cooperation of local elites and opportunists. Financial officers responsible for overseeing collection of these taxes for the Ptolemaic administration in Alexandria were installed at every level of organization down to the village, the last of these almost certainly being drawn from the local population rather than imported.[16] One finds evidence also of incentivizing locals to inform against tax evaders,[17] a none-too-subtle erosion of solidarity among the subject population as greater loyalty to the imperial rulers would bring tangible rewards.

---

[14] Berlin 1997:11.
[15] Tcherikover 1959:69; Grabbe 2008:216–217.
[16] Grabbe 2008:197.
[17] Grabbe 2008:215.

The Ptolemies' other principal interest in Coele-Syria was as a military buffer zone between its heartland and the Seleucid empire. Indeed, the Ptolemies appear to have sought to preserve their hold on Coele-Syria, Cyprus, Cyrenaica, and the southern coast of Asia Minor as a means of defending the possession that was of genuine importance to them: Egypt.[18] Significant attention was given to the rehabilitation of the coastal cities after the wars of succession—for example, Acco, Dor, Strato's Tower (later to be refounded as Caesarea Maritima), Jaffa, Gaza, and Raphia, all of which served military as well as commercial purposes. Several of the cities that would become known as the "Decapolis" were refounded during this period. Pella, Dion, and Gerasa appear to have served chiefly as military colonies for Macedonian veterans. The defensive fortifications of Gadara and Philadelphia suggest that these were particularly important garrisons for active military. Beth Shean took on new life also as a Greek city with a military colony, whether it was called Scythopolis or Nysa at this time. The presence of hundreds of stamped Rhodian amphora handles helps to confirm the date of reoccupation.[19] We also first learn of a certain Tobiah in connection with the military colonization of Coele-Syria. He was a local magnate in the Transjordan who was also made the head of a military cleruchy in his region—a sign of the importance of creating alliances with local elites for effective control on the part of the Ptolemaic government.[20] The settlement of Beth-Zur at the border of Judea and Idumea also appears to have been fortified at this time as part of the Ptolemaic system of defenses.

These Greek cities afforded an impetus to Hellenization, chiefly among the indigenous peoples who remained residents in these cities or who were attracted to them to engage in supportive industries for their populations, secondarily among those who visited the cities for some purpose and found themselves attracted to their relative grandeur and novel entertainments.[21] The majority of Greeks drawn to reside in these cities, however, were veterans, merchants, and

---

[18] See Polybius 5.34.2–9; Heinen 1984:443–444.
[19] Berlin 1997:13. A more complete survey of these cities can be found in Tcherikover 1959:90–116.
[20] Tcherikover 1959:64–65.
[21] Tcherikover 1959:114.

farmers—people interested primarily in making lives for themselves, not in serving as cultural ambassadors and evangelists.[22] In addition to their military, strategic value, many of these cities were important commercial centers along the trade routes that had already been well established along the coastal highway (linking Tyre, Ptolemais, Caesarea Maritima, and Lydda on the way south into Egypt) and along the "King's Highway" that ran down the Jordan Valley to the east of the river (linking Damascus, Gadara, Gerasa, and Philadelphia on the way south into Nabataea).[23] Caravan routes developed across Idumea from Petra to Marisa (another early Hellenistic foundation) to Gaza, supplying Egypt and, secondarily, other Mediterranean consumers.[24]

During the early Hellenistic period, Jerusalem was the only major city in Judea, and it remained relatively poor and small by Hellenistic standards, not enjoying the benefits of major trade traffic, whose routes largely bypassed Judea, or participating in the Mediterranean economy. Judea remained essentially an agrarian-based economy supporting the Temple state and relying mainly on locally made goods.[25] One can well imagine its elites, particularly those who traveled into the broader world, beginning to ponder how to get on the map and take part in the growing prosperity of the surrounding regions.

Joseph ben Tobiah

Josephus relates the story of one such Jewish notable from the Ptolemaic period, Joseph ben Tobiah (*Ant.* 12.154–236). The narrative's value may lie less in the specific details of the history it purports to relate than the profile it paints of one elite Jewish family's pursuit of wealth and influence through alignment with the interests of the Greek overlords of Coele-Syria.[26] According to Josephus, the high priest Onias II, father of the high priest Simon praised by Ben Sira (50:1–21), defaulted on paying the tribute he had been assigned to collect from Judea on behalf

[22] Tcherikover 1959:115.
[23] Reed 2000:147.
[24] Berlin 1997:6.
[25] Berlin 1997:3–4.
[26] See the critical review in Tcherikover 1959:127–134.

of the king, probably Ptolemy III Euergetes (246–221 BCE). Josephus blames Onias's miserliness, but one wonders if it was more an indication of his pro-Seleucid leanings and his (admittedly mistaken) anticipation that Judea would soon change hands or perhaps simply his resistance to his foreign overlords' extraction of resources.[27] Whatever the reason, his default offered an aristocratic Jew named Joseph ben Tobiah an opportunity to advance himself. Joseph's father was known to the Ptolemaic administration, having cooperated with them in the formation of a military settlement in Transjordan. Tobiah himself had shown a willingness to be all things to all people. In a letter to the finance minister Apollonius, he writes "thanks be to the gods" and inventories both circumcised and uncircumcised boys he is sending as slaves to Apollonius. The latter violated Torah on two counts: giving Jews as slaves to a Gentile and leaving slaves uncircumcised.[28] The fabulous palace built by Tobiah (or, perhaps, his youngest grandson Hyrcanus) in Transjordan—the complex of Araq el-Emir—bears witness to the family's nonchalance with regard to the second commandment's prohibition of graven images, as prominent bas reliefs of lions and jaguars adorned its entablature.

Joseph used the impending crisis of Ptolemy's retaliation to insinuate himself as the new representative of the province to the Ptolemaic court. He traveled to Alexandria and announced his commitment to make good on Onias's default if given the opportunity and support. Joseph outbid other local elites for the right to collect the taxes not only from Judea but from the whole of Coele-Syria on behalf of the Ptolemaic administration. Joseph guaranteed a certain amount; if he collected less, he would make up the difference, but if he collected more, he would retain the difference as compensation for his service. For the next twenty-two years, Joseph consistently collected more, thanks in part to his hired army and his willingness to make an example of cities that failed to provide their share of the tax burden by murdering dozens of their leading citizens. With financial responsibility passing to Joseph from Onias, the regional importance and status of the high priest were significantly diminished.[29] Joseph's sons would

[27] Grabbe 1992:196–197.
[28] See, further, Tcherikover 1959:64–65, 71, 126–142; Grabbe 1992:196–198.
[29] See Josephus, *Ant.* 12.4.1–11 §§154–241; Grabbe 1992:192–198.

continue to wield significant influence in Judea and the Transjordan, where they were based.

Josephus would remember Joseph ben Tobiah as having "brought the Jews out of a state of poverty and lowliness, to one that was more splendid" (*Ant.* 12.224)—though one might reasonably wonder whether the majority of Judeans enjoyed *any* benefit from his career.[30] The path by which he did so was telling:

> Joseph cheerfully broke any Mosaic law in the line of duty. . . . The Hellenistic world beckoned alluringly, and he followed. Many of his more ambitious contemporaries got the message. To succeed as Joseph did meant, almost by definition, rejecting the narrow code of Judaism: there was no other way. And that, again almost by definition, meant embracing the *ethos* of the conqueror. Here, in embryo, we can see the future ideology of the Jewish Hellenizing party: separatism had brought nothing but backwardness and trouble, whereas close cooperation at every level with the Gentiles would produce an economic and cultural boom. (Green 1990:507)

This ethos will emerge in full bloom in 175 BCE when, according to the author of 1 Maccabees, "renegades came out from Israel and misled many, saying, 'Let us go and make a covenant with the Gentiles, for since we separated from them many disasters have overtaken us'" (1 Macc 1:11).

The Beginnings of Seleucid Rule

The history of the third century BCE includes a series of so-called Syrian Wars representing the ongoing attempts of the "kings of the north" to remove Coele-Syria from the control of the "kings of the south" and secure it for themselves (cf. Dan 11:6–9). The first several of these did not penetrate the interior, though they wrought havoc in the coastal plains. Antiochus III, later called "the Great," would finally succeed.

---

[30] Tcherikover 1959:142; Green 1990:507.

Over the full course of his long reign (226–187 BCE), Antiochus III pursued an aggressive policy of military expansion in multiple directions, focusing first on claiming his great-great-grandfather's heritage to the south. He made his first attempt early in the reign of Ptolemy IV Philopator (221–203 BCE), having been invited to invade by a disgruntled officer of Ptolemy IV who handed over control of Ptolemais and Tyre to him. Ptolemy's councilors engaged Antiochus III in prolonged diplomacy, giving Ptolemy the time he needed to muster his troops for battle. Antiochus continued to sweep southward until he reached Raphia, a city very near the Egyptian border, in 218 or 217 BCE. There Ptolemy achieved a major victory, forcing Antiochus to accept a truce and to withdraw from Coele Syria, which Ptolemy recovered in its entirety (Dan 11:10–11; Polybius, *Histories* 5.30.8–87.8).

Over the next fifteen years, Antiochus III successfully focused his energies on expanding into Asia Minor and into the territories east of Babylon. The passing of Ptolemy IV Philopator in 204 BCE left Egypt in the hands of a child of five. Antiochus III took advantage of the relative weakness of leadership under Ptolemy V's regents to make another play for possession of Coele-Syria. He inflicted a resounding defeat upon Ptolemy's troops in a battle near Panion (Banias), some twenty-five miles north of the Sea of Galilee, in or around 200 BCE. When the surviving troops along with their general, Scopas, sought refuge in the fortified city of Sidon, Antiochus besieged and captured it (Dan 11:13–16; Polybius, *Histories* 16.18–19; Livy 33.19).[31] After this, he was able to secure the remaining fortresses of the coastal plain and Samaritis with relative ease.

Under the leadership of Simon II ("the Just"), high priest from 219 to 196 BCE, Jerusalem voluntarily submitted to Antiochus III, opening their gates to him, greeting him magnificently, and provisioning his troops. Simon also gave Antiochus military support against the Ptolemaic garrison in Jerusalem, deeply ingratiating the Judeans to their new overlord (Josephus, *Antiquities* 12.3.3 §§133–134; Dan 11:14). Antiochus III, in turn, took steps to secure the favor of his new subjects, particularly in Jerusalem, by issuing several decrees on their

---

[31] Abel 1952:72–87.

behalf, the text of which is preserved, more or less reliably, in Josephus (*Ant.* 12.138–144).[32] The multiple wars between the Seleucids and the Ptolemies took a significant toll on the disputed territory. Even when battles were not fought on their land, an army on the move—especially one equipped with elephant battalions—is worse than any plague of locusts with regard to the food supply (Polybius, *Hist.* 16.39). Antiochus was interested, first, in stimulating the economic recovery of his newly acquired territory. He therefore made allowances for repairs to Jerusalem, relieved individuals connected in any way with the government of the city or the work of the temple from an array of taxes, and remitted one-third of the nation's tribute for three years while the land recovered. He gave a special incentive encouraging the repopulation of the city and, one may suppose, its hinterlands—remission of taxes for three years. These relief measures would all be temporary: Antiochus's interest in Judea's economic recovery ultimately served his own interests in restoring its capacity to provide him with the maximum extractable resources for the long haul. Antiochus also gave the Judeans permission to govern themselves by their ancestral law and made provision for Temple sacrifices out of the royal treasury. While these provisions appear beneficent, they also introduce the uncomfortable reality that the privilege of observing their ancestral laws is extended to Judeans by royal decree—a privilege that might also, then, be withheld.[33] The Hefzibah stele shows Antiochus III also taking measures to prohibit his soldiers, now stationed throughout the region, from taking over the homes of local villagers or otherwise inflicting injury or abuse.[34]

Simon the Just enjoyed oversight of Jerusalem and its environs in both civil and religious matters. Ben Sira remembers him for having repaired the Temple, fortifying the city's walls (including the Temple's retaining walls), and increasing the city's water supply (Sir 50:1–4). During this period the population of Jerusalem began to expand to the area west of the City of David, outside the city walls. The initial

[32] Abel 1952:88–93; Tcherikover 1959:82–88; Grabbe 1992:246. Perdue and Carter (2015:177) question how far these relief measures extended to the villages throughout Judea.

[33] Portier-Young 2011:62.

[34] Hengel 1974:9; Berlin 1997:12–13.

decades of Seleucid rule appear to have brought increased prosperity to Jerusalem and nurtured a positive attitude toward the new overlords.[35] Antiochus's ambitions would be his undoing, as they conflicted with the designs of another great power in the region. He had designs on pushing Seleucid territory all the way west through Asia Minor into Greece, lands that he claimed by right of his forebears' defeat of Lysimachus, who had ruled in Thrace and Macedonia. Rome was already asserting its authority over all of Greece and looking to Asia Minor as a buffer zone between its territories and the Seleucid empire. Antiochus's advances into Greece prompted Rome to mobilize itself and its allies in the region against him, pushing Antiochus back into Asia Minor, all but destroying his naval forces, and finally inflicting a crushing defeat upon his army at Magnesia, near Ephesus, in late 190 or early 189 BCE (Livy, *Hist.* 36.42.1–36.45.9; 37.38.1–37.44.7).

The terms of peace required Antiochus to withdraw from all territory in Asia Minor north and west of the Taurus Mountains. The Seleucid Empire still stretched far east into Babylonia, but its Western limits had been soundly set, never again to be challenged. They also require him to pay an economically hobbling war indemnity of fifteen thousand talents: three thousand up front and the rest in installments over the space of twelve years. This was the heaviest schedule of war reparations imposed in the ancient world up to that time, no doubt intended to cripple Antiochus III's ability to pursue his expansionist policies. He was also required to send twenty members of the royal and other elite families as hostages to Rome.[36] His son, who would become Antiochus IV Epiphanes, was among the first (Livy 44.19). Polybius identified one of the principal lessons of his history to be that "the Romans managed everything to ensure the subjection of the entire known world to their rule" (Hist. 5.3.3). This agenda began to be strongly felt in the East during the reigns of Antiochus III and Antiochus IV.

---

[35] Berlin 1997:16.
[36] The precise terms are preserved in Polybius, *Histories* 21.13–17, 42, 45; Diodorus Siculus, *Bibl. Hist.* 29.10.1–11.1, 13.1; Livy, *Hist.* 37.45; 38.38.1–18; Appian, *Roman History* 11.7.37–39.

Antiochus III died soon after this crushing blow. Indeed, he perished in an ambush while he was attempting to plunder the funds deposited in a temple of Bel in Elymais in 187 BCE, impelled both by his debt to Rome and his unrecovered expenses waging an unsuccessful war in western Asia and Greece (Diodorus Siculus, *Bibl. Hist.* 28.3.1; 29.15.1; Dan 11:19). The ongoing financial burden would have repercussions for Seleucid policy in Judea, among other places, and was potentially an indirect factor in the disasters that would ensue in Jerusalem.

Hellenism and Hellenization

A subject of great importance during the periods of both Greek and Roman rule—and one that will continue to emerge throughout the following chapters—is the matter of the Hellenization of Judea and its surrounding territories. In what ways and to what degree did the situation of Greek and Roman domination change Judean culture, practice, and identity by means of introducing Greek culture, practices, and markers of identity—as well as by bringing other local cultures and practices throughout the eastern Mediterranean and Levant into closer interaction and exchange? The answers must be finely nuanced in several ways. Hellenization did not happen uniformly among the population: the elite and semielite members of the population were far more likely—and inclined—to adapt themselves to the dominant culture and its practices. They also had the necessary means to this end, for example, through access to and leisure for education. Correspondingly, Hellenization did not happen uniformly throughout the region: it was primarily an urban phenomenon. The rural villages and their inhabitants would be affected the least and the most slowly; merchants and artisans would likely adapt to the extent that it facilitated doing business. It should also be borne in mind that Hellenization did not mean the simple abandonment of native practices and culture for a foreign one, but, inevitably, a blending of the two together—and often the blending of elements of other cultures, as "Hellenism" itself represented not some pure Greek cultural ideal, but the sum total of the cultural exchanges and mutual interactions that Alexander's vast empire facilitated.

Hellenization can be observed operating at several levels. The first and most obvious is the acquisition of Greek on the part of native elites and semielites, even while Aramaic would remain the dominant language among the majority of the population throughout the Second Temple period and the elites themselves remained fully multilingual (Greek, Aramaic, Hebrew).[37] A retainer class of bilingual or trilingual "scribes" would emerge as an important element of Judean society during the Ptolemaic period to facilitate communication between local populations and Greek-speaking government representatives. The importance of this retainer class would not diminish in the centuries that followed, even—or perhaps especially—under the native dynasty of the Hasmonean kings as they carried on relations with foreign powers.[38]

Adopting Greek names represented a superficial level of assimilation, serving both to represent oneself as more akin to the members of the dominant culture (and less a subaltern foreigner) as well as to facilitate communication.[39] Another important facet of Hellenization involved the acquisition of cultural literacy, for example in the Greek heritage of philosophy, ethics, literature and drama, rhetoric, religion, and the like, as well as exposure to, and even participation in, Greek athletic and social practices. Elite and semielite persons throughout the kingdoms of Alexander's successors were particularly inclined to adapt themselves to their Greek overlords, learn their language, adopt Greek names, and otherwise seek to maintain and enhance their own local power and wealth through collaboration—that is, in part, through "Hellenization."[40]

None of these facets of Hellenization would be incompatible with continued observance of the Mosaic covenant in all of its particulars, that is, with traditional Jewish identity and practice. Particular Jews might have opined otherwise, even perhaps the author of 2 Maccabees, the first to pit *Ioudaismos* ("Judaism," "the Jewish way of life") against

---

[37] Horsley 1996:163; Freyne 1998:144.
[38] Hengel 1989b:30–31.
[39] We can observe something similar when immigrants to the West adopt Western names in place of their given names, which would be frequently mispronounced by their Western associates.
[40] Green 1990:503.

Hellenismos (2 Macc 4:10, 13, 15; 6:9)—all the while in the context of writing a very Hellenistic work of historiography! The Greek-speaking Diaspora, however, would provide the most extreme examples of a high degree of acculturation coexisting with uncompromising adherence to the Law of Moses—Philo of Alexandria or the anonymous author of 4 Maccabees, both of whom exhibit mastery of Greek language, literature, philosophy, and rhetoric and use this cultural knowledge in the service of promoting the nobility, even the superiority, of the Jewish way of life and the quality of the person whom the *paideia*—the "educative discipline"—of the Law of Moses shapes most fully.

Many particulars of Torah observance, however, would limit social interaction with and assimilation into the Greek world—as, indeed, the Law of Moses was strictly intended to do (see especially *Ep. Aristeas* 138, 142). The effects of observance of the dietary regulations; strict avoidance of all participation in (or even *near*) idolatrous rites; the disdain that the pious Jew's denial of the existence of any deity but his or her own and general aloofness invited from the members of the dominant culture with whom ambitious elite and semielite Jews would wish to form close and profitable connections;[41] the novelty and entertainment value of Greek practices and indulgences—all these things would problematize continued, strict observance of the Jewish way of life for some. For many of these people, the solution was indeed to leave behind these exclusive practices. Those who remained faithful to their ancestral practice, "however Hellenized they might be, . . . could never be fully at home in the Greek world."[42]

Perhaps the most influential surviving text from the end of the Ptolemaic and the beginning of Seleucid rule in Judea is the Wisdom of Ben Sira, a text from the early second century BCE that serves as something of a window into Jerusalem in the period of transition from Ptolemaic to Seleucid rule, and as an example of Hellenization within the bounds of Judaism. Yeshua ben Sira identifies himself as the author and as the head of a school in Jerusalem (Sir 51:23). Assuming that his

---

[41] On anti-Judaism in the Greco-Roman world, see Feldman and Reinhold 1996:305–396. There were, of course, strains of pro-Jewish attitudes, especially among the philosophically inclined Greeks (1996:105–122).
[42] Grabbe 2008:165.

description of the preparation and work of "the one who devotes himself to the study of the law of the Most High" reflects his own experience, Ben Sira traveled beyond Judea, probably beyond Coele-Syria, to learn "what is good and evil in the human lot" (Sir 39:1–4). The degree of his familiarity with Egyptian as well as Greek wisdom traditions and, quite probably, particular literary works, all of which would be available in Ptolemaic Egypt, all but requires this.[43] It seems probable that he had achieved facility in Greek himself in order to give himself access to these traditions. As Martin Hengel rightly observed, "the much-debated question whether ben Sira was anti-Hellenist or pro-Hellenist is based on a false antithesis."[44] True to the spirit of Hellenism, he crafts an amalgamation of Greek, Egyptian, and native Judean wisdom; true to his own purposes, he puts his multicultural erudition in the service of promoting continued adherence to the ancestral Jewish way of life where the performance of the Torah is concerned.[45]

The content of Ben Sira's collection of the essence of his curriculum suggests that he sought to prepare younger (elite) males for a life in government, in wealth management, in social networking with (other) members of the elite, and in the practice of managing one's own household (and his assumption that slaves will be part of his students' households suggests that some, at least, enjoyed semielite or elite status). He gives extensive and frank advice concerning how to comport oneself well at the symposium, or refined drinking party, that was an established custom of the Greek elite, a testimony to the extent to which he expected his students to participate in such non-native practices (31:25–32:13).

At the same time, he clearly resisted the growing tendencies among the members of the elite and semielite to regard a Torah-observant life as a hindrance to the attainment of greater honor, wealth, and influence in the Greek-dominated world. In keeping with the Jewish wisdom tradition, he insists that the "fear of the Lord"—reverence for the God of Israel—was the beginning of wisdom (Prov 9:10; Sir 1:14). He protests,

---

[43] On the influence of Greek and Egyptian wisdom texts on Ben Sira, see deSilva 2018:174–178.

[44] Hengel 1989c:225.

[45] Further on the composition, setting, and curriculum of Ben Sira, see deSilva 2012a:59–68; 2018:161–210.

going beyond Proverbs, that the fear of the Lord is also wisdom's fullness, crown, and root (Sir 1:16, 18, 20). And revering the Lord means obeying God's commandments: "All wisdom involves respecting the Lord, and in all wisdom there is the practice of the Torah" (Sir 19:20); "if you desire wisdom, keep the commandments" (Sir 1:26). He goes so far as to claim that "Wisdom" has taken on textual substance as the Book of the Law, the special (and exclusive) possession of Israel (Sir 24:1–23, esp. 24:23). Respecting the Lord and obeying God's commandments is the indispensable source of a person's honor (Sir 10:19–24). Wealth apart from such covenant loyalty brings only dishonor (Sir 11:4–6; 13:24), while covenant loyalty bestows honor even on the impoverished (Sir 25:10–11). Where a choice had to be made, it would always be advantageous to choose obedience to the Torah, even if it appeared to hinder the enjoyment of immediate rewards. This was the lesson he sought to reinforce through his carefully crafted rehearsal of the heroes of the covenant people (the "men of ḥesed," covenant loyalty, Sir 44:1)—which also incidentally served as a reminder of Israel's rich and honorable heritage, one that need never be overshadowed by the heritage of any other people group.

When we recall the path to wealth and power pursued by Tobiah and his son, Joseph, and when we look ahead to events soon to devolve following Ben Sira's own death, it becomes apparent that Ben Sira was not making these claims in a neutral environment, but rather in one in which the value of maintaining the exclusivist practices of the Torah was being weighed against the value of fuller assimilation to the practices of the dominant culture—and, by some at least, found wanting.

2

Abomination of Desolation

The Hellenizing Crisis and the Maccabean Revolution

The period of 187–141 BCE witnessed dramatic events with long-lasting impact. It opened with a bold experiment in bringing Jerusalem into the larger network of Greek cities and placing Jerusalem on the larger map of the Greek empires and their inhabitants for the purpose of elevating its prestige (and that of its elite), improving its participation in the economics of the Greek empires, and positioning its elite for improved connections within the social and political worlds of those empires. It reached its nadir with the wholesale repression of Jewish practices and markers of identity in a program of forced assimilation. It spawned a revolutionary movement that would ultimately restore Jewish practice and national independence, the latter for the first time since Nebuchadnezzar's conquest of the region in 597 BCE.

The primary sources for the events covered in this chapter are 1 and 2 Maccabees, the latter presenting an abridgement of the five-volume history of the period of 175–161 BCE by Jason of Cyrene, who might himself have been a contemporary of the events. Although the two have obvious partisan and theological interests, these are the most detailed and ancient sources for the Hellenization Crisis, the Maccabean Revolt, and establishment of the Hasmonean dynasty.[1] Josephus (*Ant.* 12.234–13.229) is only rarely an independent witness to this period, and often at his least reliable when most independent of these sources. The history and dynamics of the larger context of the competing

---

[1] 2 Maccabees may have been written prior to 124 BCE, with 1 Maccabees perhaps being written somewhat later; neither postdates 63 BCE. On the dates of these books, see deSilva 2018:268–269, 292–295; on their ideological programs, see deSilva 2018:276–286, 298–302 and the literature therein discussed.

Judea under Greek and Roman Rule. David A. deSilva, Oxford University Press.
© Oxford University Press 2024. DOI: 10.1093/oso/9780190263249.003.0003

Ptolemaic and Seleucid empires—within the even larger web of their neighbors, all under the watchful eye and increasing meddling of Rome—are recounted in detail by Greek and Roman historians. Livy (*Hist.* 41–45), Appian (*Rom. Hist.* 11), and fragments preserved from Polybius (*Hist.* 26, 31, 33) are particularly important. Archaeological discoveries, especially in the area of numismatic finds, are of significant help rendering the picture more precise, for example, by providing evidence of the movements of populations as reflected in the ebbs and flows of the distribution of imperial and local coinage.

Seleucus IV

Antiochus III was succeeded by his elder son, Seleucus IV Philopator (187–175 BCE). His younger brother, the Antiochus who would become Antiochus IV Epiphanes, had been living in Rome as one of the hostages supplied by Antiochus III as assurance for his compliance with the terms of the Treaty of Apamea. Upon Seleucus's accession, Antiochus was released, to be replaced by Seleucus's own eldest son, Demetrius. It is likely that he was principally occupied throughout his reign with raising funds from whatever sources he could find throughout his empire to refill the coffers that his father's ruinous later campaigns had emptied—and which continued to be bled for the annualized fines Rome had imposed. Indeed, Seleucus would fall into arrears, leaving it to his brother, Antiochus IV, to make the final payment to Rome in 173 BCE (Livy, *Hist.* 42.6.8–9).[2]

Jewish sources remember Seleucus only for sending "an exactor of tribute" to Jerusalem (Dan 11:20; 2 Macc 3:4–40). The so-called Heliodorus Stele, the text of a letter of Seleucus IV to Heliodorus, his finance minister, provides some administrative background for this episode (see Figure 2.1). This inscription indicates that Seleucus appointed his own officials to oversee the administration of sacred shrines throughout his realm, here particularly appointing one Olympiodorus over temples in Coele-Syria and Phoenicia. The inscription claims

---

[2] 2 Macc. 8:10, 36 is probably incorrect to claim that the Seleucids had been in such arrears that Antiochus IV was still paying installments in 165 BCE.

Figure 2.1 The Heliodorus Stele.

that Seleucus's goal was to assure proper "oversight," "maintenance," and "protection." The language likely masked a less altruistic interest in control and interference, especially with regard to the assets of these sanctuaries,[3] all the more as Antiochus III had not shied away from

---

[3] Portier-Young 2011:83; Perdue and Carter 2015:180.

outright seizure of temple funds. This is precisely what Seleucus IV is also remembered as having attempted with the temple in Jerusalem.

Internal rivalries in Jerusalem itself played a role as well, here between Onias III, the son of the Simon whose service as high priest is praised so loftily in Sir 50:1–21, and another Simon who served in some administrative capacity over the temple. The precise nature of their dispute is unrecoverable, but Simon took advantage of the Seleucid administration to discredit Onias. He informed against Onias to the Seleucid governor of Coele-Syria, suggesting that certain sums of money were being inappropriately sheltered in the Jerusalem temple and that the king could lay claim to these sums. Seleucus sent his deputy, Heliodorus, to investigate—all quite in keeping with Seleucus's assertion of "oversight" of the shrines and temples within his empire. For the reasons already mentioned, he would also welcome any lead on a financial windfall.

Upon Heliodorus's arrival, Onias explained that the greater part of the private funds in the temple belonged to Hyrcanus, the youngest son of Joseph ben Tobiah, but also asserted the time-honored tradition of respecting the sanctity of any funds placed under the protection of a deity by being deposited in a temple (essentially the banks of the ancient world). Hyrcanus had alienated the whole of his family by his extravagant use of their wealth to ingratiate himself with Ptolemy III, and it is likely that he had remained strongly aligned with the Ptolemies, which would make Seleucus's seizure of his assets all the more attractive to the king. Under circumstances that the author of 2 Maccabees describes as miraculous, however, Heliodorus returned to Antioch empty-handed. The sight of the city's inhabitants turning out en masse and praying to God to avert the desecration of God's holy place might well have made a strong impression even on a Seleucid official, if he were a person with strong scruples concerning the power of the divine and the danger of sacrilege.

The importance of this episode for the author of 2 Maccabees is that it demonstrated that diligent observance of the Law of Moses from the top echelons of Jerusalem down ensured God's protection of God's holy shrine and city. Its importance for the historian, however, may lay more in the way it reveals the connection between partisanship within Jerusalem and the purposeful leveraging of external Seleucid

interests to advance partisan interests that would lead to the disasters
that would overtake Judea under Antiochus IV.[4]

Antiochus IV

Heliodorus arranged the assassination of Seleucus IV soon after his
return to Antioch. He proclaimed Seleucus's younger son, Antiochus,
king and himself the young king's regent (Appian, *Roman History*
11.8.45). This particular Antiochus is assigned no number because
his reign was never established. Seleucus's brother, Antiochus IV
Epiphanes, learned of Seleucus's death while serving as a magistrate
in Athens. With the support both of King Eumenes II of Pergamum
and his own allies in the Seleucid court, he managed to gain control
of the government for himself. He tried to veil his blatant power grab
by marrying Seleucus's widow and claiming to rule on behalf of his
nephew. When he was securely in power, however, he ensured that his
nephew died young. He thus supplanted two rightful heirs (Demetrius
and Antiochus, the two sons of Seleucus) and, it might well have been
rumored, arranged for his own brother's death through Heliodorus—
thus the claim that this arrogant horn plucked up three other horns
(Dan 11:21).

Certain Judean elites used the king's recent accession to power as an
opportunity to advance their own progressive agenda for Jerusalem.
Indeed, the picture painted by the author of 2 Maccabees and
Josephus—and even reluctantly admitted by the author of 1 Maccabees
(see 1 Macc 1:11; *contra* 1:41–43)—is that the initiative for the struc-
tural Hellenization of Jerusalem came from the Judean elite, not from
the Seleucid king. In 175 BCE, Onias III's younger brother Jason—a
Greek name he had probably himself assumed in keeping with the program he had been preparing to advance—made an important overture
to Antiochus IV (2 Macc 4:7–10). He asked to be appointed high priest
in his brother's place, promising to raise the annual tribute from Judea
to the amount of 360 talents. Jason further requested that Antiochus
reorganize Jerusalem as a Greek city (a polis) with a new constitution,

[4] Portier-Young 2011:90.

granting Antiochene citizenship to those who would be enrolled as citizens in "Antioch-at-Jerusalem." The author of 2 Maccabees interprets this as a setting aside of the "royal concessions" granted the Judean people by Antiochus III (4:11). To some extent, he is correct. The Law of Moses ceased to have any status as a political constitution, even though the service of the temple and the piety of the people were not thereby affected. With the advantage of hindsight, however, this act sent Judea down a tragic path.[5]

The creation of a new political entity, "Antioch-at-Jerusalem," gave Jason and his party the opportunity to assure that only like-minded, progressive elites and semielites would have a voice in the citizen assembly and, more importantly, the *gerousia* ("senate"). Whether "Antioch-at-Jerusalem" replaced Jerusalem as a political entity or existed conceptually within Jerusalem,[6] it would be the high priest and council of Antioch-at-Jerusalem that would now represent the Judean population to the Seleucid state. This transformation would also involve the establishment of the typical institutions of a Greek city, including a gymnasium for the training of Jerusalem's elite youth (who would thus become "ephebes") in Greek language and literature, along with the introduction of Greek athletics for the youth and citizenry.[7] For these privileges, Jason pledged a one-time gift of an additional 150 talents, which might have been a means by which Jerusalem "self-funded" Antiochus's building and proper staffing of these structures.

Antiochus IV no doubt welcomed the additional funds as he made the final two payments of the indemnity owed Rome and began financing his own projected campaigns for expansion into Egypt and the East (Livy, *Hist.* 42.29). He would also have welcomed the enthusiasm of the Judean elite for becoming more fully integrated into his empire, hopefully rendering Judea a more secure possession. Onias III, the "prince of the covenant," was therefore removed (Dan 11:22) and would eventually succumb to foul play (2 Macc 4:32–34).

---

[5] All historical reconstruction involves imagination. For an imaginative recreation of the situation in Judea under Antiochus IV from 175 to 166 BCE, see deSilva 2015.
[6] Tcherikover 1959:165; Schwarz 2008:530–532.
[7] Tcherikover 1959:163–169. Jason's gymnasium was likely built in the area to the south of the Temple (Galor and Bloedhorn 2013:74).

A great deal lay behind these developments. First, the sums of money that Jason was able to promise—and, by all accounts, pay—suggest that he had the support of a significant portion of the Judean elite, who believed that the transformation of Jerusalem into a Greek polis would bring significant economic benefit to the region as well as position themselves for greater access to both economic and political advancement on the larger, international stage. Second, it suggests that some steps toward Hellenization had already been taken, for example in the establishment of institutions for the primary education that was preparatory to the level of education received at the gymnasium level.[8] The presence of a thousand stamped handles of Rhodian wine jugs in Jerusalem, the majority of which date to the period between 205 and 175 BCE, suggests a local population developing a taste for things Greek.[9]

Jason and his supporters could be said to have "sought to carve out a moderate accommodationist position that cooperated with the Seleucid empire in the political realm" while not abandoning their distinctive religious observances and practices.[10] Indeed, Jason's innovations would have affected the majority of people in Judea little or not at all. There might well have been a good deal of suspicion and grumbling about the direction in which matters were heading, but there is no evidence of popular outcry or resistance to these measures and, when Antiochus made his first visit to his new colony of Antioch in 172 BCE, there were no demonstrations against him (2 Macc 4:21–22). At the same time, there is evidence that some individual Jews were already willing to take a more radical approach to assimilation, ceasing to circumcise their sons and even attempting the surgical or cosmetic reversal of their own circumcision, presumably to adapt their naked bodies to Greek ideals and to engage in athletic competitions nude (*Jub.* 15:33–34; 1 Macc 1:14–15; Josephus, *Ant.* 12.241). One thing is clear: circumcision as an identity marker—and as a marker of allegiance—is underscored in a newly intense manner during this

---

[8] Hengel 1989b:22.
[9] Berlin 1997:17.
[10] Portier-Young 2011:112.

period, both in its proscription and its enforcement once the resistance movement gains ground.

Shortly after Antiochus's visit to Jerusalem in 172 BCE, a certain Menelaus, brother of the Simon who had opposed Onias III, was sent as an envoy to Antioch where he made his own bid to Antiochus IV for the high priesthood. Menelaus now had the backing of some portion of Jason's former supporters, including the still-powerful sons of Joseph ben Tobiah (Josephus, *Ant.* 12.239).[11] He recklessly promised an impossible increase in the annual tribute of three hundred talents over and above what Jason had pledged. Antiochus just as recklessly accepted the pledge and transferred the office of the high priesthood to a non-Zadokite person—a serious encroachment of foreign power upon native tradition.[12] Jason fled Jerusalem but, as events would later show, still enjoyed a significant number of supporters.

Menelaus proved unable to raise the promised sums. When he was summoned to Antioch to answer for it, he relied on bribery of court officials to secure a reprieve. He began to use the temple treasury as his privy purse, which provoked fresh accusations against his behavior, first on the part of Onias III, who had been living in exile, and then on the part of the senate of "Antioch-at-Jerusalem"—revealing that a significant number among the Hellenizing party were still concerned about the temple's sanctity.[13] Again Menelaus used bribery to secure not only his acquittal but also the murder of his accusers, including Onias. Open rioting in Jerusalem against Menelaus's administration followed, in the course of which his brother and deputy Lysimachus was killed (2 Macc 4:27–48).

The backdrop of relations between the Ptolemies and Seleucids bleeds into the foreground once again at this point. In 170/169 BCE, Ptolemy VI Philometor (181–146 BCE), urged on by his advisors, sought to reclaim Coele-Syria from Antiochus IV (his maternal uncle, as it happens). The attempt was a disaster (Polybius, *Histories*

---

[11] Mørkholm 1989:281.

[12] The Greek text of 2 Macc 3:4 calls Simon a member of the tribe of Benjamin, but the Old Latin and Armenian correct this by connecting him to the priestly clan of Bilgah, named in 1 Chron 24:14. The latter is probably more correct, given the easy accession of Menelaus to the high priesthood.

[13] Tcherikover 1959:171; Grabbe 2020:336–337.

27.19; 28.1.4–6). Antiochus IV captured Ptolemy VI. His younger siblings, Ptolemy VIII and Cleopatra II, assumed rule over Egypt from Alexandria. Antiochus then proceeded to invade Egypt on the pretext of reinstating Ptolemy VI to the throne of Egypt under his regency (cf. Dan 11:27–28; Livy, *Hist.* 44.19.8; 45.11.1–6; Diodorus Siculus, *Bibl. Hist.* 31.1.1). He gained control of most of the country outside of Alexandria, installed Ptolemy VI as king in Memphis, and withdrew, believing himself to have gained a foothold in Egypt through a willing puppet. Ptolemy VI and his siblings were reconciled, however, and he reasserted his independence of his uncle's supervision.[14]

This prompted Antiochus to return in the spring of 168 BCE for a second campaign (Livy, *Hist.* 45.11–12; Polybius, *Hist.* 28.18–23; 29.26–27; 2 Macc 5:1). He captured a good deal of Lower Egypt and was about to besiege Alexandria when Rome, having been petitioned by the Ptolemies, intervened on their behalf. A Roman legate gave Antiochus the ultimatum: desist from disturbing the balance in the eastern Mediterranean or face the prospect of war with Rome (Dan 11:29–30; Livy, *Hist.* 44.19.6–14; 45.12; Polybius, *Hist.* 29.27.1–7; Appian, *Rom. Hist.* 11.66). Antiochus acquiesced, losing all hope of taking Egypt but having gained Rome's assurance that Egypt would no longer threaten the Seleucid's possession of Coele-Syria.[15] As he prepared to return north after this humiliating encounter, however, word came to him that his authority over part of this precious consolation prize was being threatened from within (2 Macc 5:11).

The Hellenizing Crisis

During Antiochus's second Egyptian campaign in 168 BCE, Jason moved to recover his office, reportedly prompted by a rumor that

---

[14] Antiochus III had given his daughter, Cleopatra I, in marriage to Ptolemy V in the wake of Antiochus's seizure of Coele-Syria from Ptolemaic control. Whether this was a genuine olive branch or a surreptitious attempt to get a foothold in the Ptolemaic household through his daughter is unknown, though Dan 11:17 suggests the latter. Antiochus IV's sister was thus the mother of Ptolemy VI.

[15] Grabbe (2020:343–344) suggests that Antiochus was quietly glad to have gotten out of a lengthy and costly siege, but this was not likely to have been his only feeling as he left for Antioch without possession of Egypt.

Antiochus had died in battle. He returned to Jerusalem with a small army and besieged Menelaus in the citadel that had been used to garrison soldiers since the period of Ptolemaic rule. Jason's revolt was not a war for independence from Seleucid rule, to be sure, but it was a revolution against the arrangements that the Seleucid monarch had put in place—and that could also not be tolerated. Antiochus IV mobilized against Jerusalem to suppress any revolutionary activity. Jason fled before the arrival of Antiochus's forces, but Menelaus appears still not to have been in command of the situation in Jerusalem, since Antiochus took the city by force and inflicted massive casualties upon the residents of Jerusalem (2 Macc 5:5–7, 11–14). This has led some to suggest that the strife between Jason and Menelaus also provided a catalyst for a popular revolt against both Hellenizing leaders that Antiochus eventually suppressed.[16] On the other hand, Antiochus's severe actions might have been purely punitive, motivated by a desire to terrorize his unruly subjects into general submission or to make an example of them.[17] The scope and kind of Antiochus's reprisals—massacre both in the streets and in home invasions as well as the enslavement and deportation of a large number of captives (2 Macc 5:12–14)—suggests that "state terror" played some role in these actions in either case.

Antiochus IV entered the temple and its treasuries, escorted by Menelaus, to appropriate the funds deposited there—quite likely with a view to recovering the amounts owed by Menelaus, who was deeply in arrears.[18] Here, Antiochus IV's motivations seem quite understandable—though perhaps his personal inspection was meant to carry the message that the temple space was part of his domain, whatever the God of Israel might think about it. For the population of Judea, however, this was an act of unspeakable desecration, especially since Antiochus appears not to have spared either votive offerings or

---

[16] Tcherikover 1959:186–188.

[17] Portier-Young 2011:128–129, 138, 140. Gruen (2018:354–356) suggests that his humiliation at the hands of the Romans particularly disposed Antiochus IV to react with undue severity towards Jerusalem, which became a vicarious venue for reasserting his power and restoring his pride.

[18] It is possible that this occurred after Antiochus's first campaign in Egypt, since Dan 11:28 says that the king took some unspecified action "against the holy covenant" at that time (Mørkholm 1989:283). 1 Macc 1:20–23 and 2 Macc 5:1–22, however, locate this after the second campaign.

temple furnishings to make up the deficit in Judea's back tribute (2 Macc 5:15–21). It was either at this time or in the following year that Antiochus ordered the construction of a new fortress—the "Akra," or "Summit"—at a position south of the temple in the north end of the City of David (1 Macc 1:33–38; Josephus, *Ant.* 12.252) and stationed a peacekeeping force of his own soldiers.[19] The preceding massacre would have made a good deal of property available for reallocation, so as to provide for this new population. Together with an improved system of defensive walls surrounding some portion of the Lower City, the Akra would provide protection for the garrison, Menelaus, and the citizens of "Antioch-at-Jerusalem" and play a strategic and symbolic role in the Seleucid domination of Jerusalem for more than twenty-five years.

In the following year (167 BCE), Antiochus appears to have launched a second punitive campaign against Jerusalem (2 Macc 5:24–26; 1 Macc 1:29–32). Some view this as a response to a resurgence of resistance, but the sources present it rather as an unprovoked act of state terror.[20] On the other hand, there are hints that resistance groups—for example, a shadowy group of "mighty warriors of Israel" known as "Hasideans" (1 Macc 3:42; 2 Macc 14:6)—were active prior to their coalescence under the leadership of Judas Maccabaeus.[21] In connection with this second campaign, Antiochus authorized a number of measures that show that he had come to a desperate conclusion: If the experiment of "Antioch-at-Jerusalem" that had been set in motion eight years before—and the full integration of Judea into his empire that had appeared so promising—was to succeed, the inhabitants of Judea would need to be forcibly distanced from the exclusivist practices and ideology that hindered that goal.[22]

---

[19] The precise location of the Akra remains a matter of considerable debate. See especially Bar-Kochva 1989:445–465; Zilberstein 2021:37–52 for promising possibilities.

[20] Tcherikover 1959:188 and Green 1990:514 vs. Portier-Young 2011:159–162 and Gruen 2018:247.

[21] Tcherikover 1959:195, 198. Further on the Hasideans or Hasidim, see Grabbe 2020:135–137, who rightly advises caution concerning what we affirm in regard to this group about which we have so little direct information, and Kampen 1988.

[22] It is a telling indication of the anti-Judaism that existed in the later, Roman period that Tacitus (*Hist.* 5.8) can look back with regret upon Antiochus IV's failure in this endeavor.

Scholars have been accustomed to considering Antiochus's actions under the rubric of "religious" persecution, but such an approach inevitably distorts both Antiochus's motives and the realm of the "religious" in the Greco-Roman world. There is nothing in Antiochus's decrees that would distinguish them as "religious persecution" as opposed to the elimination of the distinctive practices of an indigenous population that, by giving them such a strong sense of distinctive identity, made them uncommonly resistant to submitting to the policies of their king in cooperation with their local, appointed leaders (like Menelaus).[23] The degree to which religion is a factor in legitimating and maintaining a distinctive identity may make the policy *look* like "religious persecution," but it is really more a matter of "forced assimilation" as a (perceived) last resort in order to undermine ongoing, tiresome resistance to foreign domination—made worse by attacks on those members of the subaltern people who willingly embraced assimilation.[24] These actions are not an indication of Antiochus's own missionary zeal for the cult of Zeus or his particular disdain for Judaism, since his decrees were limited to the population of Judea and not imposed upon Jews throughout the Seleucid empire (for example, the large communities in Babylonia, Cilicia, or Syria).[25]

A related question concerns the role of Hellenizing Jewish leaders like Menelaus in advising Antiochus concerning the roots of resistance on the ground and plausible strategies for undermining it. While some scholars are content to lay all of the blame at Antiochus's door, depicting Menelaus as a reluctant accomplice,[26] it seems more probable that Antiochus would have relied upon his deputy's insider understanding of his own people in the formulation of the new policy.[27]

---

[23] His actions have more in common with the expanding United States' treatment of indigenous peoples, enrolling their young in American schools, outlawing the indigenous peoples' practices, and the like, than with the persecution of Jews in Medieval Europe or the murder and trafficking of Christians in modern Nigeria by Boko Haram.

[24] See also Mørkholm 1966:186; Grabbe 1992:256.

[25] Abel 1952:124–125; Bickermann 1988:61–68; Grabbe 1992:248–249; Gruen 2018:344–345.

[26] Zeitlin 1962:90; Stern 1976a:204–205; Millar 1978. Gruen (2018:349–351) suggests that Menelaus was an opportunist, not a radical Hellenizer, but this alone would be sufficient to explain his desire to direct Antiochus IV's efforts in eliminating threats to his position as Antiochus IV's appointee.

[27] Bickerman 1979:76–90; 2007:1117; Mørkholm 1989:284–285; Grabbe 1992:284; Ma 2012.

A number of ancient sources also leave no doubt as to Menelaus's responsibility "for all the trouble" (2 Macc 13:4; Josephus, *Ant.* 12.384).

In keeping with the new, multiethnic population of "Antioch-at-Jerusalem," the first action involved the transformation of its temple into a worship center for all of its citizens.[28] Exactly what this entailed remains unclear. Ancient sources allege a wide variety of changes: the cessation of the daily offering to the God of Israel, which would surely have aroused horror and despair for the pious, covenant-keeping Jews throughout Judea (1 Macc 1:44–45; Dan 9:27; 11:31); the re-dedication of the temple to Zeus Olympios (2 Macc 6:2); the offering of unclean animals like swine, perhaps with a view to purposefully "de-sacralizing" the space, so as to ritually sever its connection to the exclusivistic, Jewish cult there (1 Macc 1:46; 2 Macc 6:4–5; Diodorus Siculus, *Bibl. Hist.* 34–35.1.3–4); the setting up of a "desolating sacrilege" or, more poetically, "the abomination of desolation," specifically on the great altar of burnt offering (1 Macc 1:54; Dan 11:31; 12:11), which is remembered as a new, pagan altar appropriate for foreign cultic rites (1 Macc 1:59; Josephus, *Ant.* 12.253). Whatever the particulars, for most Judeans, including many of the elites that had supported Jason's more moderate reforms, the temple was rendered hopelessly polluted and no longer available as a vehicle for the mediation of God's favor and forgiveness. The transformation of the central temple was accompanied by the construction of other shrines involving cult images and foreign rites elsewhere in Jerusalem and Judea (1 Macc 1:47, 54–55).

The second action involved the proscription of traditional Jewish practices, most especially those that set them apart from people of other ethnic groups. Parents were forbidden to circumcise their male infants. Possession of copies of scrolls of the Torah was forbidden. The inhabitants of Jerusalem were forced to participate in Greco-Syrian forms of religious cult, such as the cult of Dionysus and the sacrifices offered to honor the king on his birthday, and to participate in the cultic meals that followed such sacrifices—involving the ingestion not only of meats offered to idols, but the flesh of swine. Failure to comply with these measures meant summary execution (1 Macc 1:44–50,

[28] Tcherikover 1959:194–196.

57–63; 2 Macc 6:1, 8–11; 6:18–7:42; Josephus, *Ant.* 12.253–256).[29] While the particular stories of the martyrdoms related in 2 Maccabees 6:18–7:42 may be fictitious, we need not doubt that they represent a level of brutality in the enforcement of Antiochus's decrees that was not atypical in the ancient world. This led to widespread desertion of the defiled and dangerous city and its hinterlands, creating a displaced population that would become a prime recruiting ground for active resistance (1 Macc 2:28–30, 42–43). At this point, the process of Hellenization had overstepped the limits of the people's tolerance, and a full-scale revolution against Menelaus's leadership and Syrian rule ensued. Antiochus had by this time prepared—and launched—a massive campaign to reassert Seleucid domination over the eastern provinces, seeking to restore his empire's dimensions in a direction that would not concern Rome. He therefore set out for the east with the bulk of his armies, leaving his heir apparent, the young Antiochus V Eupator, in the care of Lysias, his prime minister. It would fall to his deputies in Antioch and, more immediately, in Judea to deal with the fallout of his repressive measures.

The Samaritans appear to have taken steps to avoid coming under negative scrutiny by Antiochus. Josephus alleges that they disavowed any ethnic or cultic connection with Jerusalem and proactively requested that their sanctuary be dedicated to Zeus Xenios, "Zeus the friend of strangers" (Josephus, *Ant.* 12.257–264; see also 2 Macc 6:2). This would not suggest that they were ready to apostatize or worship foreign gods, but only that they were eager not to come under fire for actions perpetrated in Jerusalem against Seleucid domination.[30] One cannot help but suspect Josephus's account of reflecting his own anti-Samaritan bias, however. There were significant Gentile populations in the near vicinity of Gerizim, including the Macedonian colonists in the city of Samaria. The possibility exists that the initiative for this change of name came from a Hellenizing elite population among the Samaritans who worshiped on Gerizim, perhaps in conjunction with their Macedonian neighbors, as a means of unifying the

---

[29] See also 2 Macc 11:27–38 and 11:23–26, which refer to a policy of suppression of indigenous practices—and to the eventual rescinding of the repressive decrees.
[30] Grabbe 2020:207.

two populations. The stationing of Andronicus there by Antiochus (2 Macc 5:22–23) could have been directed against more conservative Samaritans with the full support of Macedonians and Hellenizing Samaritans. Thus, one could imagine a scenario very similar to what one finds in Jerusalem at this same time, though it remains admittedly speculative.

The Maccabean Revolution

The two primary sources for the Maccabean revolt—1 and 2 Maccabees—differ significantly in their details concerning the order of events, making a secure historical reconstruction impossible.[31] What is clear, however, is that resistance finally coalesced under the leadership of a priestly family from the village of Modein, fourteen miles northwest of Jerusalem. According to 1 Maccabees, Mattathias, the patriarch of the family, initiated the rebellion when he killed both an agent of Antiochus who was calling for the village elders to offer sacrifice to a foreign god along with the first elder who stepped forward to oblige (2:15–25). The obvious parallel with the story of Phinehas (Num 25:1–13) suggests that the story has some element of the legendary, told in the service of legitimating the dynasty of priest-kings that would arise among his descendants. Nevertheless, it appropriately captures the fundamental motivation that drove the rebellion in its initial stages—zeal for the Law of Moses and the covenant that it embodied (1 Macc 2:26–27, 50).

Leadership quickly passed to Judas, the third of Mattathias's five sons, who would earn the nickname "Maccabaeus" or "the Hammer." Judas and his growing band of insurgents first targeted apostate Jews, employing domestic terrorism to curtail collaboration (1 Macc 2:44–47; 3:1–9). In the process they circumcised the male children that had been left uncircumcised, an act that particularly shows their zeal for the covenant and their belief that Israelites were not free to choose whether to maintain the covenant into which they had been born, and upon which the well-being of the whole nation depended.

---

[31] For a detailed exploration of the military history of the revolt, see Bar-Kochva 1989.

They also made effective use of guerilla tactics against small Seleucid forces while building up their army, their arms, and their resources—as well as distributing some portion of the spoil as aid for the survivors of Antiochus's persecutions or surviving family members of martyrs (2 Macc 8:28, 30). While the latter might be dismissed as a pious fiction, it would also have been an astute means of securing widespread loyalty and continued support among the traditionalist population. Judas's early victories against the forces sent against him gave significant momentum to his resistance movement, such that he was able to meet the larger armies sent out against him with an ever-increasing force of his own.

The escalating clashes eventually brought Judas's forces against a significant Seleucid force commanded by Lysias himself at Beth-Zur in 165 BCE. Lysias withdrew from the battle (1 Macc. 4:29), perhaps because he was getting the worst of it, as the author of 1 Maccabees claims (4:34–35), or perhaps because he was already considering a negotiated settlement. It is perhaps to this moment that at least one of the documents preserved in 2 Maccabees 11 belongs, in which Antiochus IV promises amnesty to any Judeans who are willing to lay down their arms and return to their homes—an amnesty negotiated by Menelaus himself—and permission to all who do so to practice their native customs as before (11:27–33).

If this offer does, in fact, date to the early months of 164 BCE, the offer was insufficient for Judas, his brothers, and their armies. Freedom to practice their ancestral laws was not compatible with conditions in Jerusalem and, above all, in the temple that had become "a house of prayer for all nations" in a manner that Isaiah would never have approved. Judas and his forces therefore continued the fight and, in late 164 BCE, entered Jerusalem, besieged the Akra, and regained control of the temple precincts.[32] The foreign cultic paraphernalia were dismantled, the spaces ritually cleansed, and the exclusive worship

---

[32] Grabbe (2020:371) would say 165 BCE. Maccabean-era dates present a general problem due to the use of two calendars within the Seleucid Empire: one used in the eastern empire that began the year in April and a second used in the western territories beginning a year in October. It is not always clear which dating system is being used by our sources—or any of the documents embedded in each—at any given point. See, further, Grabbe 1991:59–74; 2020:13–21; Bartlett 1998:36–53.

of the God of Israel in keeping with the rites prescribed in the Torah resumed. The choice of the 25th of Chislev—the third anniversary of the rededication of the temple as a center for foreign cults—was likely deliberate (1 Macc 4:36–59; 2 Macc 10:1–9). Judas also fortified Jerusalem and numerous Judean fortresses, including the important site at Beth-Zur, during this respite (1 Macc 4:60–61; 2 Macc 6:7).

Judas also came to the aid of Jews in cities in the territories neighboring Judea who were said to have been experiencing the hostility of the non-Jewish majorities around them. According to 1 Maccabees, this involved detachments of Judas's army—and, indeed, it could be called an "army" at this point based on the experience and training his fighters had achieved—in operations against populations in Idumaea, Transjordan, Gilead, and northwest Galilee, in the hinterlands of the coastal cities of Tyre and Ptolemais (1 Macc 5:1–2, 9–15, 26–27, 30–31).[33] The Jews appear to have been few enough in number to be relocated from these hostile areas to Judea (1 Macc 5:23, 45–54).[34] It is noteworthy that these efforts involved significant violence against these neighboring populations as well as sacking the territories of the offenders to procure food, supplies, and weapons for his army's ongoing efforts (1 Macc 5:3, 22, 28, 35, 51, 68; 6:6; 2 Macc 8:30–31). These activities were no doubt giving the administration in Antioch every incentive to return to pacify the region.

Sometime in late 164 BCE or early 163 BCE, Antiochus IV died while campaigning in the east to reassert Seleucid control over Armenia, Bactria, and Persia.[35] His deputy Lysias, however, moved once again to pacify Judea. This time, he is remembered to have executed Menelaus as "the cause of all the evils" (2 Macc 13:4, CEB). He engaged Judas's forces once again at Beth-Zur. During the course of a series of indecisive melees, Lysias received word that Philip, another high-ranking minister under Antiochus IV, was returning from the east to take over

---

[33] Dąbrowa 2010:24. Dąbrowa (2010:41) rightly emphasizes an easily overlooked accomplishment of Judah, namely providing military training and experience to a large number of the Judean population.

[34] Reed 2000:54.

[35] More specifically, Antiochus IV died following an attempt to raid the treasury of another temple—the sanctuary of Artemis at Elymaïs (Polybius, *Histories* 31.9; Diodorus Siculus, *Bibl. Hist.* 31.18a.1).

as regent, ostensibly on the deceased king's authority. Lysias therefore made a hasty truce with Judas, issuing a letter in the name of the young Antiochus V rescinding his father's decrees and restoring the Jews' freedom to practice of their ancestral customs (1 Macc 6:55–59; 2 Macc 14:22–26; cf. the letter quoted in 2 Macc 11:22–26) so that he could return north and give his full attention to maintaining his and the young king's positions.[36] The new terms included the agreement that the restored cult of the God of Israel would be allowed to continue without encroachment (2 Macc 11:22–26).

Antiochus IV's usurpation of the throne from his brother's eldest son, Demetrius I, would prove to be a watershed event for the Seleucid dynasty. After Antiochus IV's death, internal strife and civil wars between rival claimants would never depart from the empire, leading to its steady decline and eventual absorption by the expanding Roman empire. Demetrius I, the eldest son of Seleucus IV and the man who ought to have succeeded him in 175 BCE, had been seeking leave from the Roman Senate to return to his father's kingdom to assert his rights. While he was officially denied permission on several occasions, he finally escaped from Rome with the contrivance of friends—including the historian Polybius (Polybius 31.11–15)—and established himself in Antioch. He had Lysias and the young Antiochus V executed and began his rule in 163 or 162 BCE (1 Macc 7:1–4; 2 Macc 14:1–2; Polybius, *Histories* 31.2.1–6; 31.11–15).

Both primary sources claim that hostilities were renewed at the instigation of some leaders of Antioch-at-Jerusalem with a priest named Alcimus at their head. Whether this was part of a play to become high priest or to maintain his hold on the office in the wake of Lysias's settlement with Judas, he brings the complaint against Judas and his forces and asks for Demetrius's military intervention to reassert control and to reestablish Alcimus's Hellenizing party as the body representative of Seleucid governance in Judea (1 Macc 7:5–7; 2 Macc 14:3–10). The Hasidim or Hasideans appear a second time in this history, this

---

[36] On the particular question of the authenticity (and actual context) of the diplomatic correspondence preserved in 1 and 2 Maccabees, and therefore their value for historical reconstruction, see especially Bartlett 1998:83–97; Tcherikover 1959:213–218; Habicht 1976; and the overview in deSilva 2018:273–275, 297–298.

time either as the particular subject of Alcimus's complaint (2 Macc 14:6) or as the victims of his treachery, when a representative group of them sought just terms with the new high priest (1 Macc 7:12–18). The execution of these leaders among the Hasidim—as former, stalwart revolutionaries—is not altogether surprising. The forces sent by Demetrius, however, are defeated by Judas and his men and their general, Nicanor, killed in a significant victory at Adasa in 161 BCE (1 Macc 7:26–50; 2 Macc 14:11–15:37). At this point, the author of 2 Maccabees ends his narrative, leaving historians to depend on 1 Maccabees and Josephus.

According to these, Judas sent an embassy to forge a treaty with Rome at some point concurrent with Demetrius I's accession and actions against him (1 Macc 8:1–32; Josephus Ant. 12.415–419). This was a bold move—one calculated no doubt to bring international recognition, and thus a greater degree of internal legitimation, to Judas as the de facto ruler in Judea. It was bold in another way, namely for any representative of a subject territory (even a legitimate representative) to enter into diplomatic relations with another nation. The fact that the Roman Senate recognized Judea as a nation with whom they might themselves legitimately enter into diplomatic relations was no doubt a slight against their escaped hostage who had set himself up on the Seleucid throne.[37] The treaty was, however, little more than propaganda to serve Rome's own interests as well as Judas's (and his successors') internal interests, since Rome would not send any military forces to aid Judea for a century—and, even then, it would not be so much to assist their "allies" as to begin to dismantle their hegemony.

The alliance with Rome certainly did not help Judas when Demetrius I took decisive action against the insurgents in *his* province to the south. He quickly sent another large force under the command of Bacchides, who engaged Judas and his armies near Elasa and Beth-Horon and left Judas and two-thirds of his army dead upon the battlefield in 160 BCE (1 Macc 9:5–27). Bacchides strengthened the fortifications and garrisons at Bethel, Jericho, Beth-Zur, Gezer, Emmaus, Beth-Horon, and the Akra, strengthening the Seleucid position against the insurgents in the wake of Judas's death, as well as

[37] Green 1990:441.

taking hostages from leading families and placing them under guard in the Akra as guarantees of future compliance (1 Macc 9:50–53).

Jonathan

Their defeat of Judas "the Hammer" emboldened Bacchides and Alcimus to hunt down his colleagues and supporters, forcing many insurgents into hiding (1 Macc 9:26–27). Jonathan quickly emerges as the leader of the beleaguered rebels and gathered them in an area beside the Jordan River (1 Macc 9:28–30). Learning of their whereabouts, Bacchides mobilized against them and was surprisingly defeated (1 Macc 9:43–49). After fortifying the above-mentioned sites, he left Judea in the care of the military garrisons he installed (1 Macc 9:50–57). The sources do not explain why Bacchides left with his task unfinished, especially considering that Alcimus died of an apparent stroke at this same time, but one can readily imagine that other concerns in the Seleucid empire commanded his attention. Judea was not supposed to require that large numbers of the Seleucid army, along with an important general, be permanently stationed there.

Two years later, the deceased Alcimus's party petitioned Bacchides to return and make another attempt on Jonathan. Jonathan had apparently not allowed himself or his forces to grow unconditioned, for he defeated Bacchides a second time, even more soundly. Bacchides, enraged, executed some number of the Hellenists that had incited him to his own harm and then returned north. Jonathan followed up with Bacchides and the two struck a truce, a sign that the Seleucid general recognized that Jonathan was now the person in Judea with the real power, and thus the man with whom to negotiate to ensure quiet in the southern part of the empire (1 Macc 9:58–73): "Thus the sword ceased from Israel. Jonathan settled in Michmash and began to judge the people; and he destroyed the godless out of the land" (1 Macc 9:73). While the Hellenizing party remained in control of Jerusalem, Jonathan and his supporters established a rival government at Michmash, about seven miles north of Jerusalem. For the next seven years (159–152 BCE), he and his forces appear to have been actively reducing the numbers of the supporters of the Hellenizers living outside of the areas most heavily protected by Seleucid soldiers, which would likely have involved confiscating and redistributing their estates among his own party as well as exercising effective oversight of these territories.

Rivalries within the Seleucid dynasty again arose, to the benefit of Jonathan and his partisans. In 152 BCE, Attalus II, the king of Pergamon (an empire in the western portion of Asia Minor), produced a rival claimant to the Seleucid throne—Alexander Balas, alleged to be another son of Antiochus IV. With the blessing of Rome, still annoyed at Demetrius I for his escape, and with the support of Ptolemy VI of Egypt, for whom the prospect of a Seleucid king personally indebted to him was irresistible, Alexander Balas occupied Ptolemais and was declared king (Polybius 33.18.3; 1 Macc 10:1). In the hope of retaining power and defeating the rival, Demetrius I immediately offered concessions to Jonathan to secure him as an ally—or, at least, to secure his quiet compliance in Judea. The most important consequence of this is that Jonathan now emerged as the master of Judea. He moved his government to Jerusalem, improved the city's fortifications, and extended the city's walls to include all of Mount Zion as well as the City of David (1 Macc 10:2–11).

Alexander Balas, understanding the importance likewise of securing Jonathan as an ally, offered more enticing and important concessions if Jonathan would support his bid for the Seleucid throne. This included appointing Jonathan as high priest, sending him the accouterments of rule (a purple robe and crown), and enrolling him among the (would-be) king's "friends," a circle of favored courtiers (1 Macc 10:15–21). Jonathan accepted this offer and put his own military power behind Alexander. At this point, he became high priest and the de facto leader of the Jewish people.[38] The revolutionaries had achieved far more than the restoration of the Jews' ancestral practices; they had supplanted the Hellenizing administration of Judea (including the political entity of "Antioch-at-Jerusalem") as the power brokers in this region.

---

[38] Josephus (*Ant.* 20.237) claims the office to have been vacant for the seven years between Alcimus and Jonathan. If this is true, it is difficult to imagine the psychological burden this placed on the (pious) people of Judea as it would have precluded the performance of the rites for the Day of Atonement for this span.

Demetrius sought to regain Jonathan's support, but the die was cast. Demetrius died on the battlefield in 151 BCE and Alexander established himself as the reigning monarch over the Seleucid empire. Alexander sought an alliance with Ptolemy VI of Egypt through a marriage with Cleopatra Thea, Ptolemy's daughter. Jonathan was in attendance as an honored guest and a member of Alexander's inner circle of "friends," a sign of just how far the members of Judas's family had come from the guerilla warfare of 166 BCE. In 147 BCE, however, a new antagonist presented himself on the Seleucid stage—Demetrius II, son of the slain Demetrius I. It is evidence of Jonathan's importance as a prop for the Seleucid throne that one of Demetrius's first actions was to launch an assault against Alexander's ally. Their forces joined battle in and around the cities of the coastal plain and ended in victory for Jonathan in concert with his (last surviving) brother, Simon. As a reward, Alexander annexed the city of Ekron and its hinterlands to Jonathan's territory. These and later battles seriously weakened and depopulated the coastal cities, something Jonathan and Simon would exploit to Judea's advantage in the years to come.

The old rivalry between the Ptolemies and Seleucids also quickened, however, and Ptolemy VI sought to use the new rivalry for the Seleucid throne to his own advantage. He gained control of the coastal plain while still professing loyalty to his son-in-law, Alexander, but then shifted his allegiance to Demetrius II, dissolved his daughter's marriage to Alexander, and wedded her to Demetrius. When Ptolemy entered Antioch, he crowned *himself* king of the Seleucid empire (1 Macc 11:1–13)! His coup was not to last long, however. Although he was able to defeat Alexander in battle and cause him to flee to supposed allies who, to please Ptolemy, betrayed and beheaded him, Ptolemy himself had been mortally wounded in the battle and died himself a few days later, leaving Demetrius II the undisputed ruler of the Seleucid empire by 145 BCE (1 Macc 11:14–19).

Jonathan took advantage of the confusion to besiege the Akra—that symbol in the heart of Jerusalem not only of foreign domination, but of the civic body whose actions led to the repression of Jewish practice and the desecration of the temple—but had to desist at Demetrius's insistence. The new king might have been tempted to reassert tighter Seleucid control over Judea, but unrest among his own subjects prevented him. Demetrius II and Jonathan came to amicable terms, with the former confirming all the privileges that Alexander Balas had conferred upon him and promising more besides. In return, Jonathan brought his military power to bear against a revolt against Demetrius's rule in the city of Antioch itself. The opportunity to weaken the Seleucid overlord by decimating the population of his capital *and* be thanked by Demetrius for doing so must have been irresistible. Demetrius failed to keep several of his promises to Jonathan, however, for example leaving the garrison in the Akra and several other fortresses in Judea in place (1 Macc 11:41–52).

In the same year (145 BCE), another Seleucid challenger emerged: Antiochus, son of Alexander Balas, supported by Diodotus Tryphon, one of Alexander's partisans. Tryphon and Antiochus VI approached Jonathan with significant concessions, confirming him as high priest and "friend," allocating more territory in the region of Samaritis to his oversight—with economic benefit as well, as he would have authority over some part of its produce. Antiochus VI also granted Jonathan's brother Simon the governorship of the coastal territory from Tyre to Raphia. It is appropriate again to note the irony that those who had been the most ardent rebels against Seleucid rule were now ruling themselves through alliance with, and the favor of, the Seleucid kings.[39] Jonathan, alienated from Demetrius because the latter had not kept his promises, gave his support to Antiochus VI and engaged Demetrius's armies in the north while Simon captured the fortress city of Beth-Zur and garrisoned it with his own people (1 Macc 11:65–66).

Jonathan renewed diplomatic ties with Rome, asserting the same level of independence from the Seleucid overlords that his brother Judas had done, though now perhaps with more legitimacy and leverage. Rome's interference in the east, especially with regard to protecting the independence of Egypt, and its willingness to form alliances with the subject peoples of the Seleucid empire, notably the Maccabean party, was part of its long game in the east, undermining the power and scope of the Seleucid empire to Rome's own eventual advantage, as would become evident by 64 BCE.

[39] Rajak 1994:282.

Tryphon, however, had been planning to betray Antiochus VI and take the Seleucid crown for himself. The success of Jonathan and Simon in the coastal region of Phoenicia and Coele-Syria led Tryphon first to turn against Antiochus VI's all-too-successful ally, taking Jonathan prisoner by a ruse in 143 or 142 BCE (1 Macc 12:39–53).[40] Trypho positioned Antiochus's forces for an invasion of Judea, hoping to bring the region to heel now that their leader was in his custody.

Simon

Simon quickly stepped forward in the wake of Jonathan's capture to regroup their forces in preparation for Tryphon's advance against them. He took the important step of securing Joppa, expelling its garrison and inhabitants and settling his own troops and other Judeans there (1 Macc 12:33–34). This would give Judea its first direct outlet to Mediterranean trade. Simon met Tryphon's demands for an enormous ransom and hostages (Jonathan's two sons), but to no avail. After killing Jonathan and the young Antiochus VI, Tryphon declared himself the Seleucid king. At this point, Simon and Demetrius II realized that, despite their past antagonism, they needed one another to secure both their interests. Demetrius confirmed previous concessions made to Jonathan and offers Simon, his natural successor as high priest and governor, the important addition of the lifting of tribute—an action that provided not only economic relief but symbolized Judea's elevation to the status as an allied rather than a subjugated territory (1 Macc 13:37–40). It is probably this that explains the author of 1 Maccabees' statement concerning the removal of "the yoke of the Gentiles" in 143/142 BCE and the introduction of a new dating system in Judea ("in the first year of Simon"; 1 Macc 13:41–42).

Simon attacked the Seleucid fortress city of Gezer, located a little more than halfway between Jerusalem and the coast, since it was in the territory controlled by Trypho. He expelled the garrison and the gentile population, stationing his own forces and settling Judeans there (1 Macc 13:43–48). The discovery of houses from this period, which

---

40   Habicht 1989:366–367.

begin to be furnished with *mikvaoth*—small, stepped pools for the performance of purificatory rites by immersion in water—confirms the radical change in the character of the city's inhabitants. There is archaeological evidence for "internal colonization" at this time as well, namely the purging of Judea and Samaritis of several non-Jewish settlements.[41] Simon also lay siege once again to the Akra in Jerusalem in 141 BCE, which he successfully took (1 Macc 13:49–53), expelling the Seleucid garrison there at last. He improved the fortifications of the temple hill near the Akra and took up residence in Jerusalem. Simon renewed diplomatic ties with Rome (1 Macc 14:24), which provoked something of a response in the form of letters from the Roman Senate to the Ptolemaic and Seleucid monarchs, calling for their recognition of an independent, sovereign Judean state (1 Macc 15:15–24).

Demetrius II had set off for the east, no doubt with the understanding that Simon would keep Tryphon at bay. The author of 1 Maccabees asserts that his goal was to raise troops for his campaign against Tryphon, but the response of the Parthian king suggests that Demetrius was also intent on reasserting control over territories that the Seleucid empire had lost on its eastern front. In any event, the Parthians met Demetrius in battle, defeated his army, and took him captive.

It may be significant that the author of 1 Maccabees speaks of the *internal* confirmation of Simon as ruler and high priest in his third year (141/140 BCE), two years removed from his external appointment to the office by Demetrius II. If this is indicative of some resistance to the Hasmoneans' occupation of the high priestly office,[42] any tension appears to have been resolved, for the majority at least, on the basis of overall recognition of the family's contributions to, and investment in, the well-being of their nation—and this at great personal cost to almost every member of that family—as a resolution of the citizen body expresses (1 Macc 14:25–49). This may reflect the facts of the period or, perhaps, the desire of the author of 1 Maccabees (writing a generation later) to conjure afresh such gratitude toward the Hasmonean family as would continue to lend legitimacy to the dynasty of "the family

[41] Applebaum 1989:44; Berlin 1997:28.
[42] Atkinson 2016:35.

through whom deliverance had been given" to the nation (1 Macc 5:62). In either case, it is a marvelous piece of functional legitimation of the dynasty, drawing upon one of the most fundamental scripts of the Greco-Roman period: the necessity of rendering exceptional honor, gratitude, and loyalty for acts of exceptional benefaction.[43]

Antiochus VII Euergetes Sidetes succeeded his brother, Demetrius II, and enlisted Simon's aid against Tryphon, confirming all the concessions Demetrius had made to Simon to this end (1 Macc 15:1–9). Once he gained the upper hand over Tryphon, besieging him in the coastal city of Dor (a few miles north of Strato's Tower, which would become better known as Caesarea Maritima), he appears to have had a change of heart. He refused the military aid that Simon had sent and complained against Simon that the latter has seized Seleucid properties (Joppa, Gezer, the Akra) and devastated a good deal of Seleucid territory. Antochus VII demanded the return of these properties or the payment of significant tribute for them under threat of war (1 Macc 15:10–14, 25–31). Simon defended against the complaint by claiming to have taken nothing that did not belong to the Jewish people's ancestral land that had been unjustly taken by foreign powers—and, here, 1 Maccabees may indeed reveal something of the Hasmoneans' long-term vision (15:33).[44] He offered a much smaller sum for Joppa and Gezer, which he claimed had been acting aggressively against his people. Antiochus VII clearly did not regard Judea to be as independent as Simon and his party did. He sent his general Cendebeus at the head of a large army to reassert his sovereignty by fortifying the coastal plains and reconquering Judea for the Seleucid empire, though Cendebeus was eventually defeated under the generalship of one of Simon's sons, John Hyrcanus (1 Macc 15:25–41; 16:4–10). This incidentally says something about the practical value of Rome's letters on Simon's behalf, which the author of 1 Maccabees interjects into the narrative prior to Antiochus's change of heart (15:15–24), or, perhaps, the value of alliance with Rome, which deterred neither Demetrius II (1 Macc 10:67–73) nor Antiochus VII from attempting to reassert control over Judea.

---

[43] See deSilva 2022:96–124; on 1 Macc 14:25–49 in particular, see Gardner 2007.
[44] See also Dąbrowa 2010:188.

The author of 1 Maccabees paints a picture of life in Judea under Simon that falls somewhere between the idyllic and the truly messianic. He combines images from Zechariah, Ezekiel, and Micah to depict old men enjoying leisurely conversation as they sit in the square, people sowing their crops in peace, and everyone sitting "under their own vines and fig tress" (1 Macc 14:4–15).[45] Leaving room for exaggeration, the passage may reflect a good measure of truth concerning Simon's achievements (building upon those of Judah and Jonathan). They effectively gained control of the land and extended its borders significantly—both through military action and negotiation with desperate Seleucid contenders. Three districts in the south of Samaritis as well as Ekron and its hinterlands were granted to Jonathan; Simon took Gezer and Joppa, as well as a land bridge that ensured Judea's access to the coastal city of Joppa. This activity allowed for the resettling of many Judeans in locations where they would receive land grants. The expulsion of the garrison in the Akra meant reclaiming for Simon's soldiers as well as for other Judeans land in and around Jerusalem that had been confiscated for the use of Seleucid veterans, mercenaries, and supporters of one kind or another; the same would be true wherever other Seleucid garrisons were evicted.[46] It is possible that Jonathan's and Simon's military campaigns against one or another Seleucid pretender led to the abandonment of Seleucid fortresses and gentile-occupied villages in Galilee during the 140s as well, allowing for Judean migration into that region.[47]

It is highly likely that Jonathan and Simon maintained a standing army, rather than relying on volunteers, throughout the period of their leadership. This would have been necessary both for the manning of their fortresses and their ready mustering of large forces.[48] This would have provided steady employment for thousands of Judean males and support for them and their families. Simon no doubt retained the concept of "royal lands," a tradition that had been in place under the Ptolemies and Seleucids,[49] which would have provided the revenue

---

[45] deSilva 2018:283–284.
[46] Dąbrowa 2010:167.
[47] Leibner 2021:143.
[48] Dąbrowa 2010:62.
[49] Berlin 1997:33.

needed for a professional soldiery, the many building activities associated with his fortifications of Jerusalem, the significant improvement of the city's water supply through pools and low-level aqueducts, and the like.

In early 135 or 134 BCE, Simon, his wife, and two sons visited the fortress at Dok outside Jericho, where his son-in-law, Ptolemy ben-Abubus, had been stationed as commander. After feasting and heavy drinking had robbed his victims of their alertness, Ptolemy and his partisans treacherously murdered Simon and seized the remaining family members as hostages (1 Macc 16:11–22; Josephus, *Ant.* 13.228–229).[50] The internal strife that had plagued their Seleucid overlords had infiltrated the Hasmonean family at last. To complete his coup, Ptolemy appealed to Antiochus VII to be made ruler over Judea in Simon's place, at the same time sending men to assassinate Simon's surviving son John Hyrcanus, who was stationed in Gezer as commander of the forces there. Friends informed Hyrcanus in time for him to escape the plot, kill the assassins, and move to Jerusalem to secure what he—and, by all accounts, the majority of the population—considered to be his birthright. Events immediately following Hyrcanus's accession would show that Judeans and the Seleucid kings had different perspectives on the degree to which "the yoke of the Gentiles" had indeed been removed.

---

[50] Grabbe (2020:35–36) favors January/February 135 BCE.

3

Heirs of Phinehas

The Rise and Demise of the Hasmonean Dynasty

Roman historians give scant attention to the events in Judea prior to Pompey's intervention in 63 BCE. Tacitus makes only this brief reference to the Hasmonean dynasty: "Since the Hellenistic rulers were weak . . . the Jews established a dynasty of their own" (*Hist.* 5.8). Though in other respects he is an historian who verges into calumny in his treatment of the Jewish people, Tacitus accurately reflects the fact that it was the strife within the Seleucid dynasty that allowed for the establishment of the Hasmonean dynasty. The depopulation of Galilee, Samaritis, and the coastal plain that resulted from the ceaseless military actions between rival Seleucid claimants and occasional Ptolemaic contenders gave the Judeans opportunities for expansion through simple settling and outright conquest.[1] The strain on military and financial resources required to fight these internecine battles also prevented either kingdom from effectively reestablishing hegemony in Coele-Syria.

The more that the descendants of Simon succeeded in establishing something akin to their own Hellenistic kingdom, however, the more they appear to have departed from the ideals that gave them legitimacy in the eyes of their subjects and, thereby, alienated important portions of the population. Finally, the same power plays between rival claimants that weakened their neighbors would come home to Jerusalem and announce the beginning of the end of their dynasty with the intervention of Rome in Judean affairs in the person of Pompey the Great. The most important sources to be considered here include Josephus's *Antiquities* (13.230–14.126) and *War* (1.55–200) alongside several narratives from Diodorus of Sicily's *Bibliotheca Historia*,

[1] Berlin and Kosmin 2021:399–401.

Judea under Greek and Roman Rule. David A. deSilva, Oxford University Press.
© Oxford University Press 2024. DOI: 10.1093/oso/9780190263249.003.0004

the *Psalms of Solomon* (especially 2, 8, and 17), and several cryptic references in the Dead Sea Scrolls. Archaeological work throughout the territory provides particularly helpful supplements, correctives, and checks on the literary sources.

John Hyrcanus (134–104 BCE)

The smooth transfer of power from Simon to John Hyrcanus I appears to have been the first truly dynastic step in the consolidation of power by "the family through which deliverance was being given to Israel" (1 Macc 5:62).[2] Nothing is said either of resistance nor of a process of formal confirmation, suggesting that the majority of the Judeans had already accepted the notion of a family dynasty.

Hyrcanus led his forces against Ptolemy ben-Abubus and besieged him in the fortress of Dok, where Ptolemy had murdered Hyrcanus's father, Simon, and held his mother and two of his brothers. He had to raise the siege without achieving his objective, however. Josephus attributes this to the coming of the sabbatical year, but this was a year for the *land* to rest (and for debts to be forgiven), not a year for complete idleness (contra *Ant.* 13.234). Freed from the siege, Ptolemy killed Hyrcanus's mother and brothers before escaping himself to the city of Philadelphia, a Greek city east of the Jordan.

Antiochus VII Euergetes (ruled 139–129 BCE), nicknamed "Sidetes" because of his connection with the city of Side on the southwestern coast of what is now Türkiye, remained intent on reasserting Seleucid hegemony over Judea. He invaded Judea very shortly after Simon's death and Hyrcanus's succession. Indeed, this may have been the more substantial reason that Hyrcanus abandoned the siege of the fortress of Dok, allowing his family's murderer to escape.[3] Sidetes quickly gained the upper hand and besieged Hyrcanus in Jerusalem for a full year. The round stones found outside Jerusalem's first wall (now lying inside

---

[2] Geiger 2002:2. The regnal dates for John Hyrcanus and his successors could be pushed back by a year if Josephus or his sources were dating the beginning of the Seleucid era to 312 BCE rather than 311 BCE. Atkinson (2016:105–106) favors the earlier dating.

[3] Atkinson 2016:55.

Herod's later citadel) might have been deposited there by Sidetes's catapults.[4]

Josephus relates that, in the eleventh month of the siege, Hyrcanus petitioned Sidetes for a seven-day truce to allow the inhabitants of Jerusalem to celebrate the Festival of Tabernacles—a petition Sidetes granted, even providing animals and incense for the sacrifices. Perhaps on the strength of this magnanimous gesture, Sidetes and Hyrcanus eventually came to terms. Sidetes also faced Parthian encroachment into the eastern territories of the Seleucid empire and may have felt the need to settle matters quickly but acceptably in Judea to be free to look after Seleucid interests elsewhere. Hyrcanus offered tribute for Joppa and Gezer, the cities that Sidetes had accused Simon of annexing unjustly, rather than relinquishing them. He also pledged military support for Sidetes's campaigns and, rather than admit a fresh Seleucid garrison into Jerusalem, provided Sidetes with hostages from among the Judean elite as an alternative guarantee of good behavior. Sidetes also tore down some part of Jerusalem's fortifications as a parting symbol of the reassertion of Seleucid hegemony over Judea (Josephus, *Ant.* 13.245–247; Diodorus, *Bibl. Hist.* 34–35.1.1, 5).[5] This renewed submission is also evident in the minting of coins bearing the legend "of King Antiochus Euergetes" (rather than bearing Hyrcanus's name) in Jerusalem itself in 131–129 BCE.

Hyrcanus lent his military support to Sidetes's campaign in the east that ended in the death of Sidetes along with that of three hundred thousand of his soldiers deep in Parthian territory in 129 BCE (Diodorus Siculus, *Bibl. Hist.* 37.17.1). Hyrcanus and his forces were spared the fate of the king's principal force, possibly due to their lagging some distance behind to observe the Festival of Sukkoth (Josephus, *Ant.* 13.250–252). The defeat further diminished the resources of the Seleucid empire. The Parthians released Demetrius II to recover the Seleucid throne, now as an ally if not also as a vassal. Demetrius II launched campaigns against Egypt, the importance of which for Judea lies chiefly in the fact that it continued to subject the coastal plains to

---

[4] Berlin 1997:30.
[5] In Stern, ed. 1976b:181–183.

years of armies moving and fighting through the territory and further weakened both the Seleucid and Ptolemaic kingdoms. Rival claimants to the Seleucid throne continued to abound. With the backing of Ptolemy VIII, a pretender named Alexander II Zebinas, ostensibly a son of Alexander Balas, rose up against Demetrius II, occupying his attention from 128 to 123 BCE. This prevented Demetrius from pursuing any aggressive expansion or attempting to reassert Seleucid control in Judea. Further rivalries within the Seleucid line would occupy their attention through the end of Hyrcanus's reign and into the decades thereafter. Hyrcanus thus had the room he needed, during the latter half of his long rule, to pursue a program of substantial expansion of Hasmonean territory.[6]

Hyrcanus undoubtedly levied taxes on his subjects as the Seleucids and Ptolemies had done before him. This would have been essential to cover the costs of fielding a military force, funding campaigns of expansion, maintaining and improving fortifications along the borders, other necessary building and infrastructure projects, and his own enjoyment of the fruits of rule (seen dramatically in the construction of the palace complex near Jericho). Hyrcanus would have also received substantial funds from the produce of the "royal lands" that had fallen under the purview of his father, Simon—the vast tracts of arable land in and around the Jezreel Valley as well as the lucrative, specialty crops of Jericho and En Gedi. At the same time, there is every indication that the opportunity for wealth increased for large segments of his subjects, from the acquisition of new lands for settlers and veterans to the development of a maritime export economy thanks to Simon's seizure of several seaports. Despite the access to Mediterranean trade, however, the majority of Judea's residents continued to use locally produced wares, suggesting a policy of economic independence, if not isolationism, where imports were concerned. Of course, this was also a manifestation in the routine life of the household of the Judeans' desire to preserve their distinctive cultural and religious identity.[7] The number of

---

[6] The shrinkage of Seleucid control in Coele-Syria is reflected also in shifts in coin types struck in the cities of the coastal plain. The discontinuance of Seleucid mintings in favor of local civic coin types shows Tyre to have become "independent in 125 BCE, Sidon in 111 BCE, Akko-Ptolemais in 107/106 BCE, and Ashkelon in 104 BCE" (Berlin 1997:26).

[7] Berlin 1997:29–30.

settlements in Judea doubled between the Persian period and the end of the Hasmonean period, another sign of increased opportunity and prosperity (or, at least, reliable subsistence) for its population.[8]

Jerusalem grew significantly under Hasmonean rule. Residential neighborhoods had already expanded into the area west of the Temple enclosure—the area of the Tyropoeon Valley and western hill that would come to be known as the Upper City.[9] The city's wall had already been expanded to include the whole of the southeastern hill of the City of David and the southwestern hill of Mount Zion under Jonathan and may have come to embrace more of the western area across the Tyropoeon Valley during Hyrcanus's reign.[10] Jerusalem's elite show signs of enjoying significant wealth, seen for example in the emergence of monumental and expensive tombs such as "Jason's Tomb" west of the city and the tombs of the Kidron Valley (e.g., the Tomb of the Bene Hezir and the so-called Absalom's Pillar). The Hellenistic style of these monuments, and indeed the ethos that conduces to the building of such tomb monuments in the first place, remains a visible testimony to the ongoing Hellenization of the Jerusalem elite under the Hasmoneans.[11] Domestic architecture among the more well-to-do began to reflect Hellenistic patterns of rooms built around a central, interior courtyard, including a dedicated *triclinium* or dining room. Many of these also have bathing facilities as well as ritual immersion pools. It is also in these homes that one is likely to find delicate imported table ware alongside local Judean wares and stone vessels for rites of purification.[12] While not abandoning their religious interests with regard to purity, the owners exhibited a decidedly greater cultural openness, even imitation of non-Jewish space and practices. Small industry, however, continued to occur within domestic structures even of the wealthy, as discoveries of oil presses, pottery kilns, dyeing facilities, and the like attest.[13] Hyrcanus also renovated the old Ptolemaic fortress at the northwestern corner of the Temple, the Baris, which would

[8] Grabbe 2020:69.
[9] Halpern-Zylberstein 1989:10.
[10] Galor and Bloedhorn 2013:69.
[11] Halpern-Zylberstein 1989:21–23; Rajak 1994:298.
[12] See Galor and Bloedhorn 2013:88–97.
[13] Halpern-Zylberstein 1989:14.

also serve as the residence of the next generation of Hasmoneans until a new Hasmonean palace was built west of the Temple, across the Tyropoeon Valley.[14]

Coin finds suggest that Judeans began settling Western Galilee and Gaulanitis (the Golan) at least by the time of Hyrcanus's rule.[15] Hyrcanus's own principal energies toward expansion, however, were directed to Judea's south and west. He first annexed Idumea around the year 112 BCE. Josephus (*Ant.* 13.257–258) and Ptolemy the Historian speak of Hyrcanus's "conquest" of Idumea, asserting that the Idumeans were forced to accept circumcision and assimilate to Jewish identity and practice as the price of remaining in their land.[16] There are several reasons, however, to believe that their annexation and assimilation proceeded more consensually than these writers suggest (as in Strabo, *Geog.* 16.2.34). While there is evidence for the destruction of the principal strongholds of Maresha and perhaps Adora at this time,[17] destruction layers are otherwise lacking.[18] Moreover, forced conversion tends not to last, but Idumea produced reliable allies for the Hasmonean dynasty (most notably Antipas, his son Antipater, and his grandson Herod "the Great") and Idumeans show themselves to be every bit as invested in the fate of Jerusalem and its temple as Judeans during the First Jewish Revolt.[19]

Hyrcanus focused next on conquering those districts of the region of Samaritis that had not already been annexed by his father, Simon (Josephus, *Ant.* 13.254–256; 13.275–283). This was desirable territory with its strategic location adjacent to the coastal plains and its fertile land. Hyrcanus tasked his two eldest sons, Aristobulus (who was to succeed him) and Antigonus, with the siege of the Greek city of Samaria, which they successfully prosecuted. In the process, they

---

[14] Galor and Bloedhorn 2013:75–76.

[15] See Syon 2021 on the dispersal in this region of coins of Antiochus VII minted in Jerusalem under Hyrcanus prior to 128 BCE and coins of Hyrcanus I at Gamla.

[16] Stern, ed. 1976b:355–356.

[17] Berlin 1997:31.

[18] Atkinson 2016:68–69.

[19] Kasher 1988:46–78; Richardson 1996:55. Alexander Jannaeus will appoint Antipas to the important post of governor of Idumea, a position that Antipas's son Antipater would later occupy under Hyrcanus II. Hyrcanus II was also willing to marry an Idumean wife and to give his own granddaughter, Mariamne, to Herod, an Idumean.

defeated a force sent by Antiochus IX Cyzenicus in response to the Samarians' petition for help. Cyzenicus, however, was invested in his own attempts to secure the throne of the dwindling Seleucid empire and therefore unable to lend his full strength—again to the advantage of the Hasmoneans. Hyrcanus conquered Shechem and destroyed the temple on Mt. Gerizim. The rationale for the latter is probably to be found in the fact that Hyrcanus's own power was anchored in his occupation of the office of high priest and his final authority over the Jerusalem Temple. Allowing an alternative temple with an alternative priesthood to continue to operate would not serve to unite Samaritis to Judea.[20] However, one can hardly imagine an action that would be more likely to nurture resentment and enmity rather than unification. The annexation of Samaritis was completed between 111 and 107 BCE. During this time, Hyrcanus also conquered and annexed the Greek city of Scythopolis (Beit Shean), though he sought to destroy only its pagan religious sites and paraphernalia.[21] He was also able to make an incursion east of the Jordan to annex Madaba in the region of Moab.

The activity of Simon, Hyrcanus, and Hyrcanus's heirs suggests a larger Hasmonean program of reclaiming Israel's ancestral territory *and* making its inhabitants Jewish, by either expelling or assimilating Gentile residents, though the latter goal seems to have been applied selectively and incompletely.[22] Indeed, they appear to have been engaged in building an empire of their own even as the Gentile empires around them began to recede. It is perhaps in this context of empire building—of creating a kingdom that could compete with and establish itself alongside the surrounding Hellenistic kingdoms—that we should understand Hyrcanus's significant investment of resources in the palace complex he constructed in the oasis of Jericho. This complex included a massive main house, a heated bath, a large garden area

---

[20] Bourgel 2016.

[21] Dąbrowa 2010:74. Archaeological evidence has provided important correctives to Josephus's narrative with regard to Hyrcanus's campaigns of expansion, which Josephus dates much earlier in his reign. Shifting patterns in the presence or absence of particular coins and amphoras of Rhodian wine (datable by the stamps of the particular officials that they bear) make it clear that Hyrcanus was occupied with expansion into these areas between 113 and 107 BCE. See Berlin 1997:31; Barag 1992–1993; Magen 2008:98; 2009:193; Finkielsztejn 2021.

[22] Dąbrowa 2010:77.

Figure 3.1 A mikveh from the twin palaces of Hyrcanus II and Aristobulus II at Tulul Abu el-Alayiq, near Jericho.

with two swimming pools, and multiple small, stepped pools for the dissipation of ritual pollution (*mikvaoth*). The "purpose-built ritual immersion pool" appears to be an early Hasmonean invention, a means both of preserving their own ritual purity as the high priestly family governing the nation and of *displaying* their ability and commitment to do so through architectural means (see Figure 3.1).[23] In the juxtaposition of palace and immersion pool we catch a glimpse of two impulses that characterize the rulers of the Hasmonean dynasty—a desire to imitate neighboring Hellenistic kings' practices, architecture, and symbols (e.g., on coinage) to display their successful establishment of a kingdom of their own, coupled with a commitment to preserve the distinctive values, practices, and culture of their Judean heritage.[24]

[23] See Fatkin 2019.
[24] See, further, Regev 2017.

Hyrcanus's lavish project (and Hasmonean rule in general) would provoke strong criticism from the members of the Qumran community—whose spartan facilities and lifestyle could not contrast more markedly with the luxuries of the Hasmonean palaces. One text found near Qumran (4QTestimonia/4Q175) applies the curse laid upon anyone who would rebuild Jericho found in Joshua 6:26, namely that it would be done at the cost of his firstborn and his youngest son, to John Hyrcanus's building of the Hasmonean palace complex at Jericho. For this critic, the untimely deaths of his sons Antigonus and Aristobulus, while not precisely Hyrcanus's oldest and youngest, demonstrated that the Hasmoneans were unfit to rule the nation.[25] The point of recalling the curse is specifically to express hostility toward the dynasts: Hyrcanus did not, after all, rebuild Jericho, but rather created a palace complex a mile and a half from the ancient city site.

Hyrcanus faced criticism from other fronts as well toward the end of his reign. On one occasion, a Pharisee named Eleazar challenged Hyrcanus's fitness to serve as high priest since his mother was alleged to have been a captive during the period of Antiochus IV's repression and, thus, possibly subjected to rape. Hyrcanus was infuriated and a Sadducean companion named Jonathan told him to wait and see how Eleazar's Pharisaic colleagues would discipline him. If they judged him worthy of death, they were loyal; if they proposed a lighter punishment, they shared his position. They did, in fact, recommend flogging and, thus, Hyrcanus was alienated from the Pharisees and took the Sadducees into his confidence for the remainder of his life. The practical consequence of this is that Sadducean opinions concerning purity, pollution, and the administration of the cultic life of the temple informed everyday practice.

It bears remembering that, in a state centered upon a single temple and the administration of its rites, whose national security was believed to depend upon proceeding faithfully in line with the covenant with Judea's God, one cannot separate politics from piety. Hence, the vistas that the historical record opens up into the Pharisees, the Sadducees, their rivalries, their differing positions concerning the authority of

---

[25] See also 4Q379. Both are discussed in Eshel 2008:63–89.

particular bodies of tradition, and their contradictory visions for the performance of particular rites or the observance of the purity codes so vital to the efficacy of the cult and its personnel show us people whose interests cannot, in this period at least, be parsed into the categories of "politics" over against "religion." They are necessarily both.

Hyrcanus's success in expansion and the increased wealth and prestige this brought to the nation as a whole no doubt gave him a degree of legitimacy in the eyes of many, if not most, of his subjects. It is interesting to note several ways in which he may have fostered this legitimacy on more ideological grounds as well. The coins minted by Hyrcanus employed paleo-Hebrew script, possibly as a symbol of the revival of the Israelite monarchy of old.[26] It seems likely that 1 Maccabees was written during his rule and perhaps at his direction. The apparent authenticity of many of the documents and pieces of correspondence included in both 1 Maccabees and 2 Maccabees (and, necessarily, the original five-volume history by Jason of Cyrene of which 2 Maccabees is an abridgment) suggests that both authors enjoyed access to official archives and, thus, perhaps government sponsorship. An overarching goal of 1 Maccabees, of course, is to recall the achievements of the generation of Hasmoneans prior to Hyrcanus's own—and the incalculable debt of gratitude owed the Hasmonean house by the Judean people.[27] The spread of the observance of the festival that would become known as Hanukkah, called the "Feast of Dedication" in John 10:22, would keep the memory of national indebtedness to the family of Judas Maccabaeus alive, as well as the memory of the eventual national independence that his brothers and nephew finally achieved. Finally, Hyrcanus's renewal of diplomatic ties with Rome displays an interest in legitimating his rule by *acting* as legitimate and independent rulers do—for example, making treaties and alliances with foreign powers (as his father and uncles had done). Hyrcanus thus appears to have bequeathed to his successors a firm foundation upon which to base their own power and advance their own programs.

[26] Magness 2012:105.
[27] deSilva 2018:268–284.

Judah Aristobulus (104–103 BCE)

Hyrcanus may have intended for his wife to succeed to his civil authority while his eldest son, Judah Aristobulus, served as high priest. Whatever Hyrcanus's wishes might have been, Josephus tells the horrific tale of Aristobulus imprisoning his mother and his three youngest brothers—even causing his mother to die of starvation in her confinement. He allowed only his next youngest brother, Antigonus, freedom and some degree of partnership in his rule as a military commander. Josephus claims Aristobulus to have assumed the title "king" (*Ant.* 13.301), though the legend on his coins reads simply: "Judah the High Priest and the Assembly of the Judeans." Even if Josephus is wrong on this point, the coinage of Aristobulus's successor, Alexander Jannaeus, shows him taking the title of "king" in addition to "high priest" (cf. Strabo *Geog.* 16.2.40). At or near this point, then, the Hasmoneans could be accused of usurping not only the high priesthood (traditionally belonging to the priestly clan of Zadok) but also the kingship (belonging to David's line).

During his short reign, Aristobulus was able to expand his realm further into Upper Galilee and the Golan. The archaeological evidence—or the lack thereof—suggests that Galilee had been largely abandoned between the Assyrian invasion (attested by destruction layers in many sites) and the Persian and Hellenistic periods.[28] Gush Halav (Gischala) is one of the rare sites that shows ongoing occupation throughout the First and Second Temple periods.[29] The region was sparsely resettled during the Persian and Hellenistic periods by the surrounding people groups, especially Phoenicia, as well as military colonists planted there by the Hellenistic monarchs. The presence of pagan artifacts in the pre-Hasmonean strata of Galilean sites provides evidence of important ethnic-cultural shifts in this region as a result first of the destabilization of Seleucid control and then of Hasmonean expansion.[30]

Josephus credits Aristobulus with annexing Iturea and requiring any Itureans who wished to remain in the territory to accept

[28] Aviam 1993:453; Reed 2000:33 vs. Horsley 1996:22–23.
[29] Reed 2000:33.
[30] Aviam 2004:7–14.

circumcision and adopt the Jewish way of life. The Itureans, how-ever, chiefly inhabited territory to the north of Galilee—further north than any Hasmonean or even Herodian extended his reach. There is also a lack of clear evidence of extensive Iturean settlement in Galilee proper,[31] though the possibility exists that they exerted some form of control over some portion of the land (e.g., as extended farmlands for the benefit of their actual territory), which Aristobulus, or more likely Antigonus on his behalf, loosened from their grasp. This would align with the statement by Strabo (as quoted in Josephus, *Ant.* 13.319) that Aristobulus won control over "a portion of the Iturean nation."

Jewish settlements existed by this time in Capernaum, Hammath Tiberias, Arbel, Jotapata, Nazareth, Sepphoris, and Gamala (the latter two having a history of prior settlement—Sepphoris in the Persian and Gamala in the Seleucid periods).[32] The surge of Hasmonean coinage in the region around this time and the dwindling presence of local mintings from the coastal cities show that Galilee's political and ec-onomic focus had shifted decisively toward Jerusalem and favor the view that Galilee was populated largely by the descendants of Judean settlers by the start of the Roman period. This would both account for the continuity in material culture and argue for a greater homogeneity of religious thought throughout the regions of Galilee and Judea.[33]

According to Josephus, Antigonus fell victim to a court intrigue and Aristobulus himself died of an unspecified illness, whether or not brought on by remorse for matricide and fratricide, after only a year's rule (*Ant.* 13.318).

Alexander Jannaeus (103–76 BCE)

Upon Aristobulus's death, his widow, Salome Alexandra, released his remaining three brothers from their confinement. She married Alexander Jannaeus, the eldest of these, making him king and high priest (Josephus, *Ant.* 13.320). While this second marriage could be

---

[31] Berlin 1997:37.
[32] Reed 2000:40.
[33] Regional dialect may have been another matter, of course (see Matt 26:73).

understood as an example of the ancient Israelite practice of levirate marriage (although Alexander's sons would never be said to continue, in any way, the line of Aristobulus), it seems more appropriate to understand it in terms of the practice of the neighboring Hellenistic kingdoms, which frequently involved marrying one's predecessor's wife as a means of establishing legitimate succession.[34] Jannaeus executed one of his surviving brothers after an unsuccessful coup; the last brother receded into a discrete, private life (Josephus, *Ant.* 13.323; 14.71). The story of Aristobulus I and his four brothers differs remarkably from that of Judas Maccabeus and his own just two generations before. Coins minted by Jannaeus with inscriptions in Greek and Hebrew bear clear witness to his use of the title "king" as well as "high priest,"[35] an important and controversial step in defining Hasmonean rule. There is evidence, however, that he later drew back from the practice, reissuing coins featuring only the title of "high priest," perhaps in response to resistance to his assumption of the title "king."[36]

Alexander also pursued a policy of aggressive expansion, though he appears to have suffered more serious setbacks than his father and grandfather. His first attempt was a disaster. With rival claimants to the Seleucid throne engaged in fresh civil wars, Alexander sought to capture the coastal city of Ptolemais (modern Acre, twelve miles north of Mount Carmel), the hinterlands of which were a fertile bounty. He had entered, however, into territory of interest to the feuding Ptolemies and was repelled by Ptolemy IX Lathyrus, whose realm had been limited to Cyprus by his mother, Cleopatra III of Egypt. Lathyrus's armies swept through Galilee and Judea, jeopardizing much that Alexander's predecessors had gained and costing the lives of thousands of Alexander's soldiers. Only the military intervention of Lathyrus's estranged mother caused him to retreat from Jannaeus's

---

[34] Geiger 2002:8, 11 (though he also views it as an example of levirate marriage). Atkinson (2016:85–86) proposes that the wife of Aristobulus (referred to as Salina Alexandra in some mss. of Josephus) was not the same person as the wife of Alexander Jannaeus (referred to as Salome Alexandra), but his is the minority view (contrast Dąbrowa 2010:86; Geiger 2002; Grabbe 2020:419–420).

[35] Berlin 1997:37.

[36] Atkinson 2016:103.

territory.[37] Whether by virtue of Jannaeus's gifts and supplication or out of fear of overstepping the boundaries set for the Ptolemies by Rome, Cleopatra III allowed Jannaeus to retain his position and his realm its sovereignty.[38]

Alexander was undeterred by this inauspicious beginning and, indeed, followed it up with some important successes. By 95 BCE, he extended Judea's control over all the coastal cities from Gaza to Dor. He also successfully expanded into the Transjordan area east of Galilee, establishing control over several of the "Decapolis" cities: Gadara, Hippos, Dium, Pella, and Gerasa. Notably, his program did not include the expulsion or conversion of the Gentile inhabitants, but merely their submission. He constructed or renovated several fortresses, including Dok, Hyrcania, Alexandrium, Machaerus, and Masada. The fortress-cities of Beth-Zur, Gezer, or Marisa appear to have fallen out of use, to judge from the absence of coin finds from the period, which is in keeping with the historical record. Alexander had significantly pushed the boundaries of his territory beyond these southern and western frontier forts, rendering their ongoing occupation unnecessary.[39] Alexander had successfully expanded the territory of the Hasmonean kingdom to the dimensions once attributed to the empire of Solomon. His ambition led him into further overreaching, however. His incursions into Arab and Nabataean territory led to a military disaster and further opposition in Jerusalem among a population increasingly unwilling to bear the costs of his military aspirations—let alone tolerate defeat in the same.

Opposition against Alexander had already erupted in Jerusalem on an earlier occasion. Josephus recounts that demonstrations against him broke out one year while he was officiating at the Festival of Tabernacles. Some of the crowd that had gathered in the temple court began to pelt Alexander with their citrons and to denounce him as unfit to hold the office of high priest since his genealogy was open to question (recalling the allegation made a generation before concerning

[37] Josephus, *Ant.* 13.324–355. These events also appear to be reflected in *Pesher on Isaiah A* (4Q161 = 4QpIsaᵃ; so Eshel 2008:95–100).

[38] Atkinson 2016:115–116.

[39] Halpern-Zylberstein 1989:8.

John Hyrcanus's mother). Was this truly the heart of their concern? Or was it a pretext that hid other causes for discontent with Alexander's—or even *Hasmonean*—rule?[40] Whatever the truth on that occasion, Alexander responded by setting his mercenary forces upon the crowd to suppress the dissent, which they did vigorously. Josephus reports a death toll in the thousands (*Ant.* 13.372–373). Granted that Josephus tended to exaggerate his figures significantly, Alexander nevertheless showed himself to be the sort of ruler who would respond to opposition out of all proportion to the offense.

More serious opposition arose in the year 89/88 BCE after Alexander's unsuccessful raid on Arabia, resulting in a civil war that would last six years.[41] His rule had proven so intolerable that a faction in Judea petitioned the Seleucid king Demetrius III to intervene. These opponents are often identified as Pharisees, but the numbers suggest a coalition of multiple disaffected groups (perhaps led by Pharisees).[42] It is easy to imagine Demetrius welcoming the opportunity to reassert Seleucid control over Judea and its environs. Judea had come a long way from relying on the Hasmoneans to *deliver* them from the Seleucids! Joining forces with the Judean rebels, Demetrius quickly put Alexander on his heels and would have succeeded in unseating him, but for two developments. First, according to Josephus, large numbers of the rebels suddenly defected to help Alexander when the latter was down, whether because they felt a renewed sympathy for him or because they came to realize the danger of a victory by Demetrius for Judean independence. Second, and perhaps more importantly, Demetrius also faced an attempted—and, eventually, successful—coup by his brother, Philip, in the Syrian heartland.[43] Once Demetrius withdrew, Alexander pursued, besieged, and captured the Judeans who continued to resist him. In an act of cruelty that left its mark even

---

[40] Grabbe 2021:421.

[41] Schäfer 2003:75.

[42] Grabbe 2021:514. *Pesher Nahum* speaks of Alexander's victims as the "seekers after smooth things," where "smooth things" (*halaqoth*) suggests a pun on the *halakoth*, or legal rulings, that scribes and experts in the Torah would seek to derive from existing laws of the Torah to cover circumstances not explicitly addressed by the Torah. These experts are most often identified with the Pharisees, who would thus be regarded as far too lenient by the members of the Qumran sect.

[43] Atkinson 2018:78.

upon the sectarian writings of the Qumran community, Alexander crucified or impaled eight hundred of his enemies and slaughtered their wives and children before their eyes (Josephus, *Ant.* 13.379–380; *War* 1.96–97, 113; *4Q169* [*p. Nah.*] 1.6–7).[44] Displaying the corpse of an executed victim until sunset was considered permissible (Deut 21:22–23), but not crucifying living people—something previously unknown in Israel, according to the *Commentary on Nahum* (4Q169).

This brutal innovation appears to have achieved its desired effect: we hear no more of opposition to Alexander during his reign. Rather, the disaffected appear to have quit the boundaries of his kingdom until after his death. This freed Alexander to continue his campaigns of expansion in the Transjordan, where he finally died of disease and exhaustion.

Salome Alexandra (76–67 BCE)

Alexander entrusted the reins of his kingdom to his widow and initial sponsor, Salome Alexandra, which might suggest that she was involved to some extent in the responsibilities of government during his reign as well. Their elder son, John Hyrcanus II, acceded to the high priesthood immediately, while their younger son, Judah Aristobulus II, reluctantly remained in the wings. Nevertheless, Salome ordered the construction of twin palaces for her two sons beside the new palace that Alexander had built atop his father's in Jericho. The careful architectural parallelism of these nearly symmetrical palaces shows the lengths to which she went to assure her younger son of his equal stature in all matters of his private enjoyment of the perquisites of royalty.

According to Josephus, Salome reconciled the dynasty with the Pharisees on her deceased husband's advice, due to their popular influence. They used their newfound position to (re-)establish their traditions concerning the application of the Torah as the official practice in the Temple and beyond. They also used their restored influence and power to seek revenge against those who, it was alleged, embittered Jannaeus against them and other revolutionaries, resulting

---

[44] On 4Q169, see Eshel 2008:117–131.

in the brutal executions of the eight hundred families. These targets of the Pharisees' ire, whom Alexandra regarded also as loyal subjects deserving some measure of protection and on whose behalf Aristobulus II advocated forcefully, were removed from harm's way in Jerusalem and entrusted with the border fortresses apart from Hyrcania, Machaerus, and Alexandreion (Josephus, *Ant.* 13.405–415; *War* 1.111–114).[45] They would become the backbone of Aristobulus II's party in his contest with Hycanus II, who remained aligned with the Pharisees.[46]

Salome was able to maintain the boundaries of the kingdom established by her husband. She also built up the standing army and the mercenary contingents,[47] but she was reticent to employ them, preferring bloodless diplomacy to the uncertain and costly outcomes of war. This is evident in her use of diplomacy when faced with the prospect of the invasion of her territory by Tigranes of Armenia, who by 72 BCE had expanded as far south as Damascus as Seleucid power receded further. Diplomacy proved the wise strategy: Roman actions against Armenia in 69 BCE, part of the Roman Republic's plan for the reorganization of the east into a reliable and more stable buffer between its empire and that of the Parthians, fully occupied Tigranes and eliminated any further threat.

As Salome's health declined, she shared the powers of regency with Hyrcanus II, who was to succeed her as king while retaining the office of high priest. Aristobulus II, the younger son, had other plans. Before Salome died in 67 BCE, she witnessed him organizing a coup with the cooperation of his supporters, particularly those entrusted with the border fortresses. The soldiers garrisoned in these fortresses—and the weapons and money deposited in each that allowed him to hire and arm many more—provided him with superior military strength and an adequate war chest. With the eruption of civil war between the rival claimants to the throne, the Hasmonean dynasty had completed its journey toward becoming a true Hellenistic kingdom.

[45] Grabbe 2021:515.

[46] Atkinson 2016:136–137; Dąbrowa 2010:93–94. A core of Aristobulus's supporters are likely to have been aligned with the Sadducean party (Rajak 1994:307; Schaper 1999:415).

[47] Josephus, *War* 1.112; *Ant.* 13.409; Dąbrowa 2010:96.

Excursus: Partisan and Sectarian Judaism

Josephus first mentions the famous triad of Pharisees, Sadducees, and Essenes in connection with his treatment of Jonathan's high priesthood and asserts that they were already in existence in his time, though our sources give no sure reports concerning how any one of these parties originated (*Ant.* 13.171–173). The chaos surrounding the high priesthood and temple during the period between 175 and 152 BCE certainly provided fertile soil for widespread discontent and partisan agendas for resolving the perceived problems. Regaining independence, or at least the hope for independence, could also be considered an impetus to partisanship: once matters were back in Judean hands, there was the real possibility for influencing practice in the Temple and the land.[48] All three appear to have their origins either in the priestly class or the circles of the scribes, a literate, retainer class of growing importance throughout the Hellenistic and Hasmonean periods.[49]

Despite the attention always given to these groups in treatments of the Second Temple period, it is important to remember that the majority of Jews did not identify with any of these parties. Josephus, who is rarely accused of *underestimating* his figures, would put membership in both the Pharisaic and Essene movements at about six thousand and four thousand members, respectively, at given points (Josephus, *Ant.* 17.42; 18.21; cf. also Philo, *Quod omnis* 75). One should also never lose sight of the far larger areas of overlap in terms of convictions and practice shared by all, or almost all Jews, including those who further identify themselves with one or another partisan or sectarian group within Judaism.

The Sadducees and Pharisees are more properly thought of as partisan groups than as religious "sects." Both groups had an agenda for the nation as a whole, including how the nation's central institution— the temple—and its rites should be administered, and sought to attain the political influence required to advance that agenda. When the identity, ethos, and even convictions about the security of the nation are bound up with the keeping of a covenant with the nation's God,

---

[48] Baumgarten 1997:191–192.
[49] Schaper 1999:403; Grabbe 2020:166–167.

influencing how that covenant is put into practice is as much a political as a religious agenda.

Pharisees

The name "Pharisees" is an anglicization, by way of the Greek, of the Hebrew *perushim*, "separate ones."[50] The early Christian Gospels show Pharisees to be concerned about ritual purity, particularly around meals (and, therefore, with whom one eats), tithing, and careful observance of the Sabbath.[51] This profile aligns with traditions associated throughout the Mishnah with pre-70 CE figures, the majority of which concern ritual purity, proper tithing (particularly assuring that what is available to be consumed has been properly tithed and properly processed), and proper observance of Sabbaths and festivals.[52] These were, of course, shared concerns among many Second Temple period Jews. What set the Pharisees apart—as also the Essenes, for whom these were also lively concerns—was the degree to which these concerns were put into action, as the Pharisees sought to extend Levitical levels of purity appropriate for the Temple to laypersons and ordinary life far outside Jerusalem.[53] They could quite fairly be described as concerned with spreading holiness throughout the land. This required them, however, to restrict their table fellowship to fellow Jews who were similarly committed to maintaining these higher standards with regard to ritual purity and tithing.[54] Thus, they formed "associations" (*haburoth*) and spoke of their "associates" (*haberim*). For all this, however, they were not a separatist group (like the community at Qumran or the Essenes as a whole), but rather actively sought to win people over to their way of walking in the covenant (hence proselytizing among other Jews; cf. Matt 23:15).

---

[50] Saldarini 2001:220–225.
[51] See, e.g., Mark 2:15–28; 3:1–6; 7:1–13; Green 2007:415; Grabbe 2020:157.
[52] Neusner 2007:299–302, 309.
[53] On the concepts of purity and pollution and related ritual practices in the Second Temple Period, see deSilva 2022:272–312.
[54] Schiffman 1994:76; Rajak 1994:304.

The ancient sources agree that Pharisees ascribed a high degree of authority to the halakhic decisions passed down from their forebears, which may provide the precursor to the "oral law" of rabbinic Judaism.[55] They believed in postmortem judgment, resurrection, and the enjoyment of rewards for a life faithfully lived or endurance of punishment for a life lived in disregard for God and God's law. They assigned responsibility for events and their consequences both to God's providence and human choice.

Early Christian writers give the impression that the Pharisees were unduly stringent in their rulings concerning how to walk in alignment with the Torah (Matt 23:4; Acts 26:5). They were indeed interested in determining how to "walk" in alignment with the Law of Moses in new circumstances, hence the relationship between the Hebrew verb "to walk" (*halak*) and the term for the "rulings" that Pharisees (and other groups) derived from Scripture based on their principles of interpretation (*halakhoth*). Essenes, however, took the Pharisees to task for being too *lax* in their application of the Torah. Several writings from Qumran or the larger Essene movement call the Pharisees "the seekers after smooth things," where the word for "smooth things" (*halaqoth*) is a derogatory pun on "legal rulings" (*halakhoth*).[56] For example, Pharisees permitted "taking two wives during their lifetimes," which could be heard to permit polygamy but more practically permits divorce and remarriage, whereas the Essenes and Jesus did not (CD 4:21; 11QTemple 57:17–19; Matt 5:31–32). The prescriptions for purification in the Pentateuch typically called for a ritual bath and the passage of time, namely the arrival of evening, for purity to be restored (see, e.g., Lev 15:5–8, 10–11). According to the Pharisees, however, the immersion in and of itself restored sufficient purity. Such leniency won for them the sobriquet "seekers of smooth things," since this ruling sought to make life a good deal easier and purifications more practical for the demands of daily life.[57] The Pharisees of Herodian and Roman times appear to have become less interested in achieving political

---

[55] Schiffman 1994:77. See, e.g., Gal 1:14; Josephus, *Ant.* 13.297; Mark 7:1–13; Matt 15:3–9.

[56] 1QH 10:15, 32; 4QpNah 3–4 I 2, 7; CD 1:18. Schiffman 1994:78; 2010:328.

[57] See also Josephus, *Ant.* 13.298, on the Pharisees' greater leniency and reasonableness as a source for their popularity (Schaper 1999:412).

power, focusing instead on their own practice and on teaching their manner of living out the covenant in everyday life.[58]

Sadducees

No texts survive that can confidently be attributed to Sadducean authors, so that we must rely on the representations of Sadducees by outsiders who, in some cases, were hostile to Sadducees. Their name— *Tsedoqim*—suggests that they were themselves related to or supportive of the Zadokite high priestly line. Their origins as a group might well have predated the second century, but the events of the second century would have nurtured their formation as a specifically *partisan* group as they now found themselves having to contend for the influence that they once enjoyed as a given. They regained this influence under Hycanus I and lost it again under Salome and Hyrcanus II. Josephus and early Christian texts suggest that they regained their status in the transition to direct Roman rule in 6 CE as natural (elite) powerbrokers for the new administration.[59]

One gets the sense from Josephus that the Sadducees derived their influence as members of the elite courting the elite, whereas the Pharisees derived their influence from their popular reputation as expert interpreters—and careful adherents—of the covenant (Josephus, *Ant.* 13.298).[60] The Pharisees' popular influence may be substantiated by the archaeological record. The presence of stone vessels (including vessels of sufficient size for the immersion of other vessels) and ritual immersion pools suggests widespread concern for maintaining purity at a level beyond the requirements of the Torah itself.[61] Ritual immersion pools have also been found in close proximity to olive press and winepress facilities at twenty sites in Judea, as well as at Gamla, dating to the Second Temple period, suggesting a high level of interest in guaranteeing the ritual purity of the liquids produced by guaranteeing

---

[58] Neusner 1973; 2007:301.
[59] Schaper 1999:423. See Acts 4:1; 5:17.
[60] Mason 2009:373.
[61] Strange 2007:250–251.

the ritual purity of the workers producing the liquids.[62] This becomes evidence for the widespread, popular acceptance of a distinctive halakhic teaching of the Pharisees, namely that of *tevul yom*, since this principle alone would support the efficacy of a ritual purificatory immersion at the *beginning* of the workday.[63]

The literary sources also provide some indications as to the distinctive beliefs of the party as it existed in the first century CE: a rejection of belief in a resurrection from the dead or an afterlife, a rejection of a belief in angels (at least in regard to the extravagant developments of angelology that one witnesses in the literature of the Greek and Roman periods, such as Tobit and *1 Enoch*), and an affirmation of human choice and responsibility as the primary cause of events rather than fate or providence.[64] They regarded the Torah and, no doubt, the other written scriptures as authoritative and accorded no special authority to the rulings and interpretative traditions of earlier generations, a point of major difference with the Pharisees (Josephus, *Ant.* 13.297).[65]

Essenes

The name "Essene" might have been derived from the Hebrew *ḥasēn*, "pious ones," or possibly from a similar Aramaic word meaning "healers," as clearly was the case for the similar sect known as the Therapeutae in Greek-speaking Egypt.[66] Unlike the Pharisees and Sadducees, the Essenes have left a significant collection of firsthand literary witnesses to their beliefs, practices, worship, and way of life—if it is accepted that the sectarian texts found among the Dead Sea Scrolls are Essene documents. Though this remains a matter of debate, the many points of overlap between the evidence of the scrolls (written by insiders) and the descriptions of the movement by outsiders (Pliny the Elder, Philo, Josephus) suggest that the communities that variously regulated their life together by the *Damascus Document* (CD) and by

---

[62] Adler 2008:63–65.
[63] Adler 2008:69–71.
[64] Stemberger 1999:441. See Josephus, *War* 2.164–165; Mark 12:18; Acts 23:8.
[65] Stemberger 1999:436.
[66] Betz 1999:445–446.

the *Rule of the Community* (1QS), for example, were indeed Essene communities.[67]

There is a great deal of overlap in the practice envisioned by both rules, but they envision different kinds of communities. Most Essenes lived in communities scattered throughout the towns of Judea and Galilee, married, and raised families, engaging in sexual intercourse strictly for procreation rather than pleasure (Josephus, *War* 2.120–121, 160–161; CD VII.7–9; see *T. Iss.* 2.1–3). They lived simply, working the land and sharing their possessions (Philo, *Omn. Prob. Lib.* 76, 79). They appear to have continued to send offerings to the Temple, despite their criticisms concerning how the cult was being administered (Josephus, *Ant.* 18.19). Some Essene communities, such as the community that inhabited the site of Qumran, were more radical in their rejection of family life and of the Jerusalem Temple altogether, which their own bloodless offerings of righteousness and devotion to the covenant temporarily replaced (1QS VIII.8–12; IX.4–6). The community at Qumran, in particular, may have functioned as a kind of spiritual elite among the larger movement, aiming for "perfection of way" on behalf of the whole movement.[68] At any rate, the preservation of both rules in multiple copies among the Dead Sea Scrolls suggests that the two kinds of communities existed in a cooperative rather than antagonistic relationship.[69]

The early history of the sect remains shrouded in mystery. An earlier consensus held that the movement emerged as a consequence of the non-Zadokite Hasmonean family's takeover of the office of the high priesthood. The shadowy references to the figures of the "Teacher of Righteousness" and the "Wicked Priest" in a number of sectarian writings—and their mutual enmity—were

---

[67] Collins 2010:209; vs. Baumgarten 1997:1–2; Mason 2009:276–277. Ancient sources on Essenes and their various manifestations include Philo, *Quod Omn. Prob.* 75–91; *Apol.* 11; Josephus, *War* 2.119–161; *Ant.* 13:171–172; 18:11, 18–22; Pliny, *Natural History* 5.70–73; and, of course, the Dead Sea Scrolls.

[68] 1QS 8:14–16; Collins 2010:73, 78–79. Pliny the Elder, *Nat. Hist.* 5.73, locates a similarly isolated community beside the Dead Sea near Ein Gedi, the remains of which have been uncovered.

[69] Betz 1999:447; Collins 2010:2–6, 48–50, 122–156, 209; vs. Garcia Martinez and Barrera 1995:64–65, 77, 86–96; Boccaccini 1998:166, 178–185.

thought to fit into and support this scenario.[70] An emerging consensus, however, acknowledges that, where specific issues are named as the cause of criticism and separation, these issues revolve not around *who* is administering the temple cult, but *how* the temple cult is being administered and the specific regulations of the Law of Moses are being observed.[71] An important document in this regard is a letter that appears to have been written by a leading representative of a disenfranchised group to a person in highest authority over the Jerusalem temple who has been won over to the practice of a rival group.[72] Scholars have given this letter the name "Some Works of the Law" (4QMMT) on the basis of a recurring phrase in its contents. The positions that the writer advocates typically clash with positions that would later be identified as Pharisaic interpretations and practices. The writer's own positions align at several points with rulings that would later be attributed to Sadducees.[73] This does not mean that the writer would have self-identified as a Sadducee, "only that they shared a tradition of legal interpretation with the Sadducees."[74] The fact that several copies of this letter were found among the Dead Sea Scrolls demonstrates that its author was embraced by the Essene movement.

There were two moments in the Hasmonean period at which the leadership (potentially) shifted its allegiance and adherence to Pharisaic interpretation and practice. The first is the accession of Jonathan to the high priesthood. Onias III, Jason, and Alcimus had all been Zadokite high priests. By the time of John Hyrcanus I, however, the Pharisees enjoyed tremendous influence with the high priest, an influence that would come to an abrupt end later in his reign. Jonathan's accession, as the first incumbent of the Hasmonean high priestly line, presents an opportune time for a shift from Zadokite/Saducean to Pharisaic practices. The second, and frankly more certain, is the death of Alexander Jannaeus and the accession of John Hyrcanus II to the

---

[70] On the identification of Hyrcanus II as the "Wicked Priest" of Qumran literature, see Collins 2010:103–121; Atkinson 2018:114–122.

[71] Eshel 1996; Baumgarten 1997:33, 75–80; Collins 2010:8–9, 95–98.

[72] Schiffman 2010:117, 120; Collins 2010:20–21.

[73] Schiffman 1994:78; 2010:322.

[74] Collins 2010:45.

high priesthood under the regency of Salome Alexandra.[75] This was a moment at which significant influence, even power, returned to the Pharisaic sages after three or four decades of the Hasmonean high priest aligning himself with Sadducees and their practice. 4QMMT shows that, whichever of these events it refers to, it was a milestone in the life of the sect or, at least, in the life of one of its leaders, perhaps the figure remembered only as the "Teacher of Righteousness." The sect revered the Teacher of Righteousness as the inspired and authoritative interpreter of the Torah and the words of the prophets (1QpHab 7.4–5). In a manner that has parallels in the practice of the early Jesus movement, the Essenes applied prophecies of the Hebrew Bible to episodes in the life of the Teacher of Righteousness and the ongoing life of the sect, legitimating these as the working out of God's plan that had been announced long ago but hidden from the majority.

One particular point of dispute between the sect and the administrators of the Jerusalem temple concerned the calendar. The temple followed a lunar calendar of 354 days (with the addition of a thirteenth month essentially every third year); the sect believed that God's people were called to follow a solar calendar and to calculate the proper times for the annual festivals based on the greater, rather than the lesser, light, with the result that major religious festivals fell on different days among the Essenes vis-à-vis other Jews. They believed themselves, and not their fellow Israelites in the Temple, to be in sync thereby with the rhythms of worship in the heavenly sanctuary (and thus walking in truer obedience to the Law). This debate reveals, incidentally, the authoritative status of books like 1 Enoch and Jubilees for the sect (cited in CD 16.2–4; 4Q320–330; 1QS 10.1–6), as these prescribe a solar calendar.

The sect followed an admission process for new members that spanned two or three years. If, at the end of this period, they were deemed reliable and committed in regard to the sect's standards of covenant loyalty and ritual purity, they were admitted into full connection, which included participating in the common meal of the sect. Membership was sealed with an oath that included the promise of love for one's fellow Essenes and hatred for the wicked and a commitment to conceal the teachings of the sect from outsiders—an obvious explanation of the differences between the accounts of the Essenes in outside sources and what we find in the scrolls themselves.[76] They held all their property in common and were committed to simplicity in regard to possessions and lifestyle. They had a highly deterministic view of history and of individual destiny and, thus, whether a person would prove to be a member of God's elect people. At the same time, the individual member was challenged to demonstrate his or her place among the elect through obedience to the Law and "perfection of way," all the while acknowledging his or her utter dependence upon God's help and mercy.

Like many Jews, they believed in life beyond death and in postmortem rewards and punishments. But they were also a sect on high eschatological alert, awaiting the war between the sons of light and the sons of darkness, which would culminate in God's renewal of Israel and new ordering of the Temple in true holiness. In the meanwhile, they maintained critical distance from the corrupt ordering of the present. They regarded themselves as the community of "the new covenant," whose members kept the Law of Moses aright (CD 3:12–16; 8:22; see Jer 31:31). They studied the Law and its interpretation in shifts night and day, and it no doubt formed the principal subject at their communal meals. The strictness of the sect's observance of the Torah can be seen in its regulations for the Sabbath: "No man shall assist a beast to give birth on the Sabbath day. And if it should fall into a cistern or pit, he shall not lift it out on the Sabbath" (CD 11:11–17; contrast Matt 12:11–12). They even avoided defecating on the Sabbath, as this required the digging and filling in of a hole in the ground, hence work. While they maintained the distinction between priestly and lay castes among their members, they also extended priestly degrees of purity to all members of the sect to become "a kingdom of priests" before God (Exod 19:6), offering the spiritual sacrifices of worship, prayer, and perfect obedience, in part to make atonement for "Israel" (1QS 8:6; 9:4–6).[77]

---

[76] 1QS 1:9–10; 4:6; cf. also 9:16–17. Collins 2010:148.
[77] Betz 1999:450.

Hyrcanus II and Aristobulus II

Aristobulus II's army of Judean supporters and recruited mercenaries easily defeated Hyrcanus II's forces at Jericho. The latter fled to Jerusalem, where he nevertheless surrendered and gave up the titles and powers of king and high priest in favor of his younger brother. Josephus blames Hyrcanus for a lack of ambition, but he might rather be praised for not prolonging a losing cause—and multiplying unnecessary loss of life—for the sake of ambition.

An Idumean named Antipater, the governor of Idumea and the son of Antipas, who had been Alexander Jannaeus's and later Salome Alexandra's appointee over Idumea, now rises to prominence in Judean politics. Antipater rekindled Hyrcanus's ambition for his birthright and arranged for him to take refuge with, and seek support from, the Nabataean king Aretas III in his capital city of Petra (Josephus, *War* 1.123–124; *Ant.* 14.11–14). Hyrcanus won Aretas's support with the promise that Hyrcanus, if successful, would return to Aretas twelve cities and their hinterlands in the Transjordan that his father Jannaeus had taken. Aretas marched against Aristobulus with a force of fifty thousand soldiers, driving him and his army back into Jerusalem and laying siege to the city.

This is where matters lay when Rome intervened in the affairs of their eastern "ally." Sextus Pompey had been active in the east extending Roman control over the pitiful remnants of the once-great Seleucid empire, whose disintegration had left a power vacuum. He first dealt with piracy emanating from the northeast Mediterranean coastal regions and then invested his energies in bringing Mithridates of Pontus, Tigranes of Armenia, and Antiochus I of Commagene to heel, since their ambitions to consume the remnants of the Seleucid kingdom were disturbing the peace and stability of the region. Pompey reorganized Syria as a Roman province and strengthened its eastern frontier so that the region would serve as a stable buffer against the Parthian empire.[78] Local vassal kings or ethnarchs who possessed the

---

[78] During this period, Rome is still referred to as a "republic" based on its structures of internal governance, but it ruled a multinational *empire* long before Augustus was hailed as *imperator*.

strength and the determination to safeguard Rome's interests in the region would be allowed to retain their fiefdoms; the remainder of the territory would be placed directly under a Roman governor.[79]

While Pompey was still engaged in "pacifying" Armenia, which would eventually become a client kingdom under Rome, he sent Marcus Aemilius Scaurus south into Coele Syria to reconnoiter the region. Scaurus traveled into Judea to discover the capital city under siege, whereupon both Hyrcanus and Aristobulus presented their case to him. The power dynamics of this situation are important to note: the two Judean princes submitted their affairs to Rome's representatives to be settled. Scaurus favored Aristobulus, both for the greater likelihood that he could make good on his promise of large sums of money than the exiled Hyrcanus and for the greater ease with which Aretas could be driven back than Jerusalem successfully besieged (Josephus, *Ant.* 14.29–33). Threatened with being named an enemy of Rome, Aretas III predictably withdrew to his own land.

When Pompey finished his business in the north and came to Damascus, Hyrcanus and Antipater petitioned him, asserting the justness of Hyrcanus's claim as the elder brother and the designated successor, and thus the injustice of Scaurus's settlement. Aristobulus, of course, also appeared in order to press his claim, enhancing it with marvelous gifts from the Temple treasures. A third delegation of "leading men" also brought a petition, asking Pompey that the monarchy be dissolved and rule by a high priest in concert with the Judean senate (the *gerousia*) restored. Diodorus, admittedly no admirer of the Jewish people, recalls the complaint against the Hasmoneans thus: "these men were lording it over them, having overthrown the ancient laws and enslaved the citizens in defiance of all justice; for it was by means of a horde of mercenaries, and by outrages and countless impious murders that they had established themselves as kings" (*Bibl. Hist.* 40.2).[80] Most, if not all, of these charges could, in fact, have been easily substantiated.

Pompey, however, had his own agenda and itinerary. He announced that he would give his decision when he visited Judea, but that first

---

[79] Magie 1950:1.351–378; Green 1990:659.
[80] Stern, ed. 1976b:185–186. See also Josephus, *Ant.* 14.40–41.

he was heading to Nabatea to investigate the conditions there. He therefore ordered the two parties to keep the peace in the interim. Aristobulus, however, fearing that Pompey might rule against him, reinforced his position at the fortress of Alexandrion between Damascus and Jerusalem. Pompey took this as a sign of aggression and marched against him. When confronted, Aristobulus fled Alexandrion to the more defensible and better supplied Jerusalem, which was still principally, though not fully, under his control. Pompey therefore advanced his troops further south and besieged Jerusalem. Aristobulus saw the futility of his position and surrendered to Pompey, but his partisans inside the city refused to lay down their arms or open the gates to admit him. The Roman general therefore placed Aristobulus under arrest and pressed the siege. Hyrcanus's supporters managed to gain control of one of the city gates, allowing Pompey and his troops to enter. Aristobulus's supporters retreated into the temple precincts, where the siege continued. According to Josephus, Pompey made tactical use of the Sabbath while building his siege works—and the partisans of Aristobulus were sufficiently pious not to fight on the Sabbath when not being attacked directly themselves. In the summer of 63 BCE, at the end of a three-month siege, Pompey's troops and Hyrcanus's supporters broke through the temple's defenses and captured it. They massacred many of the followers of Aristobulus along with many of the priests who continued to attend to their duties in the temple precincts (Josephus, *War* 1.149–151).

Pompey and some number of his men entered the inner sanctum of the temple, perhaps to ensure that there were no insurgents taking refuge within, perhaps to satisfy their curiosity about what kind of image the Jews *really* worshiped (cf. Tacitus, *Hist.* 5.9). They found it to be empty, however. Josephus affirms that Pompey otherwise respected the holy place by not seizing any of the temple's treasures and authorizing the priests to perform the necessary purificatory rites the following day so that they could resume their religious duties. Nevertheless, this must have made a strongly negative impression upon all Judeans, whatever their partisan affiliation. Not since Antiochus IV had a Gentile violated the sanctity of the holy places.

Pompey sent Aristobulus II and four of his children to Rome as prisoners. Thousands of his partisans that had survived the melee were enslaved and deported. Pompey confirmed Hyrcanus II as high priest but denied him the title of "king": Hyrcanus would serve as "ethnarch" and a vassal of Rome. He would enjoy authority over internal affairs in conjunction with a Judean senate, but Judea would fall under the ultimate authority of the Roman governor of Syria. Judea would begin again to pay tribute to a foreign nation, perhaps justified as a schedule of repayment for Pompey's military intervention and advance payment for any further "protection" that might be required. At the same time, Pompey stripped away a significant part of the territorial gains achieved by preceding generations of the Hasmonean line. The cities of the Decapolis and the coastal plain were restored to independence, but under the supervision of the legate of Syria as part of his province—to which they would also pay a subvention. The Greek cities of the Decapolis nevertheless greeted this as a liberation from foreign domination, from unwelcome subjection to the rulers of an ethnic group with which they had no natural and very little cultural connection, seen for example in their adoption of a new era for dating that started in 63 BCE. While it seems clear that Rome's intent was to exercise closer oversight of the entire eastern Mediterranean, one can imagine a very different outcome had Pompey encountered a stable, strong, undivided Hasmonean kingdom such as had existed under Hyrcanus I.

Hyrcanus II and Antipater, however, would prove loyal allies to the representatives of Rome in their region. They had occasion to do so almost immediately when Pompey's subordinate, Scaurus, made his expedition to Nabataea and met with significant resistance. Hyrcanus II provided supplies when the troops were in dire need and Antipater negotiated the truce whereby King Aretas would pay a modest tribute to Rome and remain an allied king (Josephus, *War* 1.80–81; *Ant.* 13.159). At the same time, they would have multiple occasions on which they would rely on their Roman overseers to maintain their own position. Hyrcanus II's image must have suffered significantly as a result. However unjust Aristobulus's original coup might have been reckoned, Hyrcanus had now joined forces with a far superior, foreign power to recover and retain his position—and Judea had lost almost all of the gains for which his family had fought for a hundred years.

Aristobulus and his family would go down fighting. The fact that Aristobulus and his sons could always rally an army of supporters from Judea and Galilee suggests that he, and not Hyrcanus, had inherited the mantle of his revolutionary forebears whose actions had justified the dynasty in the first place.[81] Hyrcanus was now the puppet of a Gentile empire; Aristobulus and his family the "underdogs" fighting for independence from Gentile puppeteers. Pompey's settlement was followed by decades of skirmishes and unrest in both Judea and Galilee as Aristobulus II and his sons continued their fight.

Responses to Dynastic Decline

A collection of prayers known as the *Psalms of Solomon* was composed in close connection with the events of 63 BCE and its aftermath.[82] Clear historical reminiscences of Pompey's siege appear in *Pss. Sol.* 2.1–2; 8.1, 4, 15–21; 17:11–13. These psalms open windows into how one circle of pious Judeans, at least, dealt with the trauma of the decline of "the family of those men through whom deliverance had been given to Israel" (1 Macc 5:62) and the fate of the temple on their watch. The fact that God did not stop Pompey in his tracks to protect God's holy places plausibly demonstrated God's deep displeasure with the Hasmonean rulers, the priestly elite, and the people as a whole.[83] Aside from the mismanagement of the temple and its sacrifices, one focal point for criticism was the Hasmonean high priests' assumption of the title of "king." The honor of the high priestly office ought to have been sufficient; God had granted the honor of kingship to an entirely different family in an entirely different tribe:

Lord, you choose David to be king over Israel,
And you swore to him concerning his line for ever,
That his kingdom would never fail before thee.

---

[81] Dąbrowa 2010:172, 184–185; Grabbe 2021:515.
[82] See Atkinson 2004; deSilva 2012a:144–152; Eckhardt 2015.
[83] For criticism of the priestly leaders, see *Pss. Sol.* 1:7–8; 2:3–4; 8:9–13; 16:18–19; 17:4–7; of the people more broadly: *Pss. Sol.* 2:11–13; 8:9–10.

But, because of our sins, sinners rose up against us:

Those to whom you gave no promise assailed us and thrust us out;

They took possession by force and did not honor your glorious name.

In their pride, they set up a kingdom in splendor,

they laid waste the throne of David in the arrogance of *their* fortune.

(*Pss. Sol.* 17:4–6)

The fate of this usurping dynasty—to be removed by "a man that is foreign to our race" (17:7–8)—leaves no doubt that the Hasmoneans are being targeted and that the handwriting is on the wall.

The authors interpret these recent developments in line with the blessings and curses of the covenant announced in Deuteronomy 28–32: faithful observance of the Mosaic covenant results in the enjoyment of its blessings, while departure from the same (here, notably, in the ritual and ethical failures of the priestly elite) invites God's punishment of the nation as a whole. Even if the causes were not clear prior to Hyrcanus and Aristobulus's civil war, the effects brought them to light. Pompey and his actions against Jerusalem and the temple become the manifestation of God's punitive discipline (*Pss. Sol.* 3:4; 7:3, 9; 8:26, 29; 10:1–4; 13:7, 10; 14:1–2; 16:4, 11–15). Steadfastness in one's observance of the covenant, or repentance and a return to the same on the part of all who are out of alignment with God's covenant, would result in God's mercy and restoration.

These psalms culminate in expressions of hope for how God would restore Judea, namely through the actions of a messianic figure—an "anointed one" (17:32; also see 18:5, 7)—whom the psalmists ask God to raise up for the purpose of deliverance. He will purify the land of Israel's inheritance from both sinful Judeans and encroaching Gentiles (17:22–24, 30b, 36b). He will also gather the righteous Judeans who have been scattered throughout the lands of the nations (17:26, 31; see also 11:1–3), restore the land to each of the twelve tribes in line with God's original distribution (17:28), and will rule them with perfect justice, keeping them centered in the fear of the Lord through his rod of discipline (17:26–27; see also 18:7). The petition for a "son of

David" who would accomplish these things is an implicit criticism of the Hasmonean line, not least for bringing Israel to such a pass that such deliverance is again required, and of every major facet of the status quo, which lies so far removed from the ideal of God's ancient promises and provisions. The contrast here with the earlier application of promises from the Jewish Scriptures to the achievements of the first generation of Hasmonean leaders could not be starker (see 1 Macc 3:3–9 and 14:4–15). And while there is no standard set of messianic expectations in early Judaism,[84] this is a paradigm that would become particularly influential in the century to follow as revolutionaries rose up, purposefully acting in line with biblical precedents as a means of announcing God's forthcoming deliverance of "Israel" through their actions.

Other noteworthy expressions of messianic hopes seem to have their origins in the Hasmonean period as well. Where a group looks to the future for the advent of agents of God's deliverance from present ills, one might justifiably hear a veiled critique of leadership and conditions in the present, since rescue is required and the present leaders are *not* the ones through whom God will bring it.[85] The "times of refreshing" promised by God in the prophets are not yet, but lie still in the future. The vision of the dual messiahs of Levi and Judah articulated in the *Testaments of the Twelve Patriarchs* (e.g., *T. Levi* 18.5, 9–12; *T. Jud* 24.1–4; *T. Dan* 5.9–11; *T. Gad* 8.1) as well as the expectation of both a Messiah of Aaron and a Messiah of Israel found in the Dead Sea Scrolls (1QS 9.11; 1QSa 2.11–24) have often been understood as a judgment upon the Hasmoneans' concentration of both high priesthood and kingship in one person, since in God's future these powers will be separate once more.[86] The accomplishments of the generation of Judas Maccabaeus would be preserved in Judean (indeed, *Jewish*) memory, not least through the growing popularity of the Feast of Dedication (Hanukkah). But perhaps the dynasty's most lasting legacy involved a renewed zeal for the restoration and secure establishment

---

[84] Rightly, Collins 1995:195–196.

[85] Dąbrowa 2010:173–177.

[86] Atkinson 2004:177. See also *Jubilees* 31.8–20, itself a text that exercised authority in the communities that produced and preserved the *Damascus Document* (CD 16.2–4). On the recovery of the original form of the *Testaments*, see deSilva 2012a:194–222.

of the Kingdom of Israel, seeing that it had been once accomplished—and that against significant odds. Even if many in Judea and its environs ceased to view the Hasmonean kings as worthy or faithful leaders, they would continue to hope for a future agent to arise who would combine the Hasmoneans' achievements with a more perfect and enduring piety, resulting in a more lasting independence under the rule of God. Thus, hopes for God's perfect (and perhaps *final*) restoration of Israel, often combined with hope for God's raising up of a specific agent through whom to accomplish this, would flourish throughout the Roman period.

4

The King of the Jews

Herod and His Heirs

The story of Hyrcanus, Antipater, and Herod is inextricably intertwined with the larger story of Rome's actions on its eastern frontier, the internal politics of Rome that produced the civil wars that dominate Roman history from about 50 to 31 BCE, and the hostilities between the two great world powers of the time: Rome and Parthia. From these cauldrons, however, boiling over on multiple burners, would come an era of relative peace, stability, and even prosperity first for the Roman empire under Augustus (31 BCE–14 CE) and secondarily for the region assigned to Augustus's loyal and capable client-king, Herod the Great (37–4 BCE). It seems likely that, were Herod to have left a single, viable heir to his kingdom to carry on as ably as he did himself, the next installment of our narrative would have spun a very different and less disastrous story. But the fragmentation of Herod's kingdom, the introduction of direct Roman governance at different times, the dashed hopes of a restored, united kingdom under Herod's grandson and great-grandson, all added unhelpful instability and unpredictability to an already difficult situation of ethnic tensions, economic inequities, and politico-religious aspirations.

Josephus remains the most consistent ancient informant (see especially *War* 1.201–2.100; *Ant.* 14.82–17.355), and for much of this material he appears to have a fairly reliable source in the lost *Universal History* of Nicolaus of Damascus, a one-time tutor in Ptolemy's court and long-time friend of Herod in his court. A bevy of Roman historians supply information about the larger canvas against which the situation in Judea and its environs plays out. Numismatic, epigraphic, and archaeological data remain important resources to ground and to supplement the literary sources in the lived world they purport to represent.

Judea under Greek and Roman Rule. David A. deSilva, Oxford University Press.
© Oxford University Press 2024. DOI: 10.1093/oso/9780190263249.003.0005

The End of the Hasmonean Dynasty and the Rise of Herod

In 57 BCE, Aristobulus's son Alexander escaped from Rome and raised a force of ten thousand soldiers and fifteen hundred cavalry from among his father's supporters in Galilee and Judea in an attempt to supplant his uncle Hyrcanus, seizing the key fortresses of Alexandreion, Hyrcania, and Machaerus. Pompey's appointee as governor of Syria, Gabinius, with a young Marcus Antonius acting as a captain under his command, brought a quick end to Alexander's rebellion. The following year, Aristobulus himself, together with his second son, Mattathias Antigonus, escaped from Rome and attempted a revolt. They were also defeated after being besieged in Machaerus, after which Aristobulus was sent back to Rome in chains. The necessity of Roman forces' intervention underscored the fact that Judea's rulers were now Rome's creatures.

Around this time, Gabinius expended significant resources restoring Samaria and the cities of the coastal plain, which had suffered in the decades of fighting, both between Seleucid rivals and as a result of Judean conquest. For reasons that remain unclear, he also stripped Hyrcanus of much of his secular authority and reorganized Judea into five districts, each with a local council (*synedrion*). These districts were centered on Jerusalem, Jericho, Amathus (in the Transjordan), Gezer, and Sepphoris (see Josephus, *War* 1.178; *Ant.* 14.103).[1] Hyrcanus might be presumed to have continued to serve as president of the council seated in Jerusalem. Gabinius's interference with the internal organization of Judea may have further fueled the anti-Roman sentiments that would give further support to Aristobulus and his line—that is, the Hasmoneans who were *not* Rome's creatures.

Hyrcanus and Antipater had occasion to return the favor of military support in 55 BCE, lending their aid to Gabinius when he set out to reestablish Ptolemy XII Auletes on the throne of Egypt. This again brought Antipater and Marc Antony together on the field of battle, where the former won the latter's admiration. Aristobulus's older

---

[1] Josephus lists Gadara rather than Gezer, which appears to be an error. Gadara in the Decapolis was removed from Hyrcanus's jurisdiction several years prior.

son, Alexander, used this occasion to stir up a further revolt in Judea, though this was suppressed in a single battle at Mt. Tabor. Gabinius once again reorganized the administration of Judea and Galilee, this time "in line with Antipater's wishes" (Josephus, *War* 1.178; *Ant.* 14.103). While Josephus does not specify what this entailed, it is important that *Antipater* is the one exercising this level of influence with Gabinius, and not Hyrcanus.[2] It seems likely that it was at this time that administration of the whole territory reverted to a single council under Hyrcanus as its president, now with Antipater as military governor and bearing a large part of the secular responsibility and power.[3]

Marcus Licinius Crassus, one of the three leading men of the Roman empire alongside Sextus Pompey and Julius Caesar, sought and won appointment as governor of Syria in 54 BCE, replacing Gabinius. His goal for the command was to take military action against the Parthian empire to the east and push back the frontiers of Rome's principal rival. To help finance this campaign, he pillaged the Jerusalem temple's treasury (as he would do also to a Temple of Atargatis in Syria). His ill-advised campaign against Parthia resulted in his own death and a disastrous defeat for his troops. His lieutenant, Cassius, who would gain fame a decade later as one of Julius Caesar's assassins, led the surviving troops back to Syria to reestablish the frontier. He arrived in time to suppress yet another revolt of Aristobulus's supporters in Galilee, particularly centered on Tarichaeae, no doubt fueled by anti-Roman sentiments stoked by Crassus's blatant affront to the sanctity of the temple. This might account for the fact that one of the revolutionary leaders was Peitholaus, once a military commander over Hyrcanus's forces, possibly turned by the costs to the nation's dignity of continued cooperation with the Romans. The result was a high death toll among the revolutionaries and an equally large number of Jews reduced to slavery and deported.

When civil war erupted in 49 BCE between the two remaining strong men of Rome, Julius Caesar and Pompey, each sought to use a Hasmonean prince as a pawn in a proxy war in the eastern theater. Pompey ordered Hyrcanus to gather troops in his support, while

---

[2] Richardson 1996:102.
[3] Smallwood 1981:35.

Caesar released Aristobulus from his imprisonment in Rome with the design of sending him east at the head of Roman troops to destabilize the region. Ironically, those who had been so concerned to ensure stability on the eastern frontier were now risking its instability in their own internal struggles for absolute power. Aristobulus, however, met his end before being able to leave Rome, poisoned by Pompey's agents. At the same time, Pompey had Aristobulus's son Alexander arrested, tried, and executed for sedition in Judea and its environs (Josephus, *War* 1.183; *Ant.* 14.123; Dio Cassius 41.18.1). Aristobulus's other offspring—Mattathias Antigonus along with two of his sisters—were taken in and given protection by Ptolemy, son of Mennaeus and king of Chalcis, a small fiefdom in southern Lebanon. This would become important a decade later as Ptolemy's son contrived with the Parthian rulers to place Antigonus on the throne of Judea as a means of shifting the axis of power in the region.

Egypt was also experiencing unrest as the alliance between co-regents, spouses, and siblings Cleopatra VII and Ptolemy XIII (aged seventeen and ten, respectively) deteriorated into civil war. Pompey's forces suffered a significant defeat against those of Caesar at Pelusium at the northeastern frontier of Egypt, and the defeated general fled to Alexandria. The guardians of Ptolemy XIII thought to curry favor with the victor by assassinating Pompey, but they were met with stern rebuke and, eventually, his enmity instead (Dio Cassius, *Roman History* 42.3–5; Plutarch, *Pompey*, 79–80). Pompey's fate was of great importance to the author or authors of the *Psalms of Solomon*, for it resolved at last the problem of God's failure to execute judgment upon the man who ravaged Jerusalem and transgressed the holy boundaries of the temple (*Pss. Sol.* 2.24–27). Instrument of punishment or not, Pompey also had to be held accountable.

After Pompey's demise, Hyrcanus and Antipater acted quickly to demonstrate their support for Caesar as the new leading representative of Roman power in the east. Hyrcanus dispatched Antipater with military support and supplies to Caesar as he moved to intervene in affairs in Alexandria, where Antipater was also helpful in galvanizing the Alexandrian Jewish community's support for Caesar's cause.[4] Caesar

---

[4] Richardson 1996:106–108.

restored a fragile peace to Ptolemy XIII and Cleopatra VII in 47 BCE, though Cleopatra would soon emerge as sole monarch of Egypt, first with Caesar's and then with Antony's support. Thus began Rome's "protectorate" over that kingdom that would lead, in less than twenty years, to the reorganization of Egypt as a province under the personal auspices of Caesar's successor, Octavian (soon thereafter to be granted the moniker of "Augustus" or, in Greek, *Sebastos*).

Caesar responded favorably to Hyrcanus and Antipater's display. He confirmed Hyrcanus as high priest and ethnarch and named him a "friend and ally" of the people of Rome. He also approved Hyrcanus's request to rebuild the fortification walls around Jerusalem that had been destroyed in Pompey's siege efforts. Antipater was granted Roman citizenship and remained the financial officer (the procurator) in the region.[5] Caesar restored Joppa to Hyrcanus's ethnarchy and, with it, access to maritime trade. The political savvy of Hyrcanus and Antipater served Jewish communities throughout the Roman world, as Julius Caesar would formally issue decrees protecting their rights (decrees that Augustus would later affirm).[6]

Antipater appointed his two eldest sons, Phasael and Herod, military governors over Jerusalem and Galilee, respectively. Even though Herod was only twenty-five, he was determined to prove himself worthy of his father's confidence. He set himself to dealing with a band of displaced "brigands," under the leadership of one Hezekiah, that had been disrupting affairs in the north. The core of these brigands might have been formed by what remained of Aristobulus's family's supporters in Galilee, as Josephus uses the term "brigand" rather indiscriminately for both revolutionary fighters and ordinary marauders. Herod succeeded in capturing and executing Hezekiah and many of his supporters. Rather than win Herod admiration in Jerusalem, however, it won him envy and enmity. The Jerusalem elites were enraged at his independence of action with regard to inflicting capital punishment and determined to hold him accountable at a trial to which

---

[5] Smallwood 1981:39.
[6] These are listed and reproduced at length in Josephus, *Ant*. 14.185–216. See also *Ant*. 14.223–264 for local decrees concerning Jewish communities throughout the eastern Mediterranean diaspora.

Hyrcanus summoned him. Sextus Caesar, a relation of Julius Caesar and then governor of Syria, appears to have intervened to ensure Herod's acquittal, given Herod's proven value as an enforcer of order in the southern part of Sextus's province. For his own safety, Sextus removed him from the territories of Judea and Galilee, to serve directly under him for a term as military governor of the Decapolis and Samaritis.[7]

In 44 BCE, Julius Caesar was assassinated by a coalition of conspirators led by Marcus Brutus and Caius Cassius. (Sextus Caesar was also killed at about the same time.) Cassius returned to the east the following year and imposed a one-time additional levy of seven hundred talents upon Hyrcanus's territory to support his war efforts against the Caesarian party. Herod was reportedly the first to raise the one hundred talents apportioned for him to raise from Galilee, winning Cassius's approval while several others failed and suffered serious consequences. For example, another local strong man named Malichus would have been executed for his failure, had not Hyrcanus and Antipater intervened and made up what was lacking in his portion. Some portion of the residents of the districts of Gophna, Emmaus, Lydda, and Thamna were sold as slaves to make up the difference in their quotas. Herod's success in raising the sum suggests the lengths to which he had gone to "court the Romans and secure their goodwill at the expense of others" (Josephus, *Ant.* 14.274), certainly a fair assessment of Herod's motivational balance sheet.

Antipater's role in Judean affairs came to an abrupt end later that same year. He was poisoned while being entertained by Malichus, despite Antipater's having rescued him from Cassius's anger. No clear motive is supplied except for ambition, perhaps to gain for himself what Antipater had so long enjoyed as the man at Hyrcanus's right hand, or simply fear of the growing power of Antipater and his sons.[8] Herod, of course, obtained permission from Cassius—and help from the Roman military tribunes at Tyre!—to exact revenge against Malichus, confirming his fears at the same time as consummating them. Some have suggested that Malichus acted out of regard for Hyrcanus, fearing

---

[7] Smallwood 1981:45.
[8] Grabbe 2020:445.

that Antipater had designs against him, but there is no evidence that Antipater was anything but a loyal lieutenant to Hyrcanus throughout his long career.[9]

Cassius withdrew most of his troops from the east to meet Octavian and Antony's forces at Philippi in 42 BCE, where he and his co-conspirator Brutus would end their lives. Supported by Ptolemy, king of Chalcis, Mattathias Antigonus, Aristobulus's surviving son, took advantage of the absence of Roman troops to make an incursion into Galilee and Judea in another attempt to unseat Hyrcanus. Herod was able to successfully fend off this incursion with his own military forces. As a consequence, Hyrcanus decided that his own and his line's best hope for the future lay in a closer alliance with Antipater's family. He therefore betrothed his granddaughter Mariamne to Herod, to "incorporate Herod into the Hasmonean family."[10] As a condition of this union (which would not be formalized until 37 BCE), Herod divorced his first wife, Doris, and sent her away along with their son Antipater, Herod's firstborn.

Marc Antony arrived in the East after he and Octavian successfully defeated the conspirators who assassinated Julius Caesar. His former acquaintance with Hyrcanus and Antipater smoothed the way for his acceptance of them as his own clients and his forgiveness of their former association with Cassius as one of necessity—an association that he had at one time shared as well. Hyrcanus showed his own loyalty and commitment to Herod and Phasael when he commended them to Antony as able leaders, resulting in their being named "tetrarchs" in Judea and Galilee, presumably still under Hyrcanus's own overall authority.

In 40 BCE, the Parthians mounted a massive invasion of Rome's eastern frontier under the command of the Parthian prince, Pacorus. Lysanias, son and successor of Ptolemy, king of Chalcis, made common cause with Pacorus and won his support for restoring Antigonus to the throne of Judea, Antigonus promising the Parthian prince a gift of one thousand talents and five hundred women for his backing.[11] Pacorus,

---

[9] Richardson 1996:117.
[10] Richardson 1996:122.
[11] Josephus, *Ant.* 14.331; *War* 1.257. (According to *War* 1.248, however, it was Lysanias who made this promise).

for his part, would have found it highly advantageous to have a client king almost at the very shores of the Mediterranean. The supporters of Aristobulus's line flocked to support the Parthian advance against Jerusalem. Under a ruse of a truce to discuss terms, Hyrcanus and Phasael were taken prisoner. Antigonus mauled his uncle's ears to disqualify him from ever returning to the office of high priest (which required the absence of any physical defect), thus removing him forever as a competitor. Hyrcanus was taken to Parthia as a captive but given an honorable retirement among the Babylonian Jewish community. Phasael committed suicide to avoid worse mistreatment. Antigonus thus became the last Hasmonean king and high priest.

Herod had no choice but to flee, leaving his family, Hyrcanus's family, and several hundred retainers and soldiers at the well-supplied and near-impregnable fortress of Masada while he made a dangerous winter sea voyage to Rome, where he appealed to Antony for help. Rome, of course, could not allow its greatest rival to the east to determine affairs in areas that had come under Rome's jurisdiction. And with the death of Antipater and removal of Hyrcanus, Herod was clearly the strongest option for the preservation of Rome's interests in Judea and the eastern frontier. With Antony's sponsorship in the Senate, Herod was named "king of the Judeans" and "an ally and friend" (*socius et amicus*) of Rome in late 40 BCE. Octavian had also lent his support, remembering Antipater's service to Octavian's adoptive father, Julius Caesar. Josephus relates that he was escorted from the Senate chamber arm in arm with Octavian and Antony, offering sacrifice with them at the temple of Jupiter Capitolinus where the record of the Senate's decree would be deposited—perhaps not the most auspicious beginning for a king of Judea, but certainly revealing with regard to Herod's disposition ("when in Rome ...").

The eastern forces of Rome were wholly occupied with repulsing the Parthians for several years. Between 40 and 38 BCE, Herod had only residual—and unreliable—support from local Roman garrisons. Herod was able, however, to subdue Galilee and to kill the partisans of Antigonus who had taken refuge in the caves of Arbel. He also made himself helpful to Antony in the latter's assaults on Parthian forces at Samosata, near the Euphrates and on the frontier between the two empires. In 38 BCE, with the Parthian threat sufficiently neutralized,

Antony sent his general Sosius with two legions to Judea with the charge of securing Herod's kingdom. Herod himself had defeated Antigonus's forces and Parthian allies at Jericho and drove the former back into Jerusalem; Sosius arrived in time to prepare for the siege of the city. While these preparations were under way, Herod finally formalized his marriage to Mariamne.

Sosius and his troops successfully broke through the walls and took Jerusalem in 37 BCE amid horrific slaughter. Herod demonstrated sincere concern for Jerusalem and its temple when he stopped Sosius's soldiers from sacking the city by personally distributing a lavish stipend to each man. Antigonus was captured and taken to Marc Antony, who ordered his immediate execution as an enemy of Rome. Whether or not Herod had urged this action, it would have been a politic move both given his alliance with Rome's great enemy to the east and the long history of his branch of the Hasmonean family acting as a lightning rod for revolution. Herod was now the unchallenged king of the Jews.

Herod immediately supported Antony in the latter's punitive invasion of Parthia—a necessary reprisal for their interference in Roman affairs. He also executed forty-five suspected supporters of Antigonus who were also members of the Sanhedrin, which Herod restocked with appointees who would be amenable to his own purposes.[12] Herod's nonpriestly (indeed, non-Judean) lineage meant that secular and religious authority would be necessarily divided going forward. Aristobulus III, the seventeen-year-old grandson of Hyrcanus and younger brother of Mariamne, was the natural and expected choice. Herod argued against bestowing this honor on someone so young, and the office was given to Hanael, a Jew of high priestly lineage from Babylon, possibly with Hyrcanus's blessing.[13]

Resentment against Herod and the authority he had recently come to enjoy—when he had formerly been destined to play a "best supporting" role to a Hasmonean ruler—became a powerful force among his in-laws. Aristobulus III's mother, Alexandra, essentially conspired with Cleopatra VII to pressure Herod to give the high

---

[12] Smallwood 1981:63.
[13] Richardson 1996:162.

priesthood to her son immediately, and Herod acquiesced. Herod also recognized that Aristobulus III would be a focal point for both family members and the popular supporters of the Hasmonean line at large to unseat Herod. One evening, when some of the youth were playing roughly in one of the great swimming pools in the Hasmonean palace complex at Jericho, Aristobulus drowned. Josephus alleges that this was the result of Herod's explicit instructions to certain other youths in Aristobulus's company. Alexandra certainly believed that it was, and she once again used her connections with Cleopatra to have Herod brought up on charges of conspiracy to commit murder before Antony, though Antony predictably acquitted his able and committed vassal. Given the difficulties Aristobulus's death caused for Herod, and the suspicions that naturally would focus on him as the effective culprit, there is cause to doubt his involvement. This is not to say that Herod was against eliminating the young man, only that he would typically have been cleverer about it. Herod then reappointed Hanael and continued to appoint and depose high priests at his whim, which degraded the dignity of the office since its incumbents had become so wholly beholden to Herod for their position.[14]

It was perhaps around this time that Cleopatra revived old Ptolemaic designs on regaining the territory of Coele-Syria, but Antony tempered her ambitions against his loyal client kings there. He allowed her to claim some parts of Arabia, some areas along the coastal plain, and the royal lands of Jericho and En Gedi. Herod leased the latter back from her at an enormous sum, but it allowed him to maintain direct oversight of these lands that he would eventually recover as his own after the Battle of Actium and the defeat of Antony and Cleopatra at the hands of Octavian and Marcus Agrippa. Indeed, Herod, ever a loyal client, would have fought on Antony's side against Octavian at Actium. He was fortunate that Antony, believing himself to have sufficient forces, dispatched him and his militia rather to resolve a disagreement between Cleopatra and the Nabatean king.

---

[14] Sharon 2017: 314–315. Goodman (1987) suggests that Herod's erosion of the integrity of the Sanhedrin and the high priesthood contributed significantly to the eventual outbreak of the First Jewish Revolt, since these institutions never regained the legitimate authority in the eyes of the people needed to control the situation.

Octavian's victory over Antony at Actium left Herod in a bind. His primary sponsor in the Senate had been declared and defeated as an enemy of Rome and all of Antony's arrangements in the east were once again on the table. Before Herod left Jerusalem, Alexandra's unending machinations gave Herod the opportunity to execute Hyrcanus, now seventy, on the charge of treason. Despite their long time and largely mutually beneficial relationship, Herod might indeed have welcomed the opportunity to remove the best living alternative to him should Octavian choose to depose a former vassal of Antony (Josephus, *Ant.* 15.163–182). Any fears that he might have had, however, were unfounded. Herod presented himself to Octavian at Rhodes without his crown or regal attire, owned his friendship with and debt to Antony, and asked to be judged not based on whose friend he had been, but what kind of friend he had shown himself to be. This struck the right chord with Octavian, who accepted Herod as his own client on the strength of Herod's former loyalty to the now-defeated (and clearly future-less) Antony. Herod's career-long track record of loyalty to Rome's interests and directives, whatever Roman was the strong man in the East, could also not have failed to recommend him. Octavian also affirmed Caesar's protection of the Judeans' right to worship their ancestral God, to the point that he subsidized sacrifices there (Philo, *Embassy*, 157, 317). He also affirmed the rights of Jews throughout the empire to collect and send money for the support of the temple and its sacrifices (Philo, *Embassy*, 311–315).

Herod accompanied and gave hospitality to Octavian and supplied his troops with provisions as they moved through Syria and Judea to Egypt, where the final confrontation with Antony and Cleopatra would end in their double suicide. Octavian responded by returning to Herod the territories Antony had stripped away from him and given to Cleopatra, adding Samaritis, several coastal cities, and the two Decapolis cities of Gadara and Hippos besides.

It is unclear whether Herod, as a client king (the actual language of the time was to call such a ruler a *socius et amicus populi Romani*, an "ally and friend of the Roman people"),[15] also paid Rome an annual,

---

[15] Gruen, *Construct*, 383–384.

fixed tribute.[16] Client kings performed a valuable service to Rome by looking after Rome's interests in their territory (and, in Herod's case, this included looking after a good stretch of eastern frontier), freeing Rome of the massive expenses of doing so at its own expense, and supplying military aid when requested (and Herod would frequently support Roman military operations in surrounding territories with supplies and troops). What is clear is that Octavian—better known as "Augustus," the honorific title he was awarded by the Senate in 27 BCE—was fully satisfied with Herod's ability to maintain both internal stability and the security of Rome's eastern frontier under his control, with the result that Augustus rewarded his loyal and effective ally with additional territories. Between 23 and 20 BCE, Augustus added the remainder of Galilee and the northeast regions of Trachonitis, Auranitis, and Batanea to Herod's kingdom, expanding his realm to one that rivaled the Hasmoneans' and even Solomon's territories at their peaks.[17] Throughout his reign, Herod would remain attentive to the ways in which he could express his loyalty and gratitude to the emperor on whose good will his own position depended. For example, he instituted an oath of loyalty to be sworn by his subjects both to himself *and* Augustus. It appears that it was early in his reign that daily sacrifices were instituted in the Jerusalem temple on behalf of the emperor as an appropriate symbol of the nation's loyalty, as the exclusive religious commitments of the Jewish people would not permit them to offer sacrifice *to* the emperor, as quickly became the norm in other parts of the empire.

Herod's Transformation of the Judean Landscape

Herod was not, like the Seleucids, forced to invest his energies and resources into struggles against rival claimants to the throne. Nor was he, like the Hasmoneans, in a position to yield to the temptation to expand his territory through costly military action. He was therefore

---

[16] Schäfer 2003:90 thinks he did; Grabbe 2020:462–463, 488 argues that he did not on the strength of the following considerations.

[17] Grabbe 2020:462.

both free *and* forced to focus his attention and ambition on developing the territory that had been allotted to him—and this he did magnificently! The broad spectrum and diverse nature of these building and development projects reflect Herod's attempts throughout his reign to honor the diversity of the populations brought together under his rule, his desire to project an image of himself as a generous and successful Hellenistic monarch in his own right, and his determination to record his loyalty and gratitude to his patrons and friends not merely in stone but in monumental structures and in whole cities.[18]

Herod refounded or expanded several cities in the predominantly Gentile areas of his realm. The most stunning of these involved the transformation of the minor anchorage of Strato's Tower into a major port city whose harbor rivaled the Piraeus harbor near Athens. He renamed this city Caesarea in honor of his patron Augustus Caesar. The harbor was entirely artificial, made by filling large wooden hulls with a special volcanic cement from Italy that could harden underwater. In size it was outclassed only by the harbors of Alexandria and Ostia and promised a dramatic increase in maritime trade for Herod's kingdom. Herod built a seafront palace on a promontory, a theater with a seating capacity of four thousand, and a hippodrome for chariot races with a seating capacity of seven thousand.[19] He also erected a monumental temple to Augustus and Roma, the deified personification of the city of Rome, atop an artificially extended platform that dominated the inner harbor to proclaim his allegiance—and to call for the allegiance of all who docked or resided in the port city—to his patron. The needs of the increased population for water were supplied by a high-level aqueduct bringing spring water from a source four miles or so to the north.

The city of Samaria had recovered its independent status under Pompey and had once again become a largely Gentile city by the time Herod came to power. It was thus another prime location in which Herod could fulfill his aspirations for honoring his great patron and the patron of the Roman world. He renamed the city Sebaste, a form of

---

[18] See, further, Richardson 1996:174–202 (especially the catalog of Herod's buildings in 1996:197–202) and the magisterial treatment in Netzer 2008.

[19] Broshi 1999:18.

the word *Sebastos*, the Greek equivalent of the Latin *Augustus*, at about the same time as Octavian received that honorific from the Senate. Herod incorporated its Hellenistic-era fortifications into a new city wall two miles in circumference. He also built a new theater, stadium, colonnaded streets, additional aqueducts to improve water supply, and another magnificent temple to Augustus and Roma. It became a respectable place for Herod to settle thousands of the non-Jewish veterans of his army and, together with Caesarea, a prime recruiting ground for new soldiers.

Herod was careful to build these temples to Augustus and Rome only in the predominantly Gentile areas of his realm, but he built them also in the areas of his realm that Augustus specifically granted to him. Herod had been king since 40 BCE, but only received Samaritis and the coastal region in 31 BCE as a gift (or, perhaps better, as a trust) from Augustus. And when he received the territories of Galilee and the regions north and northeast of the same, he also marked that territory with a monument to his gratitude—this time a third temple to Augustus and Roma built at Panias (which Herod's son Philip would rename Caesarea, and hence would come to be known as Caesarea Philippi). Herod chose a site near an already-existing pagan sanctuary—the grotto and shrine of Pan, just beyond the Jewish-occupied region of Galilee—as an idyllic location within his new territory for his new temple, making clear the link between Augustus's grant and Herod's response.[20]

Herod's most celebrated building program was his renovation and expansion of the Jerusalem Temple.[21] He worked within the constraints set for him by the priests, training members of their lineage in masonry and related skills so that no laypersons would enter the holy places for the sake of the construction work. All the materials required for the renovation of the sanctuary itself, which included a dramatic new façade and extensive ornamentation, were first gathered before any work began, and the work itself was

[20] Berlin 2015:5; Josephus, *Ant.* 15.359, 363–364.
[21] Detailed accounts from an eyewitness of the results are available in Josephus, *Ant.* 15.380–425; *War* 5.184–227.

completed within two years with no interruption of the schedule of sacrifices. The sacred precincts around the sanctuary were expanded to the north, west, and south until the space was almost doubled, reaching an area of thirty-six acres. Retaining walls with massive ashlar blocks and carefully engineered vaulted structures supported the expanded courtyard and the new, columned porticoes lining its perimeter. At some points, the top of the temple's precinct wall towered as high as forty-five meters above the streets below.[22] The water supply and drainage systems within and around the platform were dramatically improved. Four gates gave entry to the temple platform from the west, two entrances from the south, one from the north, and perhaps as many as three from the east.[23] The entrances on the south side were apertures in the retaining wall that led to staircases that ascended through the substructure and opened dramatically into the middle of the "court of the Gentiles" (or "court open to all," 4 Macc 4:11). The main features of the project were completed by 10 BCE, though work would continue in some fashion, largely on account of subsidences and repairs, through the procuratorship of Albinus in the early sixties CE (see Figure 4.1).

While the renovation and expansion of the Temple complex was the most dramatic change to the face of Jerusalem, Herod reshaped its contours in other ways (Josephus, *War* 1.401–421). Early in his reign, he replaced the Baris, the Hasmonean fortress at the former northwest corner of the temple platform, with a larger, more heavily fortified (and opulently provisioned) structure further to the north, which he named "Antonia" in honor of his then-patron, Marc Antony (Josephus, *War* 5.238–245). He built a sprawling palace complex for himself on the west side of Jerusalem and fortified the wall north of his palace with three proud towers, of which the base of one is still standing. The palace itself consisted of two symmetrical wings that he named the Caesareum and Agrippaeum in honor of Augustus and Augustus's righthand man, Marcus Agrippa. Although archaeologists have not yet located them, Herod also built a theater and hippodrome in, or in

[22] Bahat 1999:43–44.
[23] Bahat 1999:47–51.

Figure 4.1 One of the few archaeological remains of Herod's temple is this inscription from the perimeter fence separating the large, outer court that was open to people of all races from the inner courts that were forbidden to non-Jews. It reads: "No member of another race may enter within the barrier and perimeter around the sanctuary. Whoever is caught will be the cause of his [or her] own subsequent death" (Josephus, *Ant.* 15.417; *War* 5.193–194).

the vicinity of, Jerusalem, bringing Greek and Roman kinds of enter-tainment to his capital city (Josephus, *War* 2.44; *Ant.* 17.255). He also devoted significant resources to improving its infrastructure, particu-larly roads, aqueducts, and reservoirs like artificial lakes for size (for example, the third basin of Solomon's Pools outside Bethlehem and the so-called Sultan's Pool in Jerusalem).

Herod constructed two monuments in Idumean territory. The first was the Tomb of the Patriarchs over the Cave of Machpelah at Hebron (see Gen 23:17–19; 25:9; 49:29–30), from the exterior a kind of mini-ature version of the temple mount platform. The second was a sacred enclosure around the oak of Mamre, the site of an altar to God erected by Abraham (Gen 13:18). As these sites emphasized the Idumeans' shared heritage with the people of Judea, it might be surmised that Herod's goal was to enhance the unity of these populations.[24]

He also diligently maintained the network of fortresses that his predecessors had erected along the eastern border of the kingdom. At the same time, he supplied each with one or more luxurious palaces for his own use, whether he found himself there during an inspection tour, a voluntary retreat, or defending himself against hostile actions— the last being an eventuality he never had to face. These palaces were luxuriously furnished, sporting beautifully decorated *triclinia* (dining rooms), complete bath complexes in the Roman style, and often stunning vistas (see Figure 4.2). While many of the rooms were graced with geometric mosaics or Pompeian-style frescoes, none contained images of animals or human beings. This probably says something about Herod's commitment to live as a Jew—at least in Jewish territory, even in his private life—though he was willing also to live as a Roman where necessary for his own advancement or consolidation of power (as when he offered sacrifice in Rome to the Capitoline gods Jupiter, Juno, and Minerva with Antony and Octavian in 40 BCE).

Over the course of his reign, Herod also built no fewer than three palaces adjacent to or near the Hasmonean palaces alongside the Wadi Qilt outside of Jericho, the latest of which was particularly opulent. He built another vast palace, garden, bath, and pool complex at a site seven miles south of Jerusalem that he would immodestly name Herodion. The villa was the largest such complex in the Mediterranean at the time, eventually to be outdone only by Nero's "Golden House" and Hadrian's villa at Tivoli.[25] The whole was overlooked by a smaller fortified palace atop an artificially enhanced mound. Herod was not at all reluctant to expend vast resources on his own pleasure—and on the stature that he wished to project.

After the manner of other Hellenistic kings, among whom Herod wanted both to be counted *and* to distinguish himself, he gave lavish benefactions to foreign cities. For example, he subsidized the rebuilding of the Temple of Apollo at Rhodes after a devastating fire, underwrote the cost of the Olympic games and established a

---

[24] Richardson 1996:60–62.
[25] Broshi 1999:29.

Figure 4.2 An ornate, multicolored mosaic from the bath house in the western palace atop Masada.

permanent endowment for the same at Elis (for which he received the honorary title of "president of the games for life"), contributed the funds for marketplaces, temples, and various halls and porticoes at both Tyre and Berytus, and built gymnasia for Ptolemais, Damascus, Tripolis, and Delos. His benefits even reached as far as Athens, as the inscriptions on two bases that once supported statues attest.[26] At the

---

[26] "The people [honors] King Herod, Friend of Rome (*philoromaion*), on account of beneficence and good will. . . ." *IG* II² 3440 (= *OGIS* 414); "The people [honors] King

same time, he was careful to avoid being seen to compete with his own patrons for the gratitude of (and fame within) particular cities outside his realm—and if he ever benefited a city that was on Augustus's or Agrippa's radar, he made certain to give lesser gifts than they had. There were indeed some grounds for the complaint that Herod impoverished the towns and villages of his own kingdom to enrich and adorn cities abroad (Josephus, *War* 2.85–86), but the scope of his giving also brought intangible gains for the Jewish people. It could only have helped the reputation of the local Jewish communities in those foreign cities to have the "king of the Jews" acting as a benefactor of the Greeks. It also could not have hurt the international reputation of the people of Judea, often disdained as a people having "hatred of outsiders," to be represented by a king who was so thoroughly *philhellēn*, a "friend/patron of the Greeks."

In sum, Herod's extensive construction projects appear to have served multiple goals: (1) showing gratitude toward and respect for his personal patrons, while also emphasizing, for his own subjects and any rivals, his personal connections with the most powerful men in the empire; (2) providing for his personal security and comfort; (3) promoting his reputation for piety (in both Jewish and Greco-Roman eyes); (4) facilitating the economic growth and cultural integration of his kingdom; and (5) augmenting his personal reputation as a great Hellenistic monarch.[27] At the same time, Herod advanced the Hellenization (or Romanization) of Judea and its environs, introducing Roman building techniques, styles, and institutions (e.g., bath complexes, amphitheaters) into cities throughout his realm. As Mark Chancey remarks: "Ironically, Pompey, Gabinius, and the early Roman governors did less to introduce Hellenistic and Roman architecture to Palestine than did an Idumean Jew, Herod the Great."[28]

How did Herod finance all of this, not to mention his other expenses (for example, his standing militia of at least five hundred soldiers)? Herod no doubt had significant income from family lands in Idumea,

---

Herod, the pious and friend of Caesar (*philokaisara*), on account of virtue and beneficence." *IG* II[2] 3441 (= *OGIS* 427). See Richardson 1996:207–208.

[27] Richardson 1996:192–195; Gruen 2018:387.
[28] Chancey 2005:96.

as his father and grandfather were both leading figures from and in that region. He also enjoyed the income from the so-called royal estates that had supplied funds for the privy purse of the Ptolemies, Seleucids, and Hasmoneans before him. He also taxed his subjects. While the pious Jews would pay their tithes to the temple and its staff, these were not public funds, which had to be raised through a variety of taxes. These included the following: (1) a poll tax, a tax levied upon each individual aged twelve (in the case of females) or fourteen (in the case of males) to sixty-five as well as a tax on movable property, including slaves; (2) a land tax upon immovable property (assessed in cash and in produce); (3) a tax on salt, which was a necessary preservative; (4) a "crown tax," originally a voluntary contribution to the ruler but by this time a mandatory payment; and (5) a tax on goods moved across borders, including at ports, known to have been set as high as 25 percent of the value.[29] These would essentially continue under Roman rule, with the chief difference being that they were paid directly to the Roman administrators.

Herod's building projects throughout his territory also provided a major boost to the economy through providing new employment opportunities on a vast scale as well as creating the demand for support industries first for the hordes of builders and then for the new or greatly enlarged cities and their growing populations. A sign of this is the fact that eighteen thousand workers were still employed on the Jerusalem temple project (which had suffered some setbacks and required ongoing maintenance) when work was finally completed just a few years before its destruction in 70 CE. Herod's improvements to Jerusalem in particular no doubt also helped to promote its "tourist economy" in connection with the three annual pilgrimage festivals that brought worshipers not only from all corners of Herod's realm but also from many Jewish communities throughout the diaspora, for whom the journey had become more feasible thanks to the increased safety and relatively greater ease of travel under the *pax Romana*. While not everyone in his realm benefited from his rule—and while some benefited disproportionately, as the palatial mansions in Jerusalem's Upper City bear witness—Herod appears to have generally led his

---

[29] Schäfer 2003:90–91.

realm into a state of greater prosperity. And when a famine struck his kingdom and neighboring territories in the province of Syria in 28/27 BCE, Herod went to great lengths and incurred significant personal expense to relieve those who were affected. He even stripped his own palaces of their precious metal content for ready cash to purchase grain from Egypt.[30] This is not necessarily the sign of a tender heart toward his subjects, to be sure: Herod no doubt expected his extreme efforts to redound to his glory as a ruler and arouse loyalty among his subjects. It does, however, suggest that he was more concerned with having a reputation for generosity and beneficence than exploiting his subjects—something that would not prove true for several Roman procurators.

At the same time, Herod met with frequent criticism and opposition, and where there was a clear source he or she was frequently snuffed out. His introduction of Hellenistic practices and cultural events (theaters, chariot races, athletic and artistic contests) into Jerusalem itself did not go unopposed. The frequency with which bands of "brigands" arise suggests not only revolutionary activity, but the desperate measures to which uprooted peasants and dispossessed landholders could be driven by an economy whose benefits were far from universally enjoyed.[31] And while Herod appears to have restrained his artistic expression considerably so as to not give offense to his Jewish subjects (his coins, for example, generally avoid offensive images), he almost inexplicably provoked them by placing a statue of a golden eagle over one of the gates of the Temple complex. Even if this obvious nod to Roman power was placed over the gateway to which the bridge from the Upper City led, that is, the path that would be used by the most Hellenized elites and distinguished Roman visitors accompanying Herod from his palace,[32] it was an incongruous display of a graven image next to Herod's greatest monument to his regard for Jewish religious practice. When Herod was close to death, two Jewish teachers rallied their disciples to tear it down—an act of pious vandalism that would cost all those involved their lives.

[30] Richardson 1996:222–223.
[31] Richardson 1996:251.
[32] Richardson 1996:17.

Herod's Family and Heirs

Josephus gives a great deal of attention to the drama and disaster in Herod's private life. His family was inherently unstable, with children from nine or ten marriages vying for and forming coalitions with one another and with other members of this vastly extended family with regard to the succession.[33] As soon as Herod was securely on the throne, troubles began on account of lingering Hasmonean ambitions within his own family—and lingering support for a Hasmonean dynasty among the Judean population. Herod would execute his second wife, Mariamme, the granddaughter of Hyrcanus II and Herod's bid for legitimacy in the eyes of his subjects, on the charges of infidelity and suspected treason in 29 BCE. Her mother, Alexandra, instigated rebellion and was executed the following year.[34] Herod's two sons by Mariamme, Aristobulus and Alexander, emerged as the heirs apparent, but they were themselves targeted by Herod's younger siblings Salome and Pheroras and by Antipater, Herod's firstborn son by an Idumean named Doris. It is impossible to know whether the pair were really involved in plots against their father or whether Herod's mind was unjustly poisoned against them, but Herod had them tried for treason before Augustus in 12 BCE, who acquitted them and reconciled them to their father, and then had them tried a second time in Berytus in 7 BCE, resulting in their condemnation and execution. Antipater would not profit from his plots against his brothers, however, as he, too, would be convicted of plotting against Herod and executed days before Herod's own death in 4 BCE at the end of a painful, protracted illness.

Under Roman rule, client kingdoms were not automatically hereditary. As a measure of respect, Augustus had given Herod the authority to name his own heir, though the fact that Augustus would still have to ratify Herod's will opened the door for Herod's sons to contest the division of the kingdom as well as for an embassy from other sectors of the Judean population to request an end to Herodian rule tout court. The problem of succession was exacerbated by the existence of two wills written by Herod within days of each other following Antipater's execution *and* by the power vested in Augustus to make the final determination concerning which will was valid. Herod's unstable frame of mind in his final weeks, greatly exacerbated by the wasting disease that racked his body, gave good grounds for dispute.

The contenders were Herod's sons by two other wives—Archelaus and Antipas, sons of Malthace, a Samaritan woman, and Philip, son of a Cleopatra from Jerusalem. All three had been educated in Rome and were known personally to Augustus. In the earlier of the two wills, Herod named Antipas his sole heir. In the later of the two, Herod named Archelaus, his oldest surviving son, "king" of Judea, Samaritis, and Idumea, while naming both Antipas and Philip "tetrarchs" of much smaller and less lucrative regions—assigning Galilee and Peraea to Antipas and the largely Gentile territories of Gaulanitis, Trachonitis, and Batanea to Philip. Augustus allowed Herod's final will to stand and, thus, divided Herod's kingdom into three separate jurisdictions, though he gave Archelaus the title of "ethnarch" rather than "king." The relative youth of each of the candidates at the time—nineteen, seventeen, and sixteen, respectively—might have led Augustus to prefer this arrangement to entrusting the whole kingdom to seventeen-year-old Antipas.[35]

Archelaus and the Heartland

Archelaus proved the least fit to rule. Even prior to his visit to Rome for Augustus's confirmation, his folly began to manifest itself. Without assuming the crown or the name of "king," he nevertheless presented himself to the public in Jerusalem as the likely successor. He gave in to enough demands made upon him by his subjects that they naturally made more. His resistance to further concessions led to demonstrations that Archelaus's soldiers forcibly suppressed. These continued to escalate, resulting in the massacre of three thousand Jerusalem residents and pilgrims, as all of this happened during the season of Passover.

Matters grew worse in Archelaus's absence, this time in connection with the next pilgrimage festival in Jerusalem, the festival of Pentecost,

[35] Richardson 1996:29.

with memories of the massacre at Passover seven weeks before still fresh on the minds of all concerned. Sabinus, the procurator of the province of Syria (under the authority, but against the wishes of Varus, the governor of Syria), used the interregnum to try to take stock and custody of Herod's wealth and, in the clashes that resulted with the local population, created an opportunity for his soldiers and himself to plunder the sanctuary. Conflict escalated in Jerusalem while local "strong men" like Judas ben-Hezekiah at Sepphoris and Athronges and his brothers in the periphery of Judea wrought havoc, attacking and pillaging administrative centers. As their revolutionary movements gathered greater numbers of followers, each group acted as if they had some hope of installing their favorite as king. Varus, the governor of Syria, imposed peace in the typically Roman manner: a shock and awe campaign throughout Galilee and Judea ending with the crucifixion of some two thousand men in the environs of Jerusalem. An ongoing reality of Judea under Roman rule was the fragility of the security of one's life in a system where summary "justice" and punishments serving the purpose of state terror were normal.

Little else is known about Archelaus's rule, save that he was removed by Augustus ten years later, in 6 CE, in response to complaints of misrule and brutality lodged by both Judean and Samaritan delegations. The fact that these inveterate rivals could agree on any point lent significant weight to the complaint. Unable to create stable conditions as his father had done so well for so long, he was exiled beyond the Alps to Gaul in 6 CE and died a few years later (Dio Cassius 55.27). Matthew's comment about the undesirability of living under Archelaus's rule resonates, it appears, with the opinion of many (Matt 2:22).

Philip and the Northeastern Territories

Josephus recounts very little concerning Philip save that he governed well and diligently exercised his responsibility to hear cases and dispense justice, remaining in his territory for the whole of his reign and traveling a regular circuit (*Ant.* 18.106–107). His father had expended very little on the territories that fell to Philip apart from the temple of Augustus and Roma at Paneas, in the vicinity of Pan's grotto and shrine. Philip expanded Paneas and made it his capital, rebranding it as Caesarea in Augustus's honor. It would come to be known as Caesarea Philippi, "Philip's Caesarea," to distinguish it from Caesarea Maritima ("Caesarea by the Sea"). He also improved the town of Bethsaida beside Lake Gennesaret (the Sea of Galilee), transforming it into a walled city named Bethsaida Julias, after the emperor's wife, Livia Julia (*Ant.* 18.28).[36]

Because Philip's territory was largely Gentile save for some enclaves of Jewish subjects, as at Bethsaida, his coins frequently feature portraits of members of the imperial family—and sometimes even his own portrait—on the obverse and pagan religious symbols on the reverse. A favorite, unsurprisingly, is the façade of the temple of Augustus and Roma that proclaimed his father's and now, through his coinage, his loyalty and gratitude to the emperor's house. Philip continued in his position as tetrarch until his death in 33 CE—a testimony to his ability to maintain stable conditions and, thus, the goodwill both of his subjects and his imperial patrons. As he had no children, his territory was temporarily absorbed into the province of Syria after his death while awaiting a decision by Tiberius concerning its ultimate disposition—a decision that would be deferred until Gaius came to power.

Antipas and Galilee

Galilee was surrounded by Greek cities. The Decapolis cities bordered Galilee's eastern circumference, while the hinterlands of the seacoast cities of Ptolemais and Tyre bordered Galilee's northwest. Any Gentile population within Galilee itself, however, would have been drastically reduced by the many battles fought between the Ptolemaic and Seleucid armies (or between rival Seleucid armies) in the region that

---

[36] Josephus describes this Julia as "the emperor's daughter," which would be highly problematic if he meant Augustus's biological daughter, whom he exiled to the island of Pandateria for multiple adulteries in 2 BCE. Livia, however, had been adopted posthumously as Augustus's daughter and, thus, inducted into the Julian line. It would also have been proper for Philip to honor Livia after 14 CE by naming a city "Julias" (rather than "Livias") after this (and for Josephus to refer to Livia as "the emperor's daughter").

left land and villages destroyed, by Hasmonean raids and expansion, and by aggressive Judean colonization. By the time of Herod the Great, almost all Galileans would have self-identified as Jews.[37] In terms of material culture, they differ very little from the majority of Judeans. In both Judea and Galilee, one finds chalk or limestone household vessels bearing witness to a shared interest in ritual purity (cf. John 2:6); ritual immersion pools (*miqvaoth*) in the wealthier homes, beside synagogues, and near many agricultural installations like olive and wine presses; a marked preference for locally made pottery and avoidance of finer, imported (Gentile) ware; ossuaries for the collection and permanent storage of the deceased's bones after the flesh had decayed; the marked absence of pig bones, suggesting adherence to the dietary regulations of the Torah; and the absence of pagan cultic sites in the region from the Hasmonean through the early Roman periods. Indeed, the shared material culture suggests that many Galileans were descended from Judean settlers from the period of Hasmonean expansion—and that they continued to prioritize local, Jewish identity and the practices of ritual purity that helped underscore that distinctive identity.[38] By all accounts, they remained closely connected with Jerusalem and its temple, participating in its pilgrimage festivals, flocking to its defense when threatened with desecration. It is likely that some Galileans, as descendants of Judean colonists, still had family in Jerusalem and its environs.[39] The proximity of Scythopolis, Hippos, and Gadara suggests that many Galileans would have had some familiarity with pagan practice and civic life,[40] though evidence for the use of Greek or the spread of Greek culture among the population in the villages of Galilee in the first centuries BCE and CE is quite sparse.[41]

Herod the Great had done very little to develop Galilee. It remained largely a region full of villages with an agrarian economy. Many of these villages would have been small. Calculations based on acreage and probable population density suggest that Nazareth, for example, accommodated between three hundred and four hundred people

---

[37] Freyne 1998:259–304; Reed 2000:9–10; Chancey 2005:19.
[38] Berlin 2005:425, 467; Reed 2000:21.
[39] Reed 2000:57–58.
[40] Chancey 2005:222.
[41] Freyne 1998:138–145; Chancey 2005:122–165.

while a larger village like Capernaum might have accommodated between one thousand and seventeen hundred.[42] Most of the residents farmed the land, growing the grains, olives, grapes, and smaller-scale fruit and vegetable crops that they also largely consumed. Families kept a small number of animals to provide themselves with milk, eggs, and the occasional meat dish. As the agricultural cycle has natural ebbs and flows in its demands for labor, most families would also engage in some kind of "side gigs" to supplement their subsistence-level existence.[43] The Sea of Galilee (Lake Gennesaret), of course, supported a strong fishing industry.[44]

Excavations at a number of these villages provide windows into the lived spaces of their residents. These typically consist of small three-room dwellings (three hundred to six hundred square feet total) opening onto an open courtyard, which is often a common courtyard shared by the residents of three or four dwellings. The largest room was a multipurpose room for cooking, dining, and often sleeping; the smaller rooms were used to store grain, other dry goods, olive oil, and wine. Some feature an upper loft which might or might not also afford roof access, generally for sleeping, if this was not done in the multipurpose room. Most activities, including flour grinding, weaving, and other household crafts, would be pursued in the courtyard in fair weather, where livestock would also be kept at least during the night, small vegetable gardens planted, and chickens and doves raised. Cooking might be done in indoor kitchens or in corners of courtyards.[45] The walls facing the streets and alleys were typically solid for security: light came into the dwellings from the courtyard and through the internal walls, which were perforated with large openings (often called "window walls"). Roofs were made of mud and thatch laid over beams, hence the ability to "dig through" a roof (Mark 2:4).

Galilee continued to be a theater of war as the Hasmonean dynasty declined. The region suffered significant devastation during the period of the civil wars between Hyrcanus II and Aristobulus II and then

---

[42] Horsley 1996:89; Reed 2000:83.
[43] See, further, Safrai 2010.
[44] On Galilee, see also Josephus's valuable observations as a native informant in *War* 3.35–44, 516–520.
[45] Killebrew 2010:198–200; Reed 2000:157; Horsley 1996:115.

between Herod the Great and Mattathias Antigonus. In between, it was hit by the brutal and rapacious acts of Roman generals like Cassius, who reportedly devastated Tarichaeae and enslaved thirty thousand people (Josephus, *Ant.* 14.120; *War* 1.180) and later imposed a heavy tribute on Galilee and Judea, with Herod distinguishing himself by shaking down Galilee alone for a whopping one hundred talents. All of these brought dangerous disruptions to a fragile agrarian economy along with loss of life, destruction of villages and cropland, deportation of prisoners-made-slaves, and the extraction of income that was far from disposable for those affected. However secure most Galileans were upon their land at the beginning of Roman rule, many were well positioned to have lost it or to be on the precipice of losing it by the time Antipas inherited the region. It might also have indeed changed the dynamics of Galilean life to have its Roman-backed and Rome-serving ruler in the immediate vicinity rather than at some distance in Jerusalem and Caesarea.[46]

It was under Antipas that urbanization saw major advances in Galilee. Sepphoris, located in the heart of lower Galilee, equidistant from the Lake of Gennesaret and the Mediterranean coast, would have qualified as a small, fortified city from the time of the Seleucids if not the Ptolemies. It was occupied under Hasmonean rule (Josephus, *Ant.* 14.413–414; *War* 1.303) and was the administrative center of Galilee during the few years that Gabinius had divided Hyrcanus II's realm into five districts. It suffered heavy damage and depopulation, however, in the revolt of 4 BCE, during which Judas, the son of the "bandit chief" Hezekiah whom a young Herod the Great had executed, had taken over Sepphoris and made it his base of operations (Josephus, *Ant.* 17.271–272; *War* 2.56). Antipas decided to rebuild it with the goal of making it "the ornament of all Galilee," as would befit his capital city (Josephus, *Ant.* 18.27). Prior to the First Jewish Revolt, the architects and residents of Sepphoris appear to have respected Jewish sensibilities. The mosaics featuring scenes from Greek mythology and the facilities for pagan cult all date from the late Roman period.

Sepphoris appears not to have satisfied Antipas for long. Within twenty years he was breaking ground for an entirely new city where

---

[46] Horsley 1996:11.

only a cemetery had sat before. His new capital, set winsomely on the southwest shore of Lake Gennesaret and just north of some hot springs, was named Tiberias in honor of Augustus's successor, Tiberius (ruled 14–37 CE). Josephus reports that the location of the site was problematic for pious Jews, such that Antipas had to bribe new residents with land and houses, though this would not pose a problem for the rabbis who would relocate here during the third and fourth centuries CE.[47] One wonders, therefore, if Josephus was fabricating an origins story that would besmirch a city whose population would give him significant personal trouble later during the First Revolt. Antipas did cross a line, however, when he used representations of lions as decorations on his new palace, which would become a focal point for hostility during the First Revolt (Josephus, *Ant.* 18.38; *Vita* 64–65). Tiberias had a theater from its earliest occupation, but it also reportedly had a large synagogue (or "prayer house"). Antipas was clearly trying to provide both for the Jewish citizens as well as the non-Jews who would be attracted to his cities and, of course, employed in his administration. Antipas would, incidentally, have maintained and paid for his own (reasonably small) army. When we read about Jesus of Nazareth's interactions with a "centurion" in Capernaum, we should think not of a Roman soldier, but a local army officer (who might still have been Gentile, in keeping with Antipas's father's policy on recruiting).[48]

Sepphoris and Tiberias gave Antipas an outlet for his ambitions to improve his disappointingly small realm, but these remained very modest cities in comparison with Scythopolis or Caesarea Maritima. Sepphoris is thought to have accommodated a population of between six thousand and fifteen thousand and Tiberias a population of between eight thousand and twelve thousand in the first century.[49] They would have been seen as quite backward in terms of the degree of Hellenization or the presence of the typical institutions of Greek cities. Nevertheless, these projects would have required significant funding and resources, and it is unclear if Antipas enjoyed any of the income from the "royal lands" that his father had enjoyed (the Jezreel Valley

---

[47] Grabbe 2021:337.
[48] Horsley 1996:115; Reed 2000:156, 161–162.
[49] Reed 2000:80.

would have been the most likely, if he did). He might have relied almost wholly upon the various taxes in place for his subjects.

Would the building of these cities have benefited the Galilean economy or stifled it through Herod Antipas's demands for taxes and tribute from the people of his realm? On the one hand, the building projects certainly meant increased prosperity for some, for example the hundreds or potentially thousands of masons, artisans, and laborers working on the cities as well as those staffing the service industries that would arise to sustain urban life. On the other hand, these efforts would have drained a good deal of local resources and villagers' meager wealth through ongoing—and potentially increased—taxation without the benefit of the additional income.[50]

The emergence or growth of cities profoundly affects the economies of the surrounding agrarian communities, creating a large demand for produce on the part of people who do not actually work the land themselves. In the ancient world, cities were granted hinterlands— essentially the amount of land necessary to support its population. It appears that Sepphoris and Tiberias essentially acquired hinterlands as their elite populations increased their landholdings at the expense of the economically endangered landed peasantry, with the result that many found themselves renting and working the land they (or their parents or their grandparents) might have once owned. In many cases, people could find themselves entirely alienated from the land and eking out a subsistence-level living as day laborers or, when that proved impossible, descending into banditry.[51] The parables of Jesus, incidentally, feature people from every notch in this economic scale (see Matt 20:1–16; 21:33–41). The possibility also exists that villages were simply assigned to serve as hinterlands for the new or enlarged cities, as appears to have been the case for the fourteen villages that came to be considered part of the territory of Antipas's improved city of Julias (Betharamphtha) in Perea (see Josephus, *Ant.* 20.159).

---

[50] Horsley 1996:82, 123; Reed 2000:22.

[51] Horsley 1996:10–11; Hamel 2010:312; Oakman 2014. Grabbe (2021:104–105) doubts large-scale alienation of small landowners from their holdings and suggests that many day laborers were not necessarily landless peasants. Working one's own small holding might often not have required six days of labor every week of the year (particularly during the winter months; Grabbe 2021:110).

Antipas's rule appears to have been fairly stable and free of significant disturbances. The most famous critic of Antipas was no doubt John the Baptizer (or John the Immerser), whose activity as a prophet of repentance seems not to have been particularly geared toward political critique. Indeed, Josephus mentions only John's popularity and ability to draw a following—and thus the vague possibility of fomenting revolutionary action—as a cause for concern to Antipas (*Ant.* 18.109–119). Early Christian sources make it more personal, positing an attack on John's part, in true prophetic fashion, against the legality of Antipas's marriage in the sight of God (Mark 6:17–18; Luke 3:19–20). Antipas had married Herodias, the ex-wife of Antipas's half-brother (a private citizen named Herod) and, at the same time, his niece (she was the daughter of Antipas's half-brother Aristobulus, one of Mariamne's sons). Thus, according to the Law of Moses, she was forbidden fruit on two counts (a fact that was made worse by Antipas's politically harmful step of divorcing his first wife, the daughter of the Nabatean king Aretas IV, stirring up international troubles later for Antipas and for those who had to finance his battles through their taxes). These accounts appear to be complementary rather than contradictory. A popular prophetic figure who has gathered a following and started pointing out a ruler's violation of the law code embraced as holy and inviolable by the majority of his subjects would be an obvious threat justifying—in Antipas's mind, at least—incarceration and, eventually, execution for the sake of the stability of one's rule. Aretas IV would later attack Antipas's territory in Perea—on Aretas's side of the Jordan—after Philip's death in 34 CE, likely in an attempt to expand into Philip's territory. Antipas's army suffered a crushing defeat before Antipas appealed to Tiberius who, while won over to Antipas's side, died before his generals in Syria could punish Aretas.[52]

Synagogues

By the time of Herod and his heirs, the synagogue had become an important and pervasive institution in Judea and Galilee. The synagogue

---

[52] Grabbe 2021:337–338.

appears to have its origins in diaspora Jewish communities, where the need to develop organs for social and religious cohesion among Jews would have been greater and more deeply felt, and where the Temple in Jerusalem could not serve such a function on anything like a regular basis. Inscriptions from Egypt in the second half of the third century BCE attest to the existence of *proseuchai*, "houses of prayer," as a venue for bringing Jews together for the expression of their common devotion.[53] The name is suggestive of their principal purpose, though these would quickly grow to become centers serving a wide variety of community purposes.[54] Clear evidence for such structures in Judea and its environs appears by the late first century BCE and increases into the first century CE.

An important inscription, dated to the early first century CE, was discovered in the Ophel district, to the south of the Temple mount: "Theodotus, the son of Vettenus, priest and *archisynagōgus*, son of an *archisynagōgus*, grandson of an *archisynagōgus*, built the synagogue (*synagōgē*) for the reading of the Law and the study of the commandments, and a guesthouse and rooms and water installations for hosting those in need from abroad, it having been founded by his fathers, the presbyters, and Simonides" (see Figure 4.3).[55] The guest rooms attached to this particular synagogue in Jerusalem would likely be offered to diaspora Jews traveling into the city for one of the major pilgrimage festivals (as well as at other times) and so suggests symbiosis rather than competition between the synagogue and temple.[56] The title of *archisynagogos* appears in some instances to denote an active role in leadership in liturgical and other activities, in others to serve as an honorific for a local benefactor—and there is no reason that it could not be used in both senses for the same individual.[57]

More impressive evidence is to be found in the archaeological remains of buildings identified as synagogues in Gamla, Madgala, Modi'in, and the makeshift rooms in Herodium and Masada. All of these ceased to function during the First Revolt and its aftermath—but

---

53   Grabbe 1988:402–403.
54   Bloedhorn and Hüttenmeister 1999:269.
55   Translation from Levine 2002:395.
56   Magness 2012:290.
57   Magness 2012:288.

Figure 4.3 The Theodotus Inscription. It is important to note that this inscription was written in Greek, which would have been the first language of many diaspora Jews and the common language by which Jews from the Mediterranean diaspora and Judea could converse with one another.

they thereby also bear witness to the existence, even the flourishing, of this institution throughout the first century CE (see Figure 4.4).[58]

Synagogues were, first and foremost, places for the reading and study of the Torah and other scriptures, evidenced indirectly by the memory of Jesus's teaching ministry in Galilee (e.g., Mark 1:21–29; 6:1–6; Luke 4:16–37, 44; 6:6; 7:5) and Paul's teaching activity in synagogues throughout the diaspora (Acts 9:2, 20; 13:5, 14; 14:1, etc.). It was the natural place for laity to gain the level of proficiency in the Law about which both Josephus (*Ag. Ap.* 2.175) and Philo (*Vit. Mos.* 2.211–216) boast.[59] It probably did not cease to function as a place of prayer, though the only explicit evidence for what such prayer involved comes from the Mishnah (*m. Meg.* 4.1–5), which speaks of the

---

[58] Other early Roman-period synagogues have been found at Shikhin, Qiryat Sepher, Tel Rekhesh, and Beth Shemesh (Ben David 2021:182).

[59] Cohen 1999:305; Horbury 1999:364. See also the Theodotus inscription and Philo, *Leg.* 156.

Figure 4.4 The remnants of the synagogue at Gamla, displaying a common architectural footprint.

recitation of the *Shema* and the "Eighteen Benedictions" (*Shemoneh Esre*), a series of prayers couched in the forms of statements blessing God for a wide array of characteristics and interventions.[60] These are followed by the reading from and discussion of the Torah and the whole closes with a recitation of the priestly benediction where a quorum of ten is gathered.[61] Despite the common claim that women were seated in a separate section in Roman-period synagogues, no archaeological or literary evidence lends it support.[62] Ritual immersion pools (*mikvaoth*) are frequently found adjacent to synagogues, reminiscent of the same surrounding the Jerusalem temple. This might reflect merely a concern for safeguarding the ritual purity of others when gathering, though it might also indicate that those attending to prayer

[60] The form including all eighteen benedictions likely postdates the Temple's destruction (Reif 1999:350).
[61] Horbury 1999:363.
[62] Tal Ilan 2010: 61.

and study were aware that they were preparing for an encounter with the Holy One—and doing so in a manner analogous to preparation for entering the Temple precincts.

While synagogues might well have served as places of study during the other six days of the week for those who had the leisure and inclination, they were also active centers for community affairs: "Children were exposed near a synagogue; divorce warrants were drawn up; the loss and recovery of property was announced; legal witnesses could be publicly sought; visitors could eat and drink. Business was transacted, halakhic decisions were given, corpses were laid out; justice was administered; matters of general concern were announced."[63] The shift in terminology from *proseuchai* to *synagōgai* may reflect the acknowledgment of the growing range of purposes served by this institution, though Josephus still uses "prayer house" to refer to a large structure in Tiberias of Galilee that clearly also served other community functions, such as that of a community center where common concerns could be discussed (Josephus, *Life* 277–279).[64]

[63] Bloedhorn and Hüttenmeister 1999:295.
[64] Williams 1999:77.

5

Under the Eagle's Wings

Judea under Roman Rule

The early period of direct Roman rule from the first prefects through the First Jewish Revolt is, along with the Herodian period, the best documented in the literary sources. Because we know the tragic conclusion of this story, there is a great temptation to read the whole as one of ever-increasing bilateral tensions and hostility between the Judean and Galilean subjects and their Roman overlords. However, as the literary sources make abundantly clear, the period was characterized by far more complex and varied dynamics. These factors, which worked together to create the conditions that precipitated the revolt, included economic tensions within Judea and Galilee; local tensions between the Jewish and non-Jewish populations of the regions (made worse by the fact that a large number of the local Roman auxiliaries came from the Samarian and Caesarean population); the heavy-handed, often exploitative, sometimes inexplicably provocative behavior on the part of Roman prefects and, especially, the later procurators; as well as the religious heritage and memories of Judean independence that naturally fed revolutionary activity and ideology.

Josephus is again our principal historiographical source for this period, though some episodes (for example, Caligula's attempt to install a statue of himself in the Temple) are supplemented by accounts from other voices (in this case, Philo's). Josephus's presentation of the First Jewish Revolt, in particular, has to be tested against other surviving reminiscences of the revolt, archaeological evidence, and his own propagandistic purposes in writing. The latter include (1) a clear desire to place the greater part of blame for the revolt upon a revolutionary fringe within the Judean population (though his own position as a general in Galilee bears a contrary witness); (2) a clear desire to present Vespasian and Titus, his personal patrons in Rome, in the best possible light and to glorify their achievement in Judaea; and (3) a clear desire to magnify his own importance, first as a rebel commander and then as a mediator on behalf of the Roman forces with the besieged population of Jerusalem. His version was not uncontested, as his venom toward a rival historian, Justus of Tiberias, bears witness (Josephus, *Life*, 336–367). And Josephus's claim to have the imprimatur of Vespasian, Titus, and Agrippa II for his account in the *War* only means that he adequately represents the victors' perspectives on the conflict—and their desires for how they and their war would be remembered.

The Early Prefects

After the exile of Archelaus in 6 CE, Judea, Samaritis, and Idumea came under direct Roman administration. These territories did not constitute an independent province in the normal sense, for they were governed by prefects drawn from the second tier of Roman society— the equestrians, or "knights"—rather than from the senatorial class. The *prefects* and, after 44 CE, *procurators* were entrusted with the oversight of judicial, military (which often meant "policing"), and financial matters, and they had the authority to inflict capital punishment. While generally enjoying much independence, these prefects were ultimately answerable to the governor of the larger province of Syria, who was a senator and had command over one or more Roman legions, and who was ultimately responsible for the peace of the whole region. Indeed, the intervention of the governor of Syria was sought by the people within the prefect's jurisdiction on several occasions when the prefect was not seen to have properly enforced justice or given adequate protection to some part of the population. Conversely, the governor also had to intervene on the prefect's behalf when the latter's forces were insufficient for the task. Josephus lays a great deal of blame on these middlemen, the prefects (and, especially, the later procurators) sent to Judea by Rome, perhaps as a distraction from what others would name the larger problem: Roman intrusion into the Land in the first place.

The new administrative center was Caesarea Maritima, a port city with speedier access to and from Rome and the cultural amenities and religious environment more appropriate to a largely Roman and

Greek administrative staff and military. The military corps consisted of five auxiliary infantry units and one cavalry unit, about three thousand strong in all (Josephus, *War* 3.66). These were mostly recruited from the non-Jewish populations of Caesarea and Sebaste, following the practice of Herod the Great (Josephus, *Ant.* 20.176). Indeed, there appears to have been a good deal of continuity between Herod's army, which Archelaus inherited, and the Roman auxiliaries. At least one infantry unit was stationed in Jerusalem, chiefly at the Antonia fortress. Masada and several other fortresses from Herod's time also appear to have been garrisoned at least by detachments.[1] The prefects along with additional troops tended to relocate to Jerusalem during the three annual pilgrimage festivals—the concentration of so many Jews from a vast geographical distribution in one city and the swirling of religious themes being thought to require additional policing, even though the presence of increased Roman "security" forces would on occasion prove to contribute more to the volatility of the mix than to allay unrest.

As Herod and Archelaus had enjoyed the authority to appoint the high priests, the legates of Syria and the prefects of Judea assumed this prerogative as well, no doubt also continuing the policy of selecting the candidate most likely to cooperate with Rome's interests and work to assure that the Sanhedrin and people followed suit. As a perpetual reminder that the Temple service operated by the good graces of the Roman authorities and not by any inalienable right, the high priest's vestments were kept "safe" in the Antonia fortress except for the highest holy days when the priestly staff could retrieve them early enough in advance to assure their ritual purity (Josephus, *War* 6.333–335).[2] Quirinius, the legate of Syria in 6 CE, appointed Ananus I, the Annas of the Gospels, as high priest, instituting something of an unofficial dynasty of high priests that would sporadically hold the office between 6 and 66 CE. Ananus himself would hold the office from 6 to 15 CE; his more famous son-in-law, Caiaphas, would occupy it from 18 to 37 CE.

---

[1] Smallwood 1981:147.
[2] Perdue and Carter 2015:270.

Most taxes were now paid directly to Rome. Quirinius was charged with conducting a census of persons and property for the purposes of taxation, an action that makes most sense at this point of transition from Herodian to direct Roman governance in 6 CE (Josephus, *Ant.* 18.26; vs. Luke 2:1–5). The census brought home the significance of the transition: once again, Judea and its neighboring territories would be ruled by a foreign nation rather than an indigenous king, however problematic he might have been. Josephus credits Judas the Galilean with the birth of the "fourth philosophy" in connection with the census (*Ant.* 18.7–10, 23–25). These revolutionaries, according to Josephus, shared the religious convictions and many of the practices of the Pharisees, but they were also committed to national independence in the manner of the Maccabees. Josephus creates here a convenient catch-all category for religiously motivated nationalistic impulses— which did not constitute a "fourth philosophy" in anything like an organized movement. Nevertheless, pious nationalism would play an important part on the stage of Roman Judea and Galilee, beginning with revolutionary activity protesting the census itself. It is common to hear participants in all such activity given the name "Zealots," but "Zealots" only truly emerge in Josephus's narrative in connection with the war of 66–70 CE, and then only as one of several revolutionary parties who fought one another as ruthlessly as they eventually fought the Romans when the latter were finally at the very walls of Jerusalem. The early Christian Gospels consistently portray tax collectors as among the most despised members of Judean and Galilean society, which might best be explained by popular resentment toward Roman rule focused on Jewish collaborators who facilitated—and profited from!—the same (see, e.g., Mark 2:15–16; Matt 11:18–19; 18:17; Luke 19:1–7).

Josephus gives minimal information about the period of the earliest prefects—Coponius (6–9 CE), Marcus Ambibulus (9–12 CE), and Annius Rufus (12–15 CE)—and what he does report is suspect. All that is known about Valerius Gratus (15–26 CE) concerns his high priestly appointments. He removed Ananus from office, ending his ten-year tenure; appointed three short-term high priests who were clearly unsatisfactory to him; and landed finally on Caiaphas, who would prove sufficiently competent (and, one might surmise, sensitive to Roman as well as Judean interests) to remain in the office until 37 CE.

Pontius Pilatus, prefect from 26 to 37 CE, has left more of an imprint on history (see Figure 5.1). Pilate's predecessors, following the lead of Herod himself, had been careful to mint coins that bore inoffensive images. Pilate alone chose images of Roman religious cult paraphernalia—the *lituus* and *simpulum*. While these were somewhat obscure symbols, the choice nevertheless suggests a person who was more reluctant to accommodate Judean sensibilities than his predecessors or immediate successors.

Figure 5.1 A partial inscription from Caesarea bearing the name of Pontius Pilate and his title as prefect of Judea. Pilate appears to have paid for the construction of a shrine or other monument to Tiberias (a "Tiberieum").

Pilate wished to change the cohort stationed at Antonia in Jerusalem, choosing one whose standard included images of the emperor. This provoked an uproar in Jerusalem and protestors followed Pilate back to Caesarea, where they demonstrated for days. Pilate threatened them with violence if they did not desist, but they knelt on the ground and pulled their garments away from their necks, signaling a willingness to die protesting the violation of the prohibition of images—particularly images of alleged deities known to be worshiped by other nations—in their holiest city. Pilate relented at last, replacing the cohort with one whose standard did not bear offensive images. Philo (*Embassy*, 299–301, 306) relates a similar episode in which Pilate decorated the praetorium in Jerusalem (the former palace of Herod) with golden shields that bore no image, but only some kind of dedicatory inscription. If this had been "Pilate, in honor of Tiberius," it would be difficult to understand the offense; if it had been "Pilate, in honor of Tiberius, son of the deified Augustus," it would have been understandably provocative. Here, too, Pilate yielded to local protests, removing the shields to Caesarea Maritima.

He also spearheaded a project to improve the water supply of Jerusalem through the construction of an additional aqueduct, appropriating funds from the temple treasury for this purpose. It is difficult to know how Pilate justified this in his own mind. Perhaps he considered it an advance on tribute to meet a pressing need that would benefit—and ought to be embraced as a benefit by—the whole city. In any event, the response was predictable: vocal demonstrations at Pilate's next appearance in Jerusalem against his violation of the Temple's sanctity and the sanctity of whatever was deposited there to be safeguarded. Pilate ordered his troops to use their clubs to disperse the protestors; Josephus suggests that they intentionally used excessive force, resulting in many deaths. Here the latent tensions between the Sebastenes and Caesarians who made up the auxiliaries, on the one hand, and the population of Judea, on the other hand, may have been on display as the former made full use of an opportunity to inflict harm on a population they regarded as enemies. Some believe that the episode to which Jesus refers in Luke's Gospel (13:1–3), namely the deaths of several Galileans during a pilgrimage festival, is to be identified with this one, but we need not assume Josephus to be exhaustive in his catalogue of incidents during Pilate's long tenure. The group known as "Herodians" (Mark 3:6; 12:13) may well have arisen during this time, lobbying for a restoration of rule by a member of the Herodian family, someone who would be likely to show greater awareness of and sensitivity to the religious scruples of the region.[3]

The incident that brought about Pilate's recall involved a massing of Samaritans around their holy mountain, Gerizim, at the instigation of a prophet who promised to reveal the location of the sacred vessels of the historic Tabernacle that had been buried shortly after the Hebrews' occupation of the land. Pilate suspected a revolutionary movement—and the fact that some number of those gathered had arrived armed seems in retrospect to have justified his misgivings. His troops clashed with the gathered assembly, killing many on the spot and rounding up those believed to be the leaders for execution. The Samaritan elders appealed to Vitellius, then legate of Syria, accusing Pilate of excessive force against a peaceful, religious gathering. Vitellius relieved Pilate and sent him back to Rome to answer these charges. He also visited Jerusalem on this occasion, replacing Caiaphas with Jonathan, a son of Annas, and restoring custody of the high priest's vestments to the temple staff (after being authorized to do so by Tiberius). Both may reflect an awareness that Pilate's tenure had been problematic and, as a result, a desire on Vitellius's part to appease the population.

Excursus: Jesus of Nazareth

Any consideration of Judea in the time of Pilate naturally invites some consideration of Jesus and the movement that formed around him—and that spectacularly survived his execution (Tacitus, *Ann.* 15.44).[4] Jesus appears to have been impacted by the preaching and ministry

---

[3] Smallwood 1981:163.

[4] The examination of extant evidence for the reconstruction of the Jesus of history represents a major stream of biblical and historical scholarship and has created a vast body of literature. Recommended points of entry, from the more accessible to the more detailed, include Beilby and Eddy, eds. 2009; Powell 2013; Witherington 1997; Bockmuehl, 2001; Schröter and Jacobi, eds., 2022; Bock and Webb, eds. 2010; Brown and Evans 2022; Theissen and Merz 1998. Also relevant are Horsley 1993; 1996; Sanders and Davies 1999; Reed 2000; deSilva 2012a.

of John the Immerser, taking up John's call to Jews throughout the territory of "Israel" to turn toward God in repentance and in full and fresh commitment to align their hearts and lives with the covenant God made with their ancestors. He believed his message to have been urgent, for "the kingdom of God"—a central and undeniable tenet of his proclamation—was about to break in upon, and establish itself in place of, the present ordering of this world.[5] In this regard, Jesus was certainly a revolutionary, but very much unlike the revolutionaries who took up arms after the example of Judas Maccabeus in an attempt to replace one temporal administration with another. Jesus expected, rather, that God would intervene to take authority ("the kingdom") away from the present rulers and give it to God's holy ones (cf. Dan 7:1–18, 27). What was required of God's people was to take God's covenant to heart and live it out *from* the heart. Jesus stood very much in line with the Hebrew prophets in this regard. An aspect of his activity that some contemporaries regarded as scandalous was his willingness to welcome people who had become heedless of the covenant into table fellowship with him. Jesus, however, appears to have considered restoring "the lost sheep of the house of Israel" to their sense of belonging to the covenant and to loyal obedience to the covenant to have been central to his work (Matt 9:12–13//Luke 5:31–32; Matt 18:11//Luke 19:10).

He believed himself to have been anointed by God for this work—and to say this is to say no more than one would of many of the other figures that arose as spokespersons for God during this period. He was reputed to have the ability to heal and exorcise evil spirits and was remembered to have claimed that these abilities demonstrated his spiritual authorization by God to call God's people into a renewed and sincere alignment with the covenant and to teach them the particulars of what this alignment entailed (see Mark 2:7–12; Luke 11:19–20). This, of course, stands behind the many conflicts he is remembered to have had with *other* Jewish teachers trying to chart that course for their fellow Jews. And since the stakes of covenant obedience were held to be very high (the deliverance or subjugation of the nation), the emotional amplitude of these conflicts also tended to run very high.

[5] Meier 1994:396–506.

Jesus's ability to attract a large following, one that was reportedly drawn from multiple regions (Galilee, Judea, Perea, the Decapolis), brought him to the attention of the Roman peacekeeping force, quite probably in collaboration with the Judean elite that benefited from a close, working relationship with the Roman authorities. Anyone with that much power to gather a following and direct their aspirations was a bona fide danger to the Roman peace, which meant the undisturbed status quo, regardless of the particulars of his ideology and agenda. Jesus's enactment of a prophetic paradigm, entering Jerusalem upon a donkey, while being cheered and followed by significant crowds, sufficiently signaled his messianic consciousness, even if that consciousness did not include supporting a violent uprising. It did not matter whether Jesus himself ever claimed to be God's "messiah"; it was enough that he had many followers who were making that claim on his behalf. His disruption and censure of the operations of the Temple sealed his fate both as far as the priestly elite and Roman overseers were concerned. The Jewish authorities may have cooperated with Pilate by finding a way in which to arrest Jesus quietly rather than risk stirring up a mob—and thus avoid the engagement of Roman forces to quieten such a mob, which had historically tended to result in massive casualties.

Jesus was, like many others who proclaimed an imminent change of government, crucified. The titulus placed above Jesus's head on the cross specified the charge: "Jesus of Nazareth, King of the Jews," a reflection of Pilate's judgment that Jesus, remembered to have been hailed as a "son of David" (see, e.g., Matt 9:27; 12:23; 15:22; 20:30–31; 21:9, 15), represented a royal pretender, a focal point of potentially seditious activity. In Rome's calculus, but also quite plausibly that of its elite collaborators in Jerusalem, it was indeed "better to have one man die . . . than to have the whole nation destroyed" (John 11:50).

His closest followers, however, were convinced that Jesus was indeed God's righteous one and that God vindicated him by raising him from the dead. This not only validated his teaching, which continued to be recited and to shape the practice of communities of his followers throughout Judea and Galilee—and eventually throughout the eastern Mediterranean and beyond. It validated his expectations for what was still imminent, namely the coming kingdom of God, as well as his followers' expectations for the role Jesus would continue to play in that future (e.g., 1 Thess 1:9–10). The strength of this conviction allowed them finally to release any other messianic expectations that they had harbored and hoped Jesus would fulfill, but that he did not, and to return to their scriptures to discover previously "overlooked" texts that provided a framework for understanding the very unusual nature of the Messiah they embraced—one that, for all the diversity of expectations concerning God's agents of deliverance and restoration for Israel, had never previously been formulated (as reflected in Luke 24:44–47). The movement quickly became one that would rival the other Jewish sects that figure so prominently in Josephus's writings and in histories of the period.

Agrippa I

The Herodian dynasty saw a short-lived resurgence under Julius Agrippa I, a grandson of Herod the Great through Aristobulus, one of the two sons by Mariamne whom Herod had executed. Like so many members of the Herodian line, Agrippa had been raised and educated in Rome. His mother, Berenice, was a close friend of Antonia, the mother of the future emperor Claudius, and one could infer that the boys knew each other well. Agrippa's out-of-control personal spending in early adulthood eventually led to his departure from Rome in embarrassment and landed him in debt and despair. This might have led to suicide had not his sister, Herodias, persuaded Antipas to give him a position in his government and allow him to get back on solid financial footing. Antipas and Agrippa, however, appear to have clashed, with the former taunting the latter with his failures and current dependency, leading him to leave Antipas's service and find his way back to Rome. When Gaius became emperor in place of Tiberius in 37 CE, he gave his friend Agrippa the title of "king" along with his deceased uncle Philip's territory. Antipas, allegedly prompted by Herodias, complained to Caligula and requested the same title. Agrippa, however, remembering Antipas's insults more than his beneficence, cast suspicion on Antipas because the latter was stockpiling arms well beyond the requirements of his army, alleging that he was planning a revolt in collusion with the Parthians. Instead of receiving his titular promotion, Antipas was deposed and exiled to Gaul in 39 CE, with his territories being added to Agrippa's kingdom.

During the reign of Gaius, Agrippa spent more time in Rome than in his kingdom, which in the end served the Jewish people well. From there he was able to advocate on behalf of the Jewish population in Alexandria when they faced the hostility of the Greek mob over the question of equal civic rights, as well as intervene in an episode that was traumatic not only for the nation but for the Jewish people as a whole.[6] In 39–40 CE, some Gentile residents of Jamnia erected a crude altar to Gaius in response to reports of Gaius's enthusiasm for such worship. Certain zealous Jewish residents tore it down, objecting to the erection of a religious abomination in Israel. Upon hearing an exaggerated report of this, Gaius "ordered a colossal statue to be set up within the inner sanctuary" of the Temple in Jerusalem and "dedicated to himself under the name of Zeus" (*Embassy*, 188). While this exaggerated response does not provide evidence for a balanced mind, it was also not unprecedented, for Gaius had similarly given orders that the temple to Apollo under construction in Miletus should also be dedicated to him, to bind local cult to imperial cult as an expression of loyalty to the empire.[7]

Responsibility for creating and installing the image was laid upon the legate of Syria, Publius Petronius, who well knew the difficulties he would face executing such orders. After failing to persuade the Jewish leaders to submit to the emperor's will, he was met with massive protests by Jews who made it clear they would prefer to be slaughtered than passively accept the desecration of their temple. This is an episode that clearly shows Galilean Jews' attachment to the temple, for they refused to plant their crops unless the order was rescinded—a bold act of economic protest.[8] Petronius appears to have tried to protect the Judean population from Gaius, making excuses for delay and remonstrating with the emperor to desist for the sake of the peace of the region. Caligula responded harshly, as one might imagine.

---

[6] Philo's *Embassy to Gaius* (184–338) is an important source alongside Josephus.
[7] Gruen 2018:404–405.
[8] Horsley 1996:36.

Agrippa's presence in Rome at the time, and his long-standing friend-ship with Gaius, ultimately saved the day. He persuaded Gaius to desist and to continue the same policy of toleration for the Jewish people's religious scruples that his august predecessors had followed. Gaius finally relented, strictly warning the Judeans, reasonably enough from a Roman perspective, not to interfere with the worship practices and accouterments of their Gentile neighbors if they wish to have their own rights respected.[9] It is important to note that it was enough for the general population to have forestalled Gaius's attempt to give them a physical representation of their God. Despite the enormous energy invested in the attempt to head off this desecration, it was not channeled into revolt against Roman rule itself.[10]

Agrippa also played some role of note in the transition of power after Gaius's assassination in 41 CE, helping to mediate a settlement between the Senate and the military whereby Claudius would succeed to the imperial powers (Josephus, *Ant.* 19.236–45; Suetonius, *Claudius* 11). The new emperor rewarded Agrippa with the addition of the rest of his grandfather's former kingdom (namely Judea, Samaritis, and Idumea) to his own. The Jewish inhabitants of the region appear to have welcomed a return to a native, client king and to the fiction of "independence" from foreign rule. Agrippa's overt commitment to Jewish practice and piety no doubt contributed to their satisfaction with him. The Book of Acts attributes Agrippa's actions against the Jerusalem-based leaders of the Jesus movement—the execution of James bar-Zebediah and the imprisonment of Peter—to his desire to please his constituency (12:1–3). He showed some of his grandfather's instincts, lavishing benefactions on the city of Berytus and seeking to improve Jerusalem with a new wall defending the suburbs that had grown up to the north of the earlier walls. The latter project, however, was halted by Claudius, whose permission for the project—clearly one with military implications—had not been properly sought.

---

[9] Philo claims that Gaius changed his mind again and that only his timely assassination forestalled disaster. Gruen (2018:408) argues that this is pure fantasy, though Tacitus also indirectly suggests that only Gaius's death circumvented rebellion in Judea (*Hist.* 5.9).

[10] Smith 1999:565–566.

The Herodian renaissance was cut short by Agrippa's untimely, and by all accounts extremely sudden and painful, death in 44 CE (compare Josephus, *Ant* 19.343–350; Acts 12:20–23).[11] This was greeted with open celebration by the Gentile residents of Caesarea and Sebaste, with members of the auxiliary cohorts going so far as to insult Agrippa's memory and commit indecencies upon statues of his daughters that had been erected in Caesarea. When word of this reached Claudius, he was inclined to punish the auxiliaries by removing them to Pontus and replacing them with different cohorts. In the face of their petitions, Claudius relented, which Josephus believed had dreadful consequences for the subprovince on account of the longstanding ethnic tensions between them and the Jewish people (*Ant.* 19.365).

Roman Procurators after Agrippa I

Agrippa left behind three daughters and a seventeen-year-old son, too young and inexperienced to succeed to his position, and so the entire realm came under direct Roman rule in 44 CE. This would be the first time that Galilee came under *direct* Roman rule.[12] Cuspius Fadus was dispatched to serve as procurator from 44 to 46 CE. He intervened in a violent conflict between some Jewish residents of Peraea and the Decapolis city of Philadelphia (modern Amman) over some village border disputes. Fadus arrested and either executed or exiled three of the Jewish leaders for resorting to violence rather than referring the dispute to the proper authorities. Another episode of note involved a prophetic figure named Theudas, who had gathered a large following and led them to the Jordan River in expectation of a miraculous crossing. Josephus leaves us to speculate concerning the group's motives or aspirations. Was it a symbolic retaking of the promised land (were they crossing west)? Or did it represent an exodus from Roman-occupied Israel (crossing east)? In any event, Fadus treated it as a

---

[11] Schäfer (2003:113) thinks the symptoms mentioned in Josephus and Acts point to poisoning, likely by Romans who were growing suspicious of his popularity, which, going undetected, had to be explained as a consequence of divine displeasure for some offense.

[12] Goodman 1999:599.

potential revolutionary threat and dispersed it by force, killing many and executing Theudas. Fadus also sought to recover possession of the high priestly vestments, but the Jerusalem leadership appealed to Claudius, who tactfully remanded custody of the vestments to Agrippa I's brother, Herod, king of Chalcis—along with the right to appoint the high priests, which had passed to Agrippa I in 41 CE. These rights would pass on to Agrippa II when he succeeded his uncle upon the latter's death in 49 CE.

Fadus was followed by Tiberius Julius Alexander (46–48 CE), the apostate nephew of Philo of Alexandria, who appears to have governed in a manner that showed appropriate sensitivity to the sensibilities of the population. Suppression of revolutionary bands continued, with Alexander arresting and crucifying two sons of Judas the Galilean for carrying on the family business. The whole province of Syria, inclusive of Judea, suffered a serious famine at some point during Alexander's tenure, which was relieved in large part through the generosity of Queen Helena of Adiabene, a proselyte whose tomb lies a few hundred yards north of Jerusalem's present walls.[13] This is incidentally a re-minder that the ancient world offered no large-scale (or, indeed, small-scale) safety nets in time of need apart from the largesse of benefactors.

The situation became decidedly more tense under Alexander's successor, Ventidius Cumanus (48–52 CE), largely because of Judean-Samarian conflicts and the actions of his Sebastene-Caesarian auxiliaries. During one of the Passovers of his tenure, one of the auxiliaries, perched high above the rituals below, exposed his naked bottom and made a loud flatulent sound. When the protests from below verged on becoming a riot, Cumanus released his troops upon the worshipers, many of whom died in the ensuing stampede. On another occasion, an imperial slave traveling through the Beth-Horon pass with a valuable baggage train was robbed by bandits. Cumanus held the villages in the vicinity responsible, either because they were suspected of shielding the bandits, or simply to deter others from doing so. One of the auxiliaries, however, went too far by burning a scroll of the Torah. As word spread, demonstrators converged on Cumanus

---

[13] See *Ant.* 20.17–53, 20.49–53 on the famine relief in particular; compare Acts 11:27–30, which places the famine, however, prior to Agrippa I's death.

in Caesarea. This time, he complied by executing the offender for the sacrilege.

The most dramatic episode—and the one that eventuated in Cumanus's removal—occurred in 51 CE, again in connection with one of the pilgrimage festivals. Some number of Galileans traveling toward Jerusalem through Samaritan territory were murdered. It is not at all clear whether these hostilities involved Samaritans (that is, the worshipers of the God of Israel who were attached to Mt. Gerizim as a sacred site) or the Samarians (that is, the Syrian veterans, colonists, and settlers in the region)—or, indeed, whether by this point the distinction would have become meaningless given the hostility between both populations and the populations of Judea and Galilee. The majority of historians attribute this to the religious animosity between those whose center for worship was Gerizim versus those whose center for worship was Jerusalem. There was certainly mutual disdain between these groups (Sir 50:25–26; Luke 9:52–53; John 4:9; 8:48; 4Q372), and these events would indicate significant escalation of hostilities.[14] When representatives from Galilee sought justice from Cumanus, he rather inexplicably did not follow up on the crime. Galilean Jews therefore went to Jerusalem and stirred up a large mob to invade and ransack the nearest Samarian villages—an ill-aimed act of retaliation since the offending village was much further to the north. It indicates, however, something of the ever-simmering tension between Jews and Samarians/Samaritans. Cumanus now took notice, but his response was unilaterally to have his auxiliaries round up or kill the Judeans involved, no doubt because of their grossly disproportionate response. Both the Judeans and Samarians requested the intervention of the legate of Syria, Ummidius Quadratus, who sent Cumanus to Rome to answer for himself along with the ringleaders both of the Samarian and Judean parties for adjudication of their complaints. The emperor Claudius, perhaps thanks to the advocacy of Agrippa II, executed the Samarian leaders, acquitted the Judeans, and exiled Cumanus. This was the second time a prefect or procurator was dismissed by the legate

---

[14] Mason (2016:271–272) regards this as a precursor to the kind of ethnic animosities that would erupt even more disastrously in Caesarea Maritima under Antonius Felix and Gessius Florus.

of Syria in response to complaints from their subjects—a sign that the latter *could* expect redress of grievances from Rome's representatives.

Cumanus was succeeded by Antonius Felix (52–60 CE), the brother of Pallas, an imperial freedman in Claudius's court who wielded extraordinary power (Tacitus, *Ann.* 12.54). The following year, Claudius gave the maturing Agrippa II oversight of the territory that once belonged to his great-uncle, Philip. Nero would add the cities and territories of Tiberias and Trachonitis in Galilee in 54 CE. Josephus names the steady increase in banditry and its associated violence as the primary problem besetting Felix and, indeed, a major indication of the deteriorating conditions throughout the region in the decades leading up to the First Revolt. Bandit gangs had been endemic since the transition from Hasmonean to Herodian rule; the increase in their activity, raiding the estates of the wealthy, likely points to an increase in the principal cause—the economic hardship brought about by the loss of private ownership of land, chronic indebtedness, military action or confiscation of lands, and the like. The lines between the activity of bandit gangs and anti-Roman revolutionary activity would blur as the situation in the region deteriorated still further.[15] Felix and his successor, Porcius Festus (60–62 CE), were occupied with suppressing banditry and terrorism, but Josephus claims that the problems were too far gone for them or their successors to handle.[16]

Economic class conflict extended even to the priestly caste during this period, as the more powerful hierarchs no longer waited for tithes to be brought to Jerusalem (often through priestly families living out among the villages) but sent their collection agents out to the threshing floors throughout the land to take in the tithes, often omitting to give a share to the local, lower-ranking priests (Josephus, *Ant.* 20.181, 206–207). During this time, we also first hear of the activity of the group known as *sicarii*, essentially political assassins

---

[15] Horsley 1996:37.

[16] The Acts of the Apostles places the account of the riot in Jerusalem surrounding Paul of Tarsus and his subsequent arrest and hearings during the tenures of these two procurators (Acts 21:17–26:32). Apart from the importance of this account for the life and career of Paul, it is an interesting study in the volatility of Jerusalem surrounding the sanctity of the Temple, the manner in which religious partisanship could be triggered, the reality of politico-religious assassination, and the relations between the Jerusalem authorities and the procurators.

and terrorists who targeted collaborators with the Roman occupation force and whose covert tactics made their detection and capture impossible. The high priest Jonathan appears to have been an early victim (though Josephus's allegation that this was instigated by Felix is questionable).

During Felix's tenure, another of the periodic prophets arose, gathered a following, and promised a divine intervention in line with a biblical precedent. This time it was a Jew from Egypt who led his followers to the Mount of Olives in anticipation of seeing the walls of Jerusalem fall, presumably so that he and his band could take possession of the city and establish a new government. The troops sent by Felix dispersed the group and the Egyptian himself escaped (*War* 2.261–263; see also Acts 21:38). Not all such movements appear to have been motivated primarily by anti-Roman sentiments (though none would have been *pro*-Roman, certainly), but rather by a strong sense that all is not now as it ought to be and some fresh interventions by God are required to set things right. If the expectation of this movement was that the walls of Jerusalem would spontaneously fall down and that they would enter to take over the holy city, does this reflect an indictment of Rome, which has a minimal presence in the city, or of Jerusalem? It was also during Felix's tenure that a riot erupted in Jerusalem surrounding the alleged actions of Paul, a provocative figure within the early Jesus movement, resulting in his arrest, an assassination plot, and a two-year imprisonment leaving Paul in custody in Caesarea into the term of Felix's successor (Acts 21:17–26:32). The episode well reflects the volatility of Judea, the activity of vigilantes during this period, and the unreliability of the justice system under the procurators, for whom providing a speedy trial was not at all a priority.

Porcius Festus died while in office in 62 CE. The high priest at the time—Ananus II, the youngest son of the Ananus who had been the high priest under the first prefects—took advantage of the hiatus between Festus's death and the arrival of a new procurator to clean house in Jerusalem. One of his targets was James, a half-brother of Jesus and the leader of the Jesus movement in Judea, whom he arraigned and executed. Several Judeans protested against the high priest's overreach to Agrippa II, who removed him from his position after a mere three months.

The new procurator, Lucceius Albinus (62–64 CE), was also unable to regain control of the deteriorating situation. There was now violence in the streets of Jerusalem among partisans of different high priestly families and lay elite factions. Various nationalist groups, most notably the *sicarii*, were engaging in targeted kidnappings with a view to collecting a ransom or effecting an exchange of prisoners—these being brokered by a former high priest named Ananias, the father of Eleazar, the captain of the Temple (Josephus, *Ant.* 20.208–210). Work on the Temple precincts (including repairs to some portions damaged in an earthquake) was finally completed in 64 CE, which threatened the sudden unemployment of eighteen thousand people. Agrippa II solved the problem, and prevented even more economically driven anarchy, by diverting the workers to repaving Jerusalem's streets and continuing to fund the work from the Temple's assets.

Gessius Florus and the Outbreak of Hostilities

"The Jews endured such oppression patiently until the governorship of Gessius Florus, under whom war broke out" (Tacitus, *Hist.* 5.10). The Roman historian acknowledges the problematic character of the Roman administrators entrusted with Herod's kingdom and agrees with Josephus that Florus (procurator from 64 to 66 CE) bears a significant share of the responsibility for the ongoing hostilities against local and neighboring adversaries culminating in the eruption of hostilities against Rome. Even so, it is important to observe that it is the "history of conflict" between Jews and their neighbors "that reached back many generations" that led Judea to the point that it found itself at war with Rome and her legions.[17] The image of Judea as a simmering pot of anti-Roman sentiment reaching the point of boiling over in 66 CE, as if the Jewish Revolt was the consequence of a bilateral relationship that had been bad from the beginning, is a distortion of the far more complicated web of conflicts that Jews faced closer to home.

---

[17] Mason 2014:172–173. Mason 2016 is perhaps the most detailed and thoughtful study of the First Revolt available.

One such feud was particularly important—so much so that it has been identified as the decisive spark that kindled the fire that would destroy Jerusalem. While Felix was still procurator, the large Jewish population of Caesarea Maritima, arguing that the founder of the city (Herod the Great) had been a Jew, had agitated to be recognized as citizens en bloc and to be invested with political rights equal to those of the Greek and Syrian residents. This would have significantly shifted the balance in local government, and the Gentile citizens sought to block any such development, arguing that Herod's urban planning clearly showed his intent that Caesarea was to be a city for non-Jews. The matter was referred to Nero, who decided in favor of the non-Jewish citizens. The matter did not rest, however, and mutual antagonism continued, leading to violence in the streets and the intervention of Florus's auxiliaries—who, being Syrians with roots in Sebaste and Caesarea themselves, did so overwhelmingly in favor of their own kind.

Florus next used the hated Samarian-Caesarian auxiliaries to appropriate significant funds (seventeen silver talents) from the Temple treasury. In so doing, he was almost surely obeying a directive from Nero to secure funds as plentifully as possible from wherever possible in the wake of the great fire in Rome. The amount was perhaps no more than the province owed in tribute, or perhaps included an advance on future tribute because the economic situation in Rome was so dire. Dio reports that Nero even appropriated the funds in the temples of Rome to this end and Plutarch bears witness to systematic pillaging of the provinces by Nero's governors (*Galba* 4.1).[18] This could well have been a point at which resentment and hostility could crystallize against Rome itself, the ultimate instigator and beneficiary of this sacrilegious affront.

Mass demonstrations in Jerusalem followed as a matter of course. Florus appears to have been particularly piqued by some who pretended to beg copper coins for the poor procurator, mocking his apparent avarice. He demanded that these individuals be identified and handed over. When the Jewish rulers objected that this was impossible,

[18] Mason 2016:316–318.

Florus vented his anger at his injured honor upon them, unleashing his auxiliaries to punish the city and even crucifying some who claimed the status of Roman citizens, even of the equestrian order (the second highest under the senatorial class). This was a gruesome reminder of the fragility of Judeans' status and security under Roman "rule" and no doubt contributed heavily to the sense that they could no longer trust Rome's representatives.

In the aftermath, Florus may have sensed that he had provoked more hostility than his auxiliaries could handle. He consented to exchange the hated cohort in Antonia for a different one and withdrew to Caesarea, whence he sent an appeal to Cestius Gallus, the legate of Syria, alleging that Jerusalem was in revolt. The Sanhedrin also petitioned Gallus, asking him to investigate and prosecute the actions of Florus and his auxiliaries. Gallus sent an emissary to Jerusalem whose investigation showed that Judea was *not* revolting against Rome but only had grievances concerning Florus. Gallus's subsequent lack of action against Florus, however, is difficult to comprehend. His predecessors were not reluctant to inquire into charges of maladministration of the prefects and procurators; doing so at this point could have reassured the Judean population of Rome's overall reliability. Perhaps he was hindered on account of Florus's personal connection with Nero through their wives' close friendship and Nero's prioritization of extracting whatever wealth possible for problems at home, a mandate Florus fulfilled efficiently. In any event, his failure to intervene with regard to Florus and his auxiliaries-run-amok must have been regarded as an intolerable breach of trust.

At this point, several groups took a variety of actions against Roman administration. A leader of the *sicarii* named Menahem (likely a grandson of Judas the Galilean) and his band took control of Masada and slaughtered the auxiliary garrison stationed there. (One wonders *how*, given the difficulties and length of time associated with the later Roman siege of Masada!) They armed themselves and other insurgents with Herod's cache of weapons and returned to Jerusalem. Eleazar ben Ananias, the captain of the temple, suspended sacrifices on behalf of the emperor, a symbolic declaration of revolt against Roman rule. Insurgents established themselves in the Lower City and the Temple. Agrippa II sent some of his own troops into the city to try to reassert control, but they were overpowered and forced to retreat into Herod the Great's palace and citadel (the site of the praetorium).

Insurgents ransacked and burnt the homes of the ultra-wealthy in Jerusalem. There is evidence of fire damage among the excavations of the Upper City, such as the "Burnt House" and the mansions in the Wohl Museum. It is often assumed that the fire damage is the result of the Romans' activity in 70 CE, but in some cases, there is cause to suspect Judean activity in 66 CE or the years following, given the turmoil within the city already prior to the siege. They also made a point of burning the office of the records of debts, "in order to secure the support of an army of debtors and enable the poor to rise with impunity against the rich" (War 2.427–428). Symbolic or not, these actions also bear witness to significant and long-standing tensions between the haves and have-nots. They also attacked and killed the auxiliary garrison stationed in the Antonia fortress. While they allowed Agrippa's soldiers to leave the city under a flag of truce, they murdered the second auxiliary cohort that had also been trapped in the praetorium with them. In a foretaste of the internal strife that would dog the Jewish side of the great revolt, Menahem's band murdered the high priest Ananias as a traitor to the cause of revolution; Eleazar ben Ananias, though himself a champion of the revolutionary cause, led his partisans to drive out Menahem's party, killing Menahem in the process. His supporters retreated to Masada, where they would spend the next eight years avoiding the war and preying upon the neighboring villages of their co-religionists for supplies.

The violence in Jerusalem provoked reprisals in Caesarea against the Judean minority there, which was entirely exterminated. This provoked Judeans and Galileans to further reprisals against Gentile populations in the cities surrounding them, which in turn provoked actions within Gentile cities in the Decapolis and coastal plain against their Judean residents, perhaps more as a preemptive safety measure. Long-simmering ethnic tensions exploded into violence throughout the region. Gallus could not allow such breaches of the Roman peace on his watch. He assembled a sizeable strike force in Antioch and moved first into Galilee, using shock and awe tactics against a few villages in the hope of softening up resistance. He met stiffer opposition, however, all the way from the Beth Horon pass (at the hands of revolutionary gangs under the leadership of Simon ben Giora, who would become an important player in Jerusalem) to Jerusalem itself. Having gained the upper hand in the open ground, Gallus initiated a siege of the city. Whether from sound judgment or stupidity, however, he suspended the siege and withdrew to Caesarea, possibly with a view to wintering his troops there and trying afresh in the spring. As he withdrew, insurgents inflicted such significant casualties upon his rearguard that Rome was honor-bound to strike back with its full fury.

The inevitability of this retaliation prompted the formation of a provisional government in Jerusalem led chiefly by members of the priestly elite and under the military leadership of Ananus ben-Ananus, the former high priest. It is difficult to discern motives through the haze of Josephus's propagandistic interests, but his suggestion that their ultimate aim was to manage the situation throughout the region—which included making whatever preparations could be made in the face of Rome's forthcoming fury, essential both to win the trust of the more eager revolutionaries and to strengthen their position for negotiation—until acceptable terms of surrender could be worked out seems entirely plausible.[19]

The First Jewish Revolt

Josephus's portrait of the provisional government in Jerusalem making preparations for war and sending their chosen generals into the surrounding districts to carry out preparations (and regain control over the factious population) is not the portrait of people *deciding* to go to war with Rome. It is a portrait of people preparing as best they can for a Roman counterassault that they likely deeply regretted having been provoked—and did not themselves purposefully provoke. One of their early actions involved attempting to curtail the activities of Simon ben Giora and his band of insurgents raiding northeast Judea, driving them temporarily to seek refuge at Masada with the *sicarii* there. They also appointed their own hand-picked generals to take charge of preparations for the counterassault in the various regions of

---

[19] Horsley 2002:89.

Figure 5.2 A silver shekel from year one of the First Jewish Revolt (courtesy of the Classical Numismatic Group, LLC, www.cngcoins.com).

the territory—what could be called "Israel" once again in the minds of the revolutionaries, as the coins minted in Jerusalem demonstrate (see Figure 5.2). These coins, cast in silver and bronze, bear legends such as "Jerusalem the holy," "For the Freedom of Zion," and "Shekel of Israel." One motive for the silver mintings might have been practical due to Nero's introduction of inferior silver coinage from the Antioch mint and phasing out of the hitherto reliable Tyre mint,[20] but the ideological weight of the designs cannot be denied.[21]

Josephus emerges on the stage of his own history as the general selected to take charge of preparations in Galilee. While he gave energetic attention to building or improving defensive walls around several towns, the larger part of his narrative reflects his often life-or-death struggles to assert and maintain control over local strong men who were vying with him for command in their own cities or territories (such as Joshua of Tiberias and John of Gischala) as well as with bandit gangs—some of whom Josephus eventually employed as his bodyguard in order to put a stop to their raiding (as well as provide loyal protection for himself, as he would always be the highest bidder for their services). Indeed, Josephus invested far more in bringing

[20] Mason 2016:487.
[21] Goodman 2007:14–15.

other revolutionary gang leaders in Galilee to heel than in engaging the Roman forces. The frequent suspicion that Josephus was seeking "to betray the country to the Romans," a suspicion given sufficient credence to motivate attempts to kill him (*Life* 132–148; *War* 2.598–610), may well have been based in fact.[22]

By 67 CE, Vespasian, Nero's appointee for the "pacification" of the region, had assembled two legions from Syria and one from Egypt for the task. He had brought his elder son, Titus, along with him as a means of advancing the young man's career through military victories. Adding the many auxiliary cohorts and the armies of client kings like Agrippa II, Vespasian's combined forces approached sixty thousand. Setting out from the port city of Ptolemais, his first objective was to recover control over Galilee. The inhabitants of Sepphoris, the majority of whom were solidly pro-Roman, greeted him as a deliverer. Vespasian garrisoned the city and made it a base of operations for his campaign in Galilee.

While there were certainly insurgent forces throughout the region, several historians have rightly commented that not all the resistance Vespasian's forces encountered was motivated by a commitment to revolutionary ideology and aims. A good deal of it was likely motivated simply by the drive for self-preservation and the preservation of one's loved ones. Josephus's description of the majority in the town of Gischala in Upper Galilee might well have been true for most towns: "the inhabitants were inclined to peace, being mainly agricultural labourers whose whole attention was devoted to the prospects of the crops" (*War* 4.84 LCL). A foreign army deployed in what it has been told is hostile territory where it must dominate the field positions them to regard more actions as hostile than are truly hostile and to respond with deadly force more frequently and thoroughly than necessary. It also positions the indigenous people, who formerly might not have regarded Rome as an enemy, to fear the actions of this immanent army and to be radicalized by the scorched earth policy that it tends to follow. When surrender is not regarded as a survivable option, the only recourse is to fight for one's life and the lives of one's family—a stance

---

[22] Smallwood 1981:298–300; Horsley 2002:96.

quickly substantiated by reports of what these same soldiers had done elsewhere in Galilee as they began their advance.[23]

As Vespasian's armies swept through the villages and towns of Galilee, large numbers of their residents became displaced refugees, inevitably seeking the protection of the fortified towns that were preparing to resist or of the insurgents' camps.[24] In Josephus's words, "Galilee from end to end became a scene of fire and blood; from no misery, no calamity was it exempt; the one refuge for the hunted inhabitants was in the cities fortified by Josephus" (*War* 3.63 LCL). Jotapata was one of these cities. Vespasian besieged it for six weeks to two months in the summer of 67 CE, finally taking the city and slaughtering its inhabitants without regard for age or sex. Josephus and a small number of his soldiers had escaped and found refuge in a cave from which Josephus alone emerged to become a prisoner of war, though he was treated with honor for a prediction he made concerning Vespasian's destiny. The story of one other survivor merits mention. Vespasian sent Titus to besiege Gischala in Upper Galilee, where John and his insurgents had dug in. By means of a ruse concerning the requirement to rest on the Sabbath rather than consider Titus's proposals for their surrender, John escaped with two thousand of his supporters, moving to Jerusalem as the best site for a last stand. This was an occasion on which the Romans made a clear distinction between insurgents and unwilling hosts, for the city immediately surrendered and was spared after their departure.

The details of the progress of the Roman forces make for a fascinating, if tragic, read, but they are perhaps incidental to the purposes of this volume. Suffice it to say that, within a year of campaigning, Vespasian, Titus, and their armies essentially mastered all of Galilee, the coastal plains, Judea, and Idumea apart from Jerusalem and its environs as well as three fortresses—Machaerus, Herodion, and Masada—whose residents, however, could be kept contained for attention later.[25] The community at Qumran was also a casualty of the

---

[23]   Mason 2016:578–581.

[24]   Horsley 2002:99–100.

[25]   There was minimal resistance in Samaritis apart from an episode in which a group of armed Samaritans entrenched themselves on Mt. Gerizim. Roman forces settled on starving them out rather than engaging an enemy that had the high ground. The result

Romans' sweeping advance. Vespasian established military camps around Jerusalem, perhaps fifteen to twenty miles distant, in preparation for the final siege. He rightly discerned that the revolt would end in a lengthy siege of Jerusalem itself and sought therefore to isolate the rebels there and to leave no opportunities for distractions or disruptions from other nests of insurgents. Jews who surrendered to him along the way of his march through Judea were settled in Lydda, Jamnia, and Azotus near the coast, both to keep them safe and to keep them "honest" during the remaining course of the war.

Vespasian's momentum was thoroughly disrupted in July of 68 CE, however, when news reached him of Nero's suicide in Rome. In this instance, the Roman practice of holding an emperor's mandates to have lapsed upon his death proved terribly inefficient, since the empire was plunged into the chaos of civil war. Galba, a legate and general in the Spanish provinces, was the first to make a bid for absolute power, which he held for six months before being assassinated by the partisans of Otho, the Senate's favorite for the position. At the same time, however, Vitellius, legate and general of the Germanic provinces, was declared emperor by his troops and made short work of Otho and his supporters. Vespasian's attention was wholly consumed with these matters at the heart of the empire, for he, too, was in a strong position to take control. His ambitions were made official in July of 69 CE, when Tiberius Alexander, now prefect of Egypt, made his legions swear allegiance to Vespasian. The remaining legions in Judea and Syria followed suit. Vespasian's cause was fought in Italy under the generalship of his friend Mucianus. Vitellius was killed and his surviving troops swore allegiance to Vespasian, who was installed as emperor and founder of a new dynasty.[26]

Vespasian commissioned Titus to complete the pacification of Judea. Tiberius Julius Alexander was sent as his chief of staff and as a chief advisor to guide the inexperienced and often impetuous young man. Agrippa II personally accompanied and advised Titus; Josephus

was the death of the band from thirst or from last-ditch efforts to fight their besiegers (Josephus, *War* 3.307–315; Isser 1999:577).

[26] Suetonius, *Vesp.* 4–7; Tacitus, *Hist.* 2.74–86. Tacitus's *Histories* is almost fully occupied with the saga of the "Year of the Four Emperors."

was now also in tow, no longer as a prisoner, but as a client and advisor. A fourth legion and several detachments from other legions were now added to the original strike force.

The Jerusalem leadership's primary achievement in preparation for the siege was the completion of the so-called third wall around the suburb of Bezetha (which had earlier been ravaged by Gallus) begun by Agrippa I.[27] Apart from this (which, in the end, proved entirely ineffective at forestalling the inevitable), the reprieve was disastrous for the residents and growing number of refugees in Jerusalem. Partisan strife was rampant within the city as rival factions spent their precious year fighting one another to position themselves for the spoils of victory that independence could bring before fighting the actual war against the Romans itself. By the time Titus brought his strike force to bear on Jerusalem, the moderate party favoring negotiations with the Romans had been violently eliminated by Eleazar ben-Ananias and his Zealot faction. John of Gischala and his partisans, in turn, drove the Zealots into the Antonia fortress and the Temple (which was also akin to a fortress). Simon ben Giora and his militia had been allowed in by the residents as a check to the Zealots' and John's tyranny and had taken possession of the Upper City, pinning John's forces in the middle ground, but proving to be as brutal and tyrannical a warlord as the others.[28]

Food shortages in the city were made more dire both on account of the number of refugees from Galilee and Judea that had fled to the capital along with revolutionaries for whom this would represent their "last stand" and on account of the feuding rebel factions burning one another's grain supplies to weaken their position. Famine became rampant during the siege, as did the ruthless predations of the insurgents upon the civilian populations, whom they terrorized and tortured for what little food the latter might have stored away.[29] The

---

[27] The line of this wall is heavily disputed: the minimalist view places it essentially along the line of the north wall of the Ottoman city; the maximalist view extends it perhaps another fifteen hundred feet to the north. A lengthy description of Jerusalem, its buildings, and its fortifications by a contemporary witness appears in Josephus, *War* 5.136–237.

[28] In addition to Josephus, Tacitus (*Hist.* 5.12) attests to this internal division.

[29] Tacitus (*Hist.* 5.13), whose figures are less inflated that those of Josephus, numbers the besieged at six hundred thousand.

reader of Josephus's account cannot but be moved by the atrocities committed on both sides during the siege, from the unthinkable horrors of first-century psyops (crucifying prisoners of war in creative ways for the spectacle, chopping off the hands of captured civilians and sending them back as a warning) to the plain venality of holding life cheap where money might be gained (Roman auxiliaries killing and disemboweling deserters once it was discovered that some had swallowed their gold and silver coins to smuggle them past the revolutionary guards in the city and the Roman guards at the circumvallation).

The revolutionary factions in Jerusalem continued their destructive feuding while the Romans' siege efforts outside their walls were under way, with John and his partisans finally getting the better of Eleazar and his Zealots. The reality of their common danger finally led John and Simon to work together, with the former reluctantly ceding the greater authority to the latter. According to Josephus, they put up a courageous and creative resistance, but the inevitable could only be delayed so long. In May of 70 CE, Titus's forces had breached the outer two walls. In June or July, they breached the first wall on the north side (as Pompey and Sosius had done) and captured the Antonia fortress. A fierce battle for control of the Temple courts and porticoes followed, during which both rebels and Romans started fires strategically. For example, at one point the rebels set fire to a portico that the Romans were using to spill into the Temple from the fortress, killing several combatants and destroying that point of access. In August, the temple was finally taken and destroyed in the process.

Josephus makes a point of stressing Titus's desire to spare the Temple itself from harm due to its beauty as an ornament to the city—a city that he very much had wanted to preserve for Rome. It may well be that he understood the Temple's importance for *all* Jews, and not just for the Jewish revolutionaries who were misusing it as a fortress at the time. As Josephus tells the story, one of Titus's soldiers started the blaze that consumed the Temple against his strict orders, a failure of discipline that Titus decided against punishing later as both impractical and impolitic in Titus's situation—impractical, given the difficulty of identifying the precise individual or individuals responsible; impolitic, given the importance of the victory for the newly established

Flavian emperor who, it was hoped, would become the founder of a new dynasty.[30] Titus, however, was a practical Roman surrounded by practical Roman advisors. He might well have wished to avoid destroying the Temple, if possible, but was prepared to yield to the practical necessities of the siege as it developed. It is unlikely that Titus would have prioritized preserving a building in a city in revolt over the most efficient way to bring the siege to an end while minimizing expense and (Roman) loss of life.[31] Even Josephus admits that Titus ordered some of his soldiers to plunder the furniture and treasures of the sanctuary and, when this was accomplished, to purposefully complete the conflagration of the outbuildings and colonnades. Josephus tells the tragic story of several thousand citizens gathering atop one of these colonnades even as the sanctuary itself was going up in flames, persuaded by a false prophet that God would yet deliver them (*War* 6.283–285). Their fate was to perish when the soldiers set the colonnades alight, but their gathering in the first place speaks to the power and persistence of the religious fervor that could possess the people in the face of impossible odds.

After the Temple was in the hands of the legions, the reconquest of the rest of the city was relatively easy. By the end of September, the remainder of Jerusalem had been taken and largely destroyed in the process. John and Simon were both captured to be paraded about in Rome in the triumphal procession that Vespasian would share with Titus. From those taken prisoner, some were set apart also to march on display in Rome, most of the children and women were sold as slaves, the remainder of the able-bodied males were set apart for the mines or gladiatorial shows,[32] and the elderly and infirm were simply butchered. Titus ordered the destruction of the temple court's walls and the city's walls, save for Herod's citadel with its three proud towers, which would form a part of the occupation force's camp.

---

[30] Leoni 2007:46–47; see Josephus, *War* 7.12.

[31] Josephus himself indicates this in principle (*War* 6.228). See also Mason 2016:487–513.

[32] Thousands would die in gladiatorial combats Titus personally sponsored in Caesarea Philippi and Berytus during the winter of 70–71 CE (Josephus, *War* 7.37–40).

Clean-up Operations

With the fall of Jerusalem and elimination of the revolutionary forces sheltering there, the First Jewish Revolt was effectively suppressed. Small groups of revolutionaries—and the many displaced persons who had taken refuge with them—still had to be dislodged from Herodion, Machaerus, and Masada. The first proconsular governor, Sextus Lucilius Bassus, dislodged the *sicarii* and refugees sheltering at Herodion and Machaerus, encircling and killing also a band of several thousand renegades and refugees from both Jerusalem and Machaerus in the Jordan Valley. Bassus died in his post and was succeeded by Cornelius Flavius Silva, to whom fell the task of taking Masada.

Masada had been a refuge for the *sicarii* and their families since 66 CE, when this particular party, under their slain leader Menahem, had been ousted from Jerusalem. Contrary to the (possibly ironic) speech Josephus places in the mouth of Eleazar ben Yair, a cousin of Menahem who appears to have succeeded him as the leader of the band, the residents of Masada had showed no interest in fighting for the freedom of Jerusalem.[33] Granted that they embraced a vigorous revolutionary outlook at the outset of hostilities, these "freedom fighters" managed to avoid any significant conflict with the Roman army between the initial actions in 66 CE and the siege at their doorstep in 74 CE, living in their alternative society free from the rule of either Jerusalem or Rome, preying on the villages in the orbit of their fortress when the well-supplied fortress was running low on essentials. During the revolt, they were joined by other refugees fleeing the advancing Roman army. Rebels and refugees would turn the rooms inside the casemate walls of the fortress into makeshift residences and kitchens. It may have been they who converted several rooms in the wall into a synagogue.[34]

The siege is thought to have lasted anywhere from three to six months, ending in April of 74 CE.[35] The Roman force established

[33] Mason 2016:543.
[34] Magness 2019:171.
[35] Magness 2012:216.

eight camps around the mesa and built a circumvallation wall between ten and twelve feet high, the remains of which incidentally open important windows into Roman military engineering. Silva focused his troops' efforts on building a siege ramp atop a natural debris tongue on the west whereby they were able to bring an engine with battering ram to bear on the casemate wall. What happened next was probably not nearly as poetic as Josephus's narrative suggests. According to him, the residents of Masada agreed to be slaughtered by their fellow Jews rather than face the Romans the next day and face the degradations of rape, enslavement, and whatever else the Romans might impose upon them. In any event, the myth of mass *suicide* should be laid to rest. According to Josephus, each male first killed his own dependents; then ten men selected by lot slit the throats of the heads of household; one of the ten chosen by lot killed his nine fellows; finally, he alone committed suicide at the last.

Josephus also mentions seven survivors—two women and five children, who had hidden in a cistern while the slaughter was taking place. While this gives Josephus a claim to an eyewitness report, it also suggests at the very least that the death pact did not enjoy universal consensus, since these women opted out. Indeed, there may have been many more who would have preferred surrender, even if it meant slavery, to certain death, with the *sicarii* making the decision for them. A debris pile against the northern palace is susceptible to different interpretations, one of which is that some of the inhabitants, at least, made a last stand against the Romans after they breached the wall and may well have met the very fates Eleazar's speech warned about after the Romans piled up the debris that enabled them to scale the palace wall and confront the last holdouts.[36] Hundreds of Roman soldiers witnessed what actually happened, but even Roman military who knew the facts might embrace a more dramatic and even tragic conclusion since ennobling the defeated enemy would serve, in the Roman world, to ennoble the victors. Moreover, a story of

---

[36] "Maybe there is some truth in both points of view: perhaps some of the Jews took their own lives while others fought to the death" (Magness 2012:229).

Jews seeking a noble death through voluntarily submitting to mass slaughter spares the Romans another episode of butchering mostly unarmed noncombatants. In the end, one must decide the extent to which Josephus presents "the facts" over against the extent to which he creates an effective set piece to serve as a coda to his work as a whole.[37]

---

[37] For a helpful discussion of the problem, see especially Cohen 1982.

6

A Failed Messiah and a New Beginning

The Second Jewish Revolt and the Rise of Rabbinic Judaism

No Josephus told the history of post-70 Judea, and so what little can be known must be sifted from archaeological remains, numismatics, occasional and spotty literary and nonliterary texts, and later rabbinic literature. The latter presents its own special problems insofar as the earliest rabbinic texts appear to have been committed to writing no earlier than 200 CE (the Mishnah) and the bulk of the early tradition (the Talmudim) not until the fifth or sixth centuries. The historian must be careful to seek independent means of confirming the reliability of the attribution of sayings or practices to first- or second-century sages in documents written significantly later.[1] Nevertheless, the combination of sources opens several important windows, some admittedly tinted or foggy, into the period of reorganization and reconstruction following the catastrophe of 70 CE as well as into the possibly even more calamitous Second Jewish Revolt, bringing our survey to a close.

Reorganization and Recovery of the New Province

After the First Revolt, Judea, Samaritis, Peraea, and Galilee were detached from the province of Syria and made an independent province with a governor of proconsular (senatorial) rank and a legion under his command—the Legio X Fretensis, now to be permanently stationed

---

[1] Neusner 1971; 2007; Kraemer 2010:417.

Judea under Greek and Roman Rule. David A. deSilva, Oxford University Press.
© Oxford University Press 2024. DOI: 10.1093/oso/9780190263249.003.0007

in Jerusalem and its environs. Several of its divisions were encamped in the southwest quarter of the city itself, as evidenced by plentiful finds of bricks and tiles bearing the legionary stamp (made in a large kiln works discovered west of the city) as well as an early Roman-era bath house.[2] These measures were taken to remedy two defects that were clear in hindsight: the uneven quality of the equestrian prefects or procurators given responsibility for the subprovince and the inadequate military force garrisoned there.[3] The troublesome auxiliaries drawn from Sebaste and Caesarea were finally stationed elsewhere in the empire. The governor himself, together with several vexillations of the legion, resided in Caesarea, which Vespasian elevated to the status of a Roman colony, the *Colonia Prima Flavia Augusta Caesarensis*, and where he settled many of the veterans of the Jewish war. Vespasian also refounded the coastal city of Joppa, which had suffered significant damage in the suppression of Judean pirates operating from that base, and created the new city of Flavia Neapolis (modern Nablus) in Samaritis in 72–73 CE (Pliny, *Nat. Hist.* 5.14.69).

Jerusalem and its temple were left in ruins. Cultic rites there—along with the pilgrim economy that had proven so fruitful for the city—appear to have ceased entirely. Priests continued to collect tithes and assert authority, but the loss of their institutional basis meant that their influence was bound to fade over the following generations. Income from the temple "tax" was diverted to Rome. The tracts of land that had always been "royal lands" (like the date and balsam groves of Jericho and En Gedi) remained state property, to be administered by Vespasian as part of his personal estate, increased by land confiscated from revolutionaries and perhaps also the dead who were absent heirs. Many among the surviving population would have found themselves in the position of tenant farmers on imperial land. Jews who had not supported the Revolt and had surrendered in a timely fashion would likely have had their properties or estates (or some compensatory property, as in the case of Josephus) restored to them. Judea was essentially reduced once again to a subsistence-level agrarian economy.[4]

[2] Magness 2012:281.
[3] Smallwood 1981:331.
[4] Grabbe 2021:432.

Recovery of this economy in Judea appears to have been relatively quick following the Jewish War. The whole toparchy of Acraba in northern Judea, for example, has yielded no archaeological evidence of destruction prior to the Second Jewish Revolt.[5] Depopulation was a greater problem than destruction of arable land. New Jewish settlements appear in the Shephelah (the western Judean hills and foothills), including several new synagogues, in the decades following the war.[6] Galilee also appears to have been positioned well for economic recovery. During the winter of 67/68 CE, Vespasian already engaged his soldiers in rebuilding areas that had been devastated alongside setting up garrisons in the territories retaken (Josephus, *War* 4.442). The major cities of Galilee that had either entered the war as pro-Roman (Sepphoris) or surrendered in a timely fashion (Tiberias) either escaped significant destruction or were quickly rebuilt and would continue to serve as centers for Roman administration. Those Jews who had declared themselves for Rome and distanced themselves from the rebellion would have been important participants in the reconstruction of Judean and Galilean society in the decades following the war.[7]

Flavian Propaganda and Its Impact

The suppression of the First Jewish Revolt was an important achievement for Vespasian, the newly installed emperor, and his line and it would serve as a resource for Flavian propaganda for two decades. The Senate awarded Titus a triumphal procession upon his return to Rome, a procession in which John of Gischala and Simon ben Giora participated and of which the execution of the latter served as a notable spectacle. The triumph itself was commemorated first in a triumphal arch erected near the Circus Maximus (now lost), later to be joined by a second at the eastern end of the Roman Forum after Titus's death and divinization. This later triumphal arch features the famous scene

[5] Schwartz 2014:245.
[6] Schwartz 2014:246.
[7] Alon 1994:77.

Figure 6.1 A carved relief from the Arch of Titus depicting the furnishings of the Temple being carried in Titus's victory celebration.

of some of the furnishings of the Jerusalem temple—the menorah, the table of the shewbread, and the trumpets—being carried as part of the procession (see Figure 6.1). The seizure and parading of these items might have been understood to signal, in the manner of other ancient conquerors carrying away the images of the conquered people's gods, the triumph of the gods of Rome over Israel's God.[8] The placement of the spoils as trophies and artwork in Vespasian's new Temple of Peace, the centerpiece of his expansion of the forum, consecrated in 75 CE, also points in this direction: the Judean God was essentially a prisoner on display, at least from the Roman point of view.[9] The Flavian Amphitheater (or the "Colosseum") itself sported an inscription claiming it to have been financed with spoils appropriated in the wake of the Jewish Revolt.[10]

---

[8] Magness 2008:203.
[9] Magness 2008:208. See also Minucius Felix, *Octavius* 10.4.
[10] Alföldy 1995:195–226.

Figure 6.2 A bronze sesterce celebrating the suppression of the First Jewish Revolt and the incorporation of Judea into the empire as a province (courtesy of Numismatica Ars Classica NAC AG, Auction 64, lot 1140).

The propagandistic medium that spread the farthest throughout the empire, of course, was coinage, and both Vespasian and Titus exploited the victory over Judaea in their mintings throughout their reigns (particularly in 70–73 CE and again in 80–81 CE, near the beginning of each of their reigns),[11] giving the Judean defeat a long life in the public memory. These coins, proclaiming the conquest of Judaea (*Judaea Capta*) and the formation of Judaea as a new, independent province, helped to formalize the fiction that the Flavians had somehow contributed to the preservation and even the positive growth of the empire alongside inflicting significant destruction in their civil war against the armies of Vitellius.[12] Many issues feature the territory of Judea, personified as a woman, weeping beneath the date palm that was a well-established symbol of the region, or alternatively at the foot of a Roman trophy, often with a Roman military figure (Vespasian or Titus himself?) standing triumphantly behind her (see Figure 6.2).

[11] Keddie 2018:511.
[12] Josephus and his narrative account in many ways served this propagandistic purpose by making the "war" a far more momentous and heroic struggle than it likely was— "one of the greatest magnitude" (*War* 1.1.2)!

While not Flavian propaganda per se, an important—and highly symbolic—change involved the so-called Temple tax of two denarii, formerly sent to Jerusalem for the maintenance of the temple and its sacrifices. Vespasian ordered that this should continue to be collected. The funds would now be used in the first instance, however, for the restoration and renewed cultic operations of the temple of Jupiter, Juno, and Minerva, the Capitoline gods whose temple sat atop the Capitoline Hill overlooking the Roman Forum. This temple, central to the Roman state cult, had been destroyed in the fighting between the armies of Vitellius and Vespasian. Liability for the two-denarius tax, now called the *fiscus Iudaicus*, was extended from nonpriestly Jewish males over twenty to all Jews, male and female, free and slave, aged three years and older.[13] The dramatic increase in the number of Jews liable appears to have been merely opportunistic (perhaps not a surprise from the emperor who first instituted a fee for the use of public latrines, which were thereafter referred to as *Vespasiani*). In any event, this became essentially the price for the individual Jew's freedom to practice his or her ancestral faith. Rosters, of course, and records of payment would be dutifully kept to ensure compliance.

We can only speculate concerning the rationale and significance of this particular shift for both the emperor and Jews throughout the empire. It is possible that it was understood to represent, once again, the triumph of Rome's primary deities (and temple) over Judea's God (and temple).[14] Or perhaps it merely represented a means by which Vespasian believed the Jewish subjects of empire could now express their loyalty to the heads of state. The money sent to the Jerusalem Temple had symbolized participation in the daily sacrifices on behalf of the emperor (among other sacrifices), the distinctive manner in which Jews were allowed to show the loyalty that other eastern provinces' populations typically showed through emperor cult. It could thus continue to serve this purpose for *all* Jews, both in the province and throughout the Mediterranean diaspora, without Vespasian

[13] Josephus, *War* 7.218; Dio 66.7.2; Keddie 2018:522. Smallwood (1981:345) suggests that women over the age of sixty-two became exempt, but that men may have been liable for life.
[14] Alon 1994:65.

considering it to be a punitive measure—particularly since the diaspora population had not participated in the revolt in Judea. Indeed, neither Vespasian nor Titus adopted the title *Iudaicus*, perhaps out of consideration for the diaspora Jewish populations.[15] One cannot escape the sense, however, that, for many Jews, the requirement to give to Caesar what was due God caused significant vexation.

Dealing with Destruction and Reconstruction

For many survivors of the First Jewish Revolt, recovering one's property (where this was even possible), rebuilding, dealing with the trauma of the loss of family, friends, and associates, and many other such facets of the aftermath of the upheaval of 66–70 CE would have required all available physical, emotional, and spiritual energy. Whenever they were sufficiently still, however, the theological ramifications of what they had endured—and of the consequences that the nation now suffered—could not have failed to press in on many minds and raise questions that cut to the core of Jewish identity, belief, and practice. It is, in part, the gravity of these questions that makes their perseverance and recovery, particularly as seen in the work and impact of the sages who would become the founders of rabbinic Judaism, so awe-inspiring.

The apocalypse known as *4 Ezra* (2 Esdras 3–14) provides a window into the kinds of questions with which contemporary Jews were wrestling and one distinctive way, at least, in which some Jews found a way forward that affirmed the continuing meaningfulness of Jewish identity, practice, and belief. What was the significance of being a people chosen by God, a concept at the heart of Jewish identity, when the other nations of the world continued to dominate—and violently trample—God's "special possession"? Granted that Israel may have merited punishment at God's hands for its people's failures in regard to keeping their part of the covenant and perhaps even honoring the sanctity of their own temple (having made of it a haven for violent revolutionaries), such that God might use a foreign nation once again

15 Smallwood 1981:329.

as an instrument of punishment, where was the justice in allowing that foreign nation to continue to flourish rather than punishing it as well for its more egregious sins against the one God? What is the good of having a covenant with God at all when the majority of Israel seems incapable of keeping it, such that Israel continues to experience its curses rather than its promised blessings?

The author of 4 Ezra ultimately rejects the narrative spun by the Flavian emperors and set before the eyes of the world in their Judea Capta coinage. On the contrary, he presents a vision in which the mourning, desolate woman that is Judea (or, more precisely for him, Jerusalem) is transformed by God into a vast and glorious city once again (9:38–10:57). Just as this situation of devastation had turned itself around once before in the wake of the Babylonian conquest, so God would restore Jerusalem again. Furthermore, the author communicates reports of visions in which a prodigious three-headed, twelve-winged eagle—in a barely veiled allegory of the Julio-Claudian and Flavian imperial lines—is indicted and exterminated by God's messiah for its violent destruction of peaceful villages and cities and its reign of terror in general, "so that the whole earth, freed from your violence, may be refreshed and relieved" (11:1–12:47). The apocalyptic hope that the author holds out allows him to affirm for himself and his audiences that the pivotal concern of the span of this life remains the commitment to observe the Torah with one's whole heart and the fight against one's contrary inclinations to disobey God's commandments.[16] This remains the path to reward in the age to come—and it may be pursued also in the assurance that God's justice would work itself out in the present age as it draws to its close.

In the decades that separated the destruction of Jerusalem from the visionary meditations of the unknown authors of 4 Ezra and 2 Baruch (a similar enterprise in reconstructing the "larger picture" that kept the path of Torah-observance meaningful and even essential for the Jewish people), several Judeans took some very practical steps in the same direction. The most celebrated of these was Johanan ben Zakkai. Little is

---

[16] On this point, there is an essential alignment between the apocalyptists and the nascent rabbis, even though the latter would soon come to have little use for the former apart from the firm conviction about the life of the age to come.

known of his life before 70 CE, except that he was clearly a part of the learned elite, perhaps a scribe himself. He was remembered to have surrendered to the Romans before the siege of Jerusalem and to have settled—more likely, to have *been* settled—in Jamnia (Yavneh), one of the cities of the coastal plain that, together with Azotus (Ashdod), Lydda, and Gophna, were designated by Vespasian and Titus as places for settling Judeans who had surrendered to them (Josephus, *War* 4.130, 444; 6.115).

Johanan ben Zakkai sought and received permission to gather with like-minded peers and students to study the Torah and perform its commandments in quiet and peace.[17] The resulting "academy" is regarded as the moment of conception of rabbinic Judaism—the principal survivor, alongside the early Jesus movement, of pre-70 CE Judaism. It was only "the foundation of what was to become the Sanhedrin reborn," and the gestation period was to be centuries long.[18] Any influence that Johanan's circle enjoyed would have been informal and voluntarily accepted (or not) by other Jews at this time. In the wake of the destruction of Jerusalem and its temple, the office of high priest was left vacant and the Sanhedrin disappeared from the administrative structures of Judea, leaving a significant vacuum in leadership. Johanan and his circle were determined to step into this gap and provide at least the religious leadership that was very much needed. They appear to have focused on offering determinations concerning the liturgical calendar, the timing of new moons and festivals, and the calculations of the intercalation of a thirteen month into the lunar calendar—tasks once fulfilled for the worldwide Jewish community by the temple priests and for which the Jewish people were accustomed to look for authoritative guidance.[19]

Johanan himself is associated with rulings that exhibit an interest in keeping the temple's rituals alive in observances conducted far from the temple, to keep the temple that was physically absent symbolically present in the spaces where Jews continued to gather. For example, he prescribed the carrying of the lulav and etrog on each day of Sukkot,

---

[17] Alon 1994:96.
[18] Alon 1994:99; Grabbe 2021:451.
[19] Alon 1994:98.

as in the temple, rather than just on the first, as had been customary in synagogue and home celebrations. Similarly, he allowed the shofar to be blown not only in the Temple courts but in *any* courtyard when the New Year fell on a Sabbath day (so as to provide every such space with the exemption from the prohibition of what might be considered "work" on the Sabbath).[20] In a tradition preserved in the later rabbinic text, *Aboth de Rabbi Nathan* 4:5, Johanan answers an inquirer concerned about how they will be able to make atonement for sins without a temple with the words: "be not grieved; we have another atonement as effective as this. And what is it? It is acts of loving-kindness, as it is said: 'For I desire mercy and not sacrifice'" (Hosea 6:6).[21]

Johanan ben Zakkai appears either to have been displaced by, or perhaps to have stepped aside in favor of, Gamaliel II ben Simon, whose father (Simon ben Gamaliel I) had been invested with leadership authority prior to 70 CE.[22] Gamaliel appears to have sought to reestablish ties between the homeland and the diaspora, now that the annual occasions for mass pilgrimages to Jerusalem had ceased, by traveling himself to diaspora communities as well as welcoming diaspora pilgrims to Jamnia for study and consultation.[23] He and his circle created connections with towns and villages throughout Judea and Galilee as well, perhaps using synagogues as venues for carrying on an adult education program in the Torah and its prescriptions for post–70 CE life, recruiting disciples (cf. *Pirke Aboth* 1.1) to provide the same learned guidance throughout the land to those who would accept it. Rabbis made themselves available to serve as unofficial arbitrators, providing an option to Roman courts for local conflicts, a role that served no doubt to heighten their authority and stature throughout Galilean communities. One might regard them as slowly gaining authority by steadily increasing their exercise of authority. There was little if any community support for their work at this early stage: this would emerge only in the late second and early third centuries. Rabbis either were people of independent means who had the leisure for study

[20] Schäfer 2003:136; Alon 1994:114, 260.
[21] Translation from Goldin 1955:34.
[22] Alon 1994:106–107.
[23] Alon 1994:119, 131.

and teaching or supported their vocation through labor at some trade or agricultural endeavor.[24]

By this period there appears also to have been a general recognition of the basic contours of what would become the canon of the Hebrew Bible. This is reflected in Josephus's tally of twenty-two and 4 Ezra's tally of twenty-four "books"—which assume treating 1 and 2 Samuel as one book (and similarly with the books of Kings, Chronicles) and the minor prophets as a single "Book of the Twelve." Very few books actually occasioned discussion beyond this period—Song of Songs, Ecclesiastes, Esther, and the Wisdom of Ben Sira being the exceptions. Whether or not the differences in the tallies of Josephus and 4 Ezra are to be reconciled by assuming other combinations of books or received as evidence of some omissions, the degree of consensus is impressive, even if one cannot speak of a formal fixing of the canon until perhaps the third century CE.[25]

One commonly encounters the statement that the rabbis of Jamnia and their followers were the direct descendants of the Pharisees. There is cause to nuance this position, not least because the rabbis themselves sought to build an inclusive consensus rather than perpetuate the partisanship of pre–70 CE Judaism and because some nonpartisan teachers and scribes would have been attracted to their work as, essentially, the best path toward reconstruction. Nevertheless, the close alignment of the rabbis with their Pharisaic predecessors is visible in several places. The Pharisees' program of extending the sanctity of the Temple to the household table and the sanctity of the priests to all Israelite laity who were willing to give similar degrees of attention to maintaining purity and dealing in a timely fashion with pollution provided an important platform for the work of the rabbis, who would seek to do the same *in the absence* of a functioning temple and, to a large extent, as a functional replacement for the same (alongside the study of the laws of sacrifice as a substitute for the practice of sacrifice itself).[26] The religious importance of the "table"—forging connections

---

[24]   Alon 1994:490, 493–498.

[25]   See Grabbe 2008:245–253; 2020:263–268 on both development of canon and text traditions of particular books in the canon.

[26]   See also Schäfer 2003:133–134, 166; Cohen 1999:317.

with the "holy" at home—prepared the majority of Jews for a Judaism without an "altar."[27] Synagogues, of course, became all the more important an organ for social and religious cohesion. They were increasingly adorned with temple imagery in the third century CE and beyond, suggesting that they served increasingly as a functional substitute for the Temple that no longer existed.[28] The increasing lavishness of synagogues in the centuries after the destruction of the Temple also indicates their importance as a surrogate, now receiving the donations and support that might once have gone to the central shrine in Jerusalem.

Several sects that (often disproportionately) dominate discussions of pre–70 CE Judea have not left traces of continuing presence in, or impact upon, the post–70 CE landscape. The impact of the Sadducees, as of the temple priestly elite as a whole, diminished with the loss of the temple as a focal point for Jewish activity and the decimation of the landed aristocracy.[29] The elite Essene community at Qumran was destroyed in the war, but the Essenes might otherwise have been expected to remain a viable movement. However, literary testimonies to their existence cease with Josephus's narrative. Perhaps with the loss of the Temple, itself a focal point for their sectarian objections, many of their members found their way to integrate themselves once again among the more rigorist circles of their fellow Jews. Perhaps the failure of the anticipated war against the sons of darkness—indeed, the defeat of the sons of light by the sons of darkness—brought on a disillusionment that was difficult if not impossible to surmount.[30] The Samaritan community centered on Gerizim has persevered even into the twenty-first century. And, of course, the early Christian movement became, alongside the rabbinic movement, one of the two principal bearers of the Jewish tradition and scriptures, admittedly in a significantly transformed fashion.

Historians have sought particularly to understand how the separation of the early Jesus movement from Judaism came about. In the lands

[27] Schwartz 2014:250.
[28] Cohen 1999:322–323; Sharon 2017:326.
[29] Stemberger 1999:435.
[30] Collins 2010:210–213.

outside of Israel, the answer seems forthright. Christian communities were made up largely of Gentile converts who, in the circles shaped by the Pauline mission at the very least (but probably considerably more widely), showed little interest in adopting a Jewish way of life apart from rejecting idolatry and giving their allegiance solely to the God of Israel and the man they believed to be this God's anointed agent of deliverance. By the early second century, both Roman and Christian writers were able to distinguish between "Jews" and "Christians"— something that Roman prosecutions, above all else, make abundantly clear.[31]

In Palestine itself, the matter may not have been nearly so clear cut. Some have speculated that one of the prayers contained in the *Shemoneh Esre*—a liturgy of eighteen short prayers each concluding with a statement pronouncing God "blessed" for some attribute or characteristic action—was introduced as a tool to drive Jewish Christians out from the assembly of Jews gathering at the synagogues throughout the land. This so-called Benediction against Heretics (*birkhat ha-minim*) petitioned God to destroy apostates, "the insolent kingdom" (by which Rome was no doubt meant), Nazarenes, and heretics and to strike their names from the "Scroll of Life." However, the specific term "Nazarenes" appears only in very late examples and the directing of this prayer against Christians is not otherwise attested prior to the fourth century, when Epiphanius and Jerome draw attention to this subtext.[32] If this was indeed a part of the *Shemoneh Esre* from the period of Gamaliel II,[33] it was more likely directed not against any particular heretics (*minim*), but against the spirit of sectarianism, issuing a kind of declaration that the time for sectarianism within Judaism was past and a call for a united commitment to move forward from the ashes of the temple together,[34] the aim that the rabbis would generally foster (under their own auspices, of course).

Nevertheless, there is very little evidence of a Jewish Christian population standing out from the larger Jewish population in second- and

---

[31] See especially Pliny, Ep. X.96–97; 1 Pet 4:14–16; Cohen 2014:309.
[32] Cohen 2014:329–335.
[33] Schäfer 2003:140.
[34] Cohen 1987:227–228.

third-century Judea and Galilee.[35] While there are references to *minim* in the Mishnah, none appear to have Jewish Christians particularly in view.[36] The Tosefta, a less authoritative and somewhat later supplement to the Mishnah, relates a mere two stories relevant to relations between pious Jews and Jewish Christ-followers in the early second century CE, both advising avoidance of Jewish Christians.[37] Jewish Christians—apart from a few known sects like the Ebionites and Nazoreans that persevered into the fourth century—appear to have forsaken their Jewish identity in favor of blending into the Gentile majority in the early Christian communities or abandoned (or at least muted) their commitment to Jesus as the Messiah in favor of continuing to exist within the Jewish community.[38]

While the majority of Zealots and *sicarii* could be presumed to have perished in the First Jewish Revolt, the nationalist and revolutionary spirit that fueled their partisan movements certainly survived, as events in the first half of the second century would demonstrate. The last years of Trajan's reign were marked by a series of uprisings among diaspora Jews, particularly in Cyrenaica (modern Libya), Egypt, and Cyprus. These caused significant destruction (Greco-Roman religious sites were particularly targeted) and even more significant loss of life. Trajan threw the full force of several legions against these uprisings, with the result that formerly great diaspora populations, for example the massive Jewish community of Alexandria, were decimated. The question naturally arises whether the Jewish population of Judea and its environs participated in these uprisings. Most of the evidence is circumstantial. Trajan had appointed Lucius Quietus as governor of Judaea following Quietus's success as a general in Trajan's campaigns in Mesopotamia. A second legion, the II Traiana, was transferred to Judea and stationed at Caparcotna ("Legio") sometime prior to 120 CE (given the discovery of a milestone erected there by this legion at that time), a result of the elevation of the province from merely proconsular to consular status. Were these responses to active unrest? Or

---

[35] Horsley 1996:185.
[36] Cohen 2014:322.
[37] Cohen 2014:328.
[38] Cohen 2014:309–310.

do they indicate, first, Trajan's desire to reward a valuable officer and, second, an interest in shoring up the strength of the armies in a frontier province—or, at most, taking a proactive stance against revolutionary activity spreading to the Judean homeland? While the possibility of some revolutionary activity must be acknowledged, in the end any such activity was so quickly suppressed as to have left very little evidence in the literary or archaeological record.[39] The increased Roman military presence in the area would incidentally give fresh impetus to the Romanization of Galilee with the proliferation of nymphaea, baths, stadia, hippodromes, and other such Roman cultural institutions in the cities north of Judea.[40]

The Second Jewish Revolt

One episode that particularly drew the attention of later historians is the Second Jewish Revolt or Bar-Kochba Rebellion. Cassius Dio (*Roman History* 69.12.1–14.3) and Eusebius (*Eccl. Hist.* 4.6.1–4.6.4) both provide relatively brief narrative accounts, the former being the more detailed. It is difficult to discern the causes of this revolt. Eusebius offers nothing beyond a simmering rebellious spirit coming once again to a boil. Aelius Spartianus in his *Life of Hadrian* (14.2) attributes it to a general decree by Hadrian forbidding the mutilation of genitals. Castration had been forbidden in the empire since Domitian, and Hadrian reinforced this by making it a capital crime.[41] It is not clear, however, if he forbade the Jews their time-honored (and hitherto openly tolerated) practice, which would not be in keeping with his interest in preserving peace in the empire, or, if he did, whether this preceded or followed the revolt. What is known is that his successor, Antoninus Pius, would issue a clarification limiting the applicability of the ruling against *any* genital mutilation (including circumcision) to Gentiles, while respecting the Jewish people's historic freedom to

---

[39] See Alon 1994:413–429 for a maximalist view; Smallwood 1981:421–427 and Grabbe 2021:461–464 for smaller-scale revolutionary activity swiftly suppressed.

[40] Chancey 2005:223–224.

[41] Suetonius, *Domitian* 7.1; Cassius Dio 47.2–3; Ulpian, *Digest* 48.8.4.2.

follow this custom among their own ethnic group.[42] In any event, there is no reliable record of persecution of Jews who circumcised their male children (as there was under Antiochus IV) and no other evidence beyond the generally unreliable *Augustan History* that such a decree spawned a full-scale revolt.

Cassius Dio (69.12.1–2) provides the most plausible cause, namely Hadrian's refounding of the dilapidated (and probably somewhat derelict) Jerusalem as a new, Roman colony—the *Colonia Aelia Capitolina*. Such a decision was in keeping with the tenor of Hadrian's tour of the eastern provinces in 129–130 CE and his interest in their development as a "restorer" (*restitutor*). While this might have been intended as an act of general beneficence for all the people of the region, it was certainly an act of beneficence toward the legion stationed there and the veterans and their dependents settled there or in the vicinity. Such a large military and ex-military population merited living in a genuine *colonia* and not amid the haphazard makeovers of a former war zone. Eusebius claims that the founding of Aelia Capitolina was a consequence, not a cause, of the revolt, but we are not presented with a genuine "either/or" scenario here. The formal founding of Aelia Capitolina provides the flashpoint for the outbreak of the Second Jewish Revolt. The discovery of a coin hoard containing coins of Aelia Capitolina alongside coins minted under Bar Kosiba suggests strongly that the new foundation was under way before the uprising (as the hoard was never retrieved by its owners, who can be presumed casualties of the revolt).[43] An uprising of the scale that confronted the Roman forces, however, would certainly disrupt progress on new construction, with the result that the city's completion would have to await the suppression of the military threat.[44]

Hostilities broke out by 132 CE. The revolutionary forces were not divided between rival party chiefs this time, but rather coalesced under the firm-handed leadership of one Simeon bar Kosiba. Much about him remains unknown, but he was clearly a capable and charismatic

[42] Modestinus, *Digest* 48.8.11.1; Schäfer 2003:160. See also Grabbe 2021:474–475 for a sober evaluation of this tradition.

[43] Goodman 2000:673.

[44] Smallwood 1981:433.

leader—so much so that he acquired a messianic moniker, Simeon bar *Kochba*, "son of a star" (cf. Justin, *1. Apol.* 31.6). It is entirely possible that no less a figure than Rabbi Akiba acclaimed him, at some point during the revolt, as "the king messiah" or "anointed king," applying the promise of the "star" that would "rise up out of Jacob" to him (*y. Taan.* 4.8.68a, referring to Num 24:17), though another rabbi was remembered to have immediately objected.[45] Coins and documents refer to Simeon as *Nasi*, or "prince," and he clearly exercised an autocratic rule over the revolutionaries and those caught up in their domains.

The revolutionaries achieved surprising initial successes by repeating the Maccabean strategy of guerilla warfare. Galilee was largely, though not wholly, uninvolved in the Second Revolt. The greatest part of the fighting and, consequently, the destruction appears to have been confined primarily to Judea, largely to the area south of Jerusalem and Jericho. Early on in the revolt, Bar Kosiba established a kind of headquarters at Ein Gedi and was able to gain control of at least some of the state-owned property, mostly likely in Jericho (the largest concentration of "royal lands" in Judea proper), which he treated as his own property, leasing plots out to private citizens and thus raising money for the war effort.[46] Dates on documents discovered at Herodium, twenty-three miles northwest of En Gedi, show that revolutionaries secured that fortress by the second year of the revolt, though it is not known how long they were able to maintain their position.[47] It is likely that the maze of tunnels beneath the Herodian construction, similar to such tunnels dug elsewhere during this period, was the work of the revolutionaries, who made use of such strategies both for attack and escape (Cassius Dio, 69.12.3).

Did Simeon and his forces ever gain control of Jerusalem itself? The evidence is mixed. On the one hand, literary references to the destruction or capture of Jerusalem under Hadrian seem to presume that it had been the site of military action—and thus had been in the rebels'

---

[45] Grabbe 2021:485–487 favors the reliability of this tradition. The messianic application of Num 24:17 is also attested in *T. Judah* 24:1–6; CD 7.18–21; cf. also Schäfer 2003:149–150.

[46] Yadin 1971:172–183.

[47] Yadin 1971:182–183.

Figure 6.3 A silver tetradrachm from the third year of the Second Jewish Revolt (courtesy of the Classical Numismatic Group, LLC, www.cngco ins.com).

hands for at least some time (Appian, *Syr.* 50; Justin Martyr, *Dial.* 108.3; Eusebius, *Demonstratio evangelica* 6.18.10).[48] The iconography and legends on the coins minted under Simeon present ambiguous evidence. These certainly show that the revolutionaries' *aims* centered on Jerusalem and its "liberation" from Roman domination and on the Temple whose future restoration was jeopardized by Hadrian's plans for the city. The common representations of the façade of Temple and cultic objects like the palm branch, citron, or trumpets call the Temple and its rites constantly to mind, as does the mention of one "Eleazar the priest" in tandem with "Simeon, the prince of Israel." The legends "For the Freedom of Jerusalem" or simply "Jerusalem" may represent the rallying cries of the movement as a whole, though the latter has been read as an indication of the place of minting.[49] The legend "Year 1 *of* the freedom of Jerusalem" as distinct from "*for* the freedom of Jerusalem" is ambiguous: to some, it suggests the *achievement*, however temporary, of the revolutionaries' aims; to others, it remains *aspirational* (see Figure 6.3).

---

[48] Smallwood 1981:444.
[49] Alon 1994:614–616; Smallwood 1981:443–444. Yadin 1971:18 also asserts that Bar Kosiba captured Jerusalem.

In favor of the aspirational reading is the existence also of legends that read "year 2" and "year 3 of the freedom of Jerusalem" and the inherent implausibility of revolutionary forces holding Jerusalem for any part of three years when most of their initial campaigns were spent carrying on their guerilla assaults from their well-dug tunnels—and succeeding *because* of these tactics—and the last part of the war constituted a long siege of the rebels in Bethar. Moreover, the absence of any archaeological evidence *in* Jerusalem or its environs (for example, of over 15,000 coins discovered in digs in Jerusalem, only two are mintings of Bar Kosiba) argues strongly against the language being anything more than aspirational at any point during the revolt.[50] We should also remember both that Jerusalem's defenses were almost wholly destroyed or dismantled in connection with the First Jewish Revolt, rendering it indefensible in the manner that it had been defended in 70 CE, and that its southwestern quarter was the central camp of the Legio X Fretensis—a legion that remained sufficiently strong to survive the revolt and was not likely to relinquish control of its camp at any point during the same.

In addition to the resident legions X Fretensis and VI Ferrata (which had replaced the II Traiana at Caparcotna),[51] the II Traiana was brought back from Egypt, the III Gallica from Syria, the III Cyrenaica from Arabia, and detachments of infantry and cavalry from several more legions. Hadrian dispatched Sextus Julius Severus, stationed in Britannia, to Judea to lead the war effort there. The size of the Roman force and the choice of commander testify to the seriousness of the threat to Roman sovereignty in Judea. Severus pursued a cautious strategy of dividing and blockading rebel forces, starving them into submission or extermination without risking open engagements (Cassius Dio, 69.13.3). Simeon and his forces were put on the defensive and made their last stand at Bethar, about five miles southwest of Jerusalem, the site of a Hasmonean/Herodian-era fortress that was further fortified to enclose about twenty-five acres of territory. It was naturally well protected by steep grades on the east, west, and north sides. The Romans besieged the city-fortress, creating the usual

---

[50] Schäfer 2003:155; see also Magness 2012:270; Grabbe 2021:484.
[51] Sartre 2000:640.

circumvallation wall, and prepared to attack from the south by means of a siege ramp built across the moat there. The size of the two Roman army camps southwest of Bethar suggests that at least one and a half legions were occupied with the siege. The rebels ultimately succumbed in 135 CE.

The discovery of letters written in the name of Simeon Bar Kosiba in several caves above the western shore of the Dead Sea between Qumran and Masada (Wadi Murabba'at and Nahal Hever) has opened important windows into the nature of the revolt and Simeon's command—although they are all views on different and disconnected parts of a landscape and do little to help reconstruct the whole.[52] One group consists of a variety of orders sent to two subordinates at Ein Gedi, a Yehonathan ben Be'aya and Masabala ben Shimeon, whose last refuge, along with other revolutionaries and their families, had apparently been in the caves where the letters were left. One calls upon these subordinates to send some people from Tekoa and other places, who appear to have taken refuge in Ein Gedi, on to Bar Kosiba's location, most likely to support the war efforts rather than dodge the draft, as it were. At the same time, they are to disarm and arrest a certain Yeshua bar Tadmoraya and send him back to Bar Kosiba "in safe custody," which does not bode well for him. Another orders them to send one Eleazar bar Hitta to Bar Kosiba along with an unspecified amount of wheat and fruit that they are to confiscate, again suggesting that someone is being treated as an enemy of the cause and his resources appropriated. Another gives instructions simply to assist the bearer of the letter, one Elisha, in the unspecified task he is undertaking on Bar Kosiba's behalf. Another chides Yehonathan and Masabala for allegedly hoarding supplies for themselves and not making adequate provision for Bar Kosiba and his camp. Another, written in Greek by a middleman on Simeon's behalf, requests that supplies of palm branches, citrons (which are to be tithed!), myrtle, and willow—the four ingredients for the celebration of the Feast of Tabernacles—be sent to Bar Kosiba's location in large quantities, showing that he and his army remained committed to observing the prescribed festivals

---

[52] For texts and discussion, see Fitzmyer and Harrington 1978:158–162; Yadin 1971:124–139.

in some fashion. The letters also exhibit concern for observing the Sabbath, by ordering the completion of tasks prior to, or initiating their execution only after, the day of rest. Most of these letters threaten the two subordinates with punishment if they fail to comply, which raises questions about their own personal investment in the "cause" and the degree to which Bar Kosiba exercised leadership through coercive measures. It is his willingness to use violent measures against his own officers that lends credence to Justin's allegation that he also subjected Jewish Christ followers to "dreadful torments" if they refused to accept his leadership and join his cause (*1 Apology* 36.1).

The caves west of the Dead Sea also yielded documentary evidence of a very different kind in the form of the personal archives of two women who met their fate in connection with the Roman reconquest of southern Judea following Bar Kosiba's demise at Bethar. A woman named Babatha took a collection of thirty-five documents with her into the cave where her life, or at least her freedom, came to an end. These included the *ketuboth* or marriage contracts from her two marriages, a good number of documents pertaining to legal actions either initiated by her (through her male legal representation) or against her, as well as declarations of property she owned in the province of Arabia made for tax purposes.[53] Salome's smaller collection also focuses on legal disputes concerning property. These documents provide windows into matters of more typical concern for the people in and around Judea: marriages, property, the care of orphaned children, and the use of existing legal structures to settle disputes.

The human cost of the Second Revolt was enormous. It resulted in the destruction of fifty towns and 985 villages, mostly in Judea, if Cassius Dio (69.14.1) is to be believed. Judea experienced significant depopulation through death and enslavement, even if Dio's figure of 580,000 slain on the Jewish side (besides indirect casualties of famine or disease) is significantly inflated. This was exacerbated by at least some degree of emigration from Judea, whether north into Galilee, which becomes the new center of gravity for Jews in their homeland,

---

[53] Yadin 1971:222–253 remains a fine introduction to the documents and the reconstruction of the history and legal battles represented therein. See also Grabbe 2021:452–457.

or places further afield, such as Asia Minor and Egypt. The suppression of the revolt gave the victor once again the opportunity to appropriate the land of the deceased or captured revolutionaries, alienating their survivors from property and increasing the incidence of tenant farming (cf. Eusebius, *Hist. eccl.* 4. 6.1). Casualties on the Roman side were also high. One Roman legion, the XXII Deiotariana, disappeared from history at about this time. Some believe it was decimated during this war, suggesting the scope of Roman casualties, while others argue that it had been disbanded previously, by 123 CE, on account of its having been disgraced, perhaps in the Alexandrian riots of 121–122.[54] Irrespective of the fate of this particular legion, the Roman losses were significant enough that, again according to Dio, for a time Hadrian omitted from his greetings to the Senate the customary clause, "I and the legions are well" (69.14.3).

The cost to the Jewish people was also high in other ways, particularly in terms of the symbolic punishments inflicted on them at this time. First, Jews would be forbidden henceforth to enter the city limits of Aelia Capitolina. The ban was lifted, it would appear, for one day out of the year—the ninth of Ab, an occasion on which the Jews were allowed to visit the city and to mourn its fate. This, of course, would also entail the dispossession of any Jews who still owned property in the city. Second, the province acquired the new name of *Syria Palaestina*, and it is difficult to discover a rationale for this change of name other than a desire on Hadrian's part to distance the land from the Jewish ethnos, its revolutionary heritage, and the ideology of the land that sustained revolutionary ideology. However, although Hadrian was hailed as *imperator* a second time after this victory at some point in 135 CE, he did not hold a triumph in Rome nor broadly publicize the victory (quite unlike his Flavian predecessors), perhaps out of a sober awareness of the cost in Roman lives, particularly in the initial years of the revolt before Severus's arrival. Rabbinic traditions of Hadrian compelling abandonment of Jewish practice and the study of the Jewish law—acting like a second Antiochus IV (seen most poignantly in *Lamentations Rabbah*, which recasts the martyr scenes of

---

54 Grabbe 2021:482.

2 Maccabees 7 with figures from the Hadrianic period)—may reflect some degree of suppression between 135 CE and Hadrian's death in 138 CE. It is possible that Hadrian was sufficiently provoked at this point to revoke the Jewish people's exclusion from his prohibition of circumcision (as part of an empire-wide ban on genital mutilation).[55] Even if this was the case, however, his successor Antoninus Pius would act to restore these rights almost immediately. This exemption would not extend, however, to non-Jews who wished to convert to the Jewish way of life, which may reflect long-standing Roman scruples against proselytizing. Jewish leaders would compensate for this by affirming that ritual immersion would thenceforth suffice both for female *and* male gentile converts.[56]

Severus remained for two years as governor of Syria Palaestina. He and his successors oversaw the energetic expansion of the road network throughout the region to facilitate troop movement should the need again arise. It would not. Sometime during Hadrian's reign, perhaps in connection with his tour of the eastern provinces in 129–130 or his second visit during the Revolt itself, orders were given for the improvement of the water supply to Caesarea Maritima (itself a Roman colony since 70 CE). The best known of these efforts involved a second aqueduct running alongside the older Herodian aqueduct for a span of several kilometers north of the city. Plaques set into the wall commemorate the participation of vexillations of several legions, including the X Fretensis, II Traiana, and VI Ferrata. Legionnaires also constructed the larger hippodrome to the east of the city during this period. The reshaping of Jerusalem as Aelia Capitolina was also energetically resumed, resulting in a thorough reconfiguration of the northern portion of Jerusalem.[57] Not surprisingly, Herodian ashlars, available in abundance amid the ruins of the Jerusalem temple and other structures, provided the building blocks for a good portion of Hadrian's new city.

---

[55] Smallwood 1981:465.
[56] Smallwood 1981:469, 472.
[57] The definitive resource on the camp of the Legio X Fretensis and the layout of the city, its forums, and roads is Weksler-Bdolah 2020:19–125. See also Magness 2012:271–285.

Aelia Capitolina

The southwest quarter of Jerusalem, including most of the Upper City, remained the camp of the X Fretensis through 300 CE. A major east-west street (the Decumanus) ran north of the camp from the Jaffa Gate to the retaining wall of the temple mount. The principal north-south Cardo, with covered colonnades on both sides, appears to have begun its northward run at the Decumanus, terminating in a grand oval forum inside a three-arched gateway, part of which remains visible today beneath the Damascus Gate. It would only be extended to the south of the Decumanus in the Byzantine period. A secondary Cardo ran from the oval forum to the east of the principal Cardo and alongside the western wall of the temple mount, continuing south beyond the Decumanus possibly as far as the Pool of Siloam, which remained in use throughout this period.

A large forum was constructed north of the temple mount. An area larger than the defunct Antonia Fortress was leveled by erecting vaulted roofs over the Struthion Pools that once sat open to the sky. The great flagstones that are presented to modern visitors as the "Lithostratos" or "Pavement" of the Johannine account of the trial of Jesus (John 19:13) are actually part of the pavement of Hadrian's northeastern forum. Another three-arched gateway was erected as a monumental entrance to this forum, parts of which are still visible as the so-called Ecce Homo Arch, with one of the smaller entrances now enshrined behind the altar in the chapel of the Convent of the Sisters of Zion (see Figure 6.4). To the east of this forum, a shrine to Aesclepius was erected over the Pools of Bethesda, suggesting the perseverance of the legend of the healing powers of its waters (see John 5:3–7 and the variant reading that includes 5:4).

A second, larger forum was located in the area northwest of the intersection of the main Cardo and Decumanus. This space also required significant engineering and fill to create a level surface of adequate size for the project. Another triple-arched gate gave access to the forum from the east. The northern part of the forum was dominated by a basilica and a temple sitting atop a majestic podium, possible the temple to Tyche (assimilated to the local Syrian goddess Astarte),

Figure 6.4 A triple-arched, freestanding gateway constructed in the Decapolis city of Gerasa to commemorate Hadrian's tour of the province. The gates of Aelia Capitolina's north and west forums would have closely resembled this structure.

whose cult image and temple façade feature prominently on coins from Aelia during the reign of Antoninus Pius and his successors.[58]

There is no doubt that Aelia *Capitolina* also hosted a temple dedicated to the trio of gods worshiped in the original Capitolium on the Capitoline hill overlooking Rome's ancient forum, namely Jupiter, Juno, and Minerva. According to Cassius Dio (69.12.1), this temple was erected most provocatively upon the derelict temple mount, prominently overlooking the new city—and perhaps declaring afresh the victory of Rome's gods over Judea's own.[59] The ongoing use and widening of the causeway that joined the legionary camp site to the temple mount, as well as evidence of purposeful repair of Herodian walls to the height of the platform during the Roman period, suggest that the space atop the temple mount continued to play an important role in the life of the city in some form. Some seventh-century texts refer to the temple mount as the Capitolium, suggesting a historical memory. The evidence remains admittedly mixed, however, as the Bordeaux Pilgrim (333 CE) speaks of a shrine and two statues of Hadrian on the site (one of which was more likely an equestrian statue of Antoninus Pius). Jerome speaks of a statue of Jupiter and another of Hadrian on the spot in connection with his exposition of the "abomination of desolation" (*Commentary on Matthew* 24:15). These might point to a shrine of the imperial cult on the temple mount—which would have been no less offensive, to be sure. Other scholars therefore gravitate to the West Forum as the likely place for the Capitolium along with the temple of Tyche.[60] From this position, elevated by the leveling and raising of the ground through filling in a quarry (Golgotha) and cemetery (now marked by the Church of the Holy Sepulcher), the Capitolium could stand prominently above the forum and the western Cardo Maximus running alongside the forum. If this was the civic forum, as the presence of the basilica suggests, it would also have been an appropriate site for the Capitolium, or temple to Jupiter, Juno, and Minerva. At some point, a similar temple to the Capitoline trio, such as appears on early third-century coinage from Samaritis, was erected on Mt. Gerizim.

Resurgence under Rabbinic Leadership

After the Second Revolt, the leaders of the emerging rabbinic movement relocated to Galilee—first to Usha in Upper Galilee under the leadership of Simon ben Gamaliel II and then Beth Shearim in Lower Galilee under the leadership of his son Judah, who would be called *ha-Nasi* or "the Prince."[61] Simon appears to have enjoyed some degree of recognition by the Roman authorities as a representative of the Jewish people and to have reconvened the Sanhedrin. Whether their authority at this point extended beyond matters that might be considered "religious" is unclear. They had by this time successfully filled the gap left by

[60] Murphy-O'Connor 1994:407–415.
[61] Schäfer 2003:163.

the priestly authorities in the temple as far as determining the calendar and the proper dates for the observances of the cycle of festivals, both for Jews in the land and throughout the diaspora (although this met with resistance in the Babylonian diaspora).[62] Their conversations and rulings otherwise seem to have focused on matters of purity, Sabbath observance, marriage and divorce, the proper tithing of produce, the continued application of Torah's prescriptions (and proscriptions) regarding agricultural practice (such as avoiding the planting of mixed crops), and, increasingly, matters of civil and criminal law.

The period of Simon's leadership also witnessed the creation and dissemination of a new Greek translation. The project was undertaken by a gentile convert to Judaism named Aquila—reputedly (and, if true, quite ironically) a relative of the emperor Hadrian who came to Jerusalem in connection with the construction of Aelia Capitolina. His translation project, which would be followed by another undertaken by Symmachus around 200 CE, reflects long-standing dissatisfaction by Judean sages with the Greek versions that had been in use among Greek-speaking Jews for over three centuries. While the Christian movement's particular reliance upon and interpretation of certain readings in the Septuagint no doubt contributed to the perceived problem with the older Greek version, the more long-standing and pervasive problem was the variation in underlying Hebrew texts in existence in the third and second centuries BCE. Aquila produced his translation on the basis of the Hebrew texts currently preferred by the rabbinic sages and followed a distinctively wooden translation principle. While this rendered his version far less fluid, it made the underlying Hebrew text more transparent for its readers, which was no doubt deemed more important for the task of biblical interpretation.[63]

The rabbis' growing influence and reach led organically to the official delegation of authority to their leaders by the Roman administration, certainly with the naming of Judah ben Simon as the "patriarch" in the final decades of the second century. This more official collaboration between the Roman governor and the patriarch as representative of an indigenous people group may have led Judah to move his center to

---

[62] Schäfer 2003:169.
[63] Jobes and Silva 2015:26–28.

one of the urban centers of Galilee, namely Sepphoris. This move may suggest a certain degree of flexibility—or, at the very least, tolerance—on Judah's part, since Sepphoris had become thoroughly Romanized by the end of the second century. It had been renamed Diocaesarea (a combination of the names of Zeus and Caesar) in honor of Hadrian and by this time featured a temple to Jupiter Capitolinus, a theater, and a population whose elite freely decorated their villas with scenes from Greco-Roman mythology. Similarly, Tiberias—where the rabbinic movement would later move and where the so-called Jerusalem Talmud would be compiled—erected its first pagan temples in the second century, including a temple to Hadrian and, perhaps, temples to Zeus and Hygeia (the latter being appropriate to the warm, therapeutic baths south of the city), whose images were well represented on the city's coinage.[64] The recognition of the patriarch, however, was still just another important step on the longer journey to establishing the dominance of the rabbis within the larger Jewish body, one that would require several more centuries of patient and relentless work.

Under the leadership of Judah ha-Nasi, the rabbinic sages would compile the Mishnah, the foundational document of what would become Rabbinic Judaism. The six major divisions of the compendium reflect the principal concerns that occupied the rabbis to this point. The first, "Seeds," lays out a body of regulations (or, better, rabbinic *opinions* about regulations) concerning agriculture, tithing, and prayers. The second, "Festivals," is concerned with the proper observance of the Sabbath and the festivals of the liturgical calendar. The third, "Women," collects material pertinent to betrothal, marriage, and divorce, but also conversion and oaths. The fourth, "Damages," treats civil and criminal infractions and their penalties as well as judicial processes. One of the subsections of this division is the "Sayings of the Fathers" (*Pirke Aboth*), a collection principally of maxims that provides a winsome introduction to the ethos and core convictions of named rabbis. The fifth, "Holy Things," is particularly interesting for its attention to the dimensions of the Temple, the proper performance of daily offerings and other sacrifices, and other rites bound to the cultic system of the Temple—a sign, again, of the manner in which

---

[64] Horsley 1996:61, 105; Smallwood 1981:474.

the rabbis held onto this vital facet of Jewish practice through study, if not performance. The final section, "Purities," treats sources of impurity and, where applicable, the means and rites for purification. Taken as a whole, the corpus well reflects the goal of the rabbinic movement, namely the discovery of ways in which to perform the whole of the Torah, even if that performance meant only study, and thus to fulfill Israel's covenant obligations faithfully while resigned to the necessary condition of Gentile domination.

Bibliography

Abel, F.-M. 1952. *Histoire de la Palestine Depuis la Conquète d'Alexandre Jusqu'a l'Invasion Arabe. Tome I. De La Conquete D'Alexandre Jusqu'a la Guerre Juive*. Paris: Gabalda.

Adams, Samuel L. 2014. *Social and Economic Life in Second Temple Judea*. Louisville, KY: Westminster John Knox Press.

Adler, Yonatan. 2008. "Second Temple Period Ritual Baths Adjacent to Agricultural Installations." *Journal of Jewish Studies* 59: 62–72.

Alföldy, Geza. 1995. "Eine bauinschrift aus dem Colosseum." *Zeitschrift für Papyrologie und Epigraphik* 109: 195–226.

Alon, Gedaliah. 1994. *The Jews in Their Land in the Talmudic Age*. Translated by Gershon Levi. Cambridge, MA: Harvard University Press.

Applebaum, Shimon H. 1989. *Judea in Hellenistic and Roman Times: Historical and Archaeological Essays*. SJLA 40. Leiden: Brill.

Astin, A. E., F. W. Walbank, M. W. Frederiksen, and R. M. Ogilvie, eds. 1989. *The Cambridge Ancient History. Volume VIII: Rome and the Mediterranean*. 2nd ed. Cambridge: Cambridge University Press.

Atkinson, Kenneth. 2004. "*I Cried to the Lord*": *A Study of the Psalms of Solomon's Historical Background and Social Setting*." Journal for the Study of Judaism Suppl. 84. Leiden: E. J. Brill.

Atkinson, Kenneth. 2016. *A History of the Hasmonean State: Josephus and Beyond*. London: T. & T. Clark.

Atkinson, Kenneth. 2018. *The Hasmoneans and Their Neighbors: New Historical Reconstructions from the Dead Sea Scrolls and Classical Sources*. London: T. & T. Clark.

Aviam, Mordechai. 1993. "Galilee: The Hellenistic to Byzantine Periods." In *The New Encyclopedia of Archaeological Excavations in the Holy Land*, vol. 2, edited by Ephraim Stern et al., 450–453. Jerusalem: Israel Exploration Society.

Aviam, Mordechai. 2004. "First Century Jewish Galilee: An Archaeological Perspective." In *Religion and Society in Roman Palestine*, edited by Douglas R. Edwards, 7–27. New York: Routledge.

Bahat, Dan. 1999. "The Herodian Temple." Pp. 38–58 in Horbury, Davies, and Sturdy, eds. 1999.

Barag, Dan. 1992–1993. "New Evidence on the Foreign Policy of John Hyrcanus I." *Israel Numismatic Journal* 12: 1–12.

Bar-Kochva, Bezalel. 1989. *Judas Maccabeus: The Jewish Struggle against the Seleucids*. Cambridge: Cambridge University Press.

Baumgarten, Albert. 1997. *The Flourishing of Jewish Sects in the Maccabean Era: An Interpretation*. Leiden: Brill.

Beilby, James K., and Paul R. Eddy, eds. 2009. *The Historical Jesus: Five Views*. Downers Grove, IL: IVP Academic.

Ben David, Chaim. 2021. "On the Number of Synagogues and Their Location in the Holy Land." Pp. 175–194 in Bonnie, Hakola, and Tervahauta, eds. 2021.

Berlin, Andrea M. 1997. "Between Large Forces: Palestine in the Hellenistic Period." *Biblical Archaeologist* 60: 3–51.

Berlin, Andrea M. 2005. "Jewish Life before the Revolt: The Archaeological Evidence." *Journal for the Study of Judaism* 36: 417–470.

Berlin, Andrea M. 2015. "Herod, Augustus, and the Augusteum at the Paneion." Pp. 1–11 in *Eretz-Israel: Archaeological, Historical and Geographical Studies, volume 31 (Ehud Netzer Volume)*, edited by Zeev Weiss. Jerusalem: Israel Exploration Society.

Berlin, Andrea M., and Paul J. Kosmin, eds. 2021. *The Middle Maccabees: Archaeology, History, and the Rise of the Hasmonean Kingdom*. Atlanta: Society of Biblical Literature.

Berlin, Andrea M., and J. Andrew Overman, eds. 2002. *The First Jewish Revolt: Archaeology, History, and Ideology*. New York: Routledge.

Betz, Otto. 1999. "The Essenes." Pp. 444–470 in W. Horbury, W. D. Davies, and J. Sturdy, eds. 1999.

Bickerman, E. J. 1979. *The God of the Maccabees: Studies on the Meaning and Origin of the Maccabean Revolt*. Translated by H. R. Moehring. Studies in Judaism in Late Antiquity 32. Leiden: Brill.

Bickerman, E. J. 1988. *The Jews in the Greek Age*. Cambridge, MA: Harvard University Press.

Bickerman, E. J. 2007. *Studies in Jewish and Christian History: A New Edition in English including The God of the Maccabees*. 2 vols. Edited by Amram Tropper. Leiden: Brill.

Bloedhorn, Hanswulf, and Gil Hüttenmeister. 1999. "The Synagogue." Pp. 267–297 in Horbury, Davies, and Sturdy, eds. 1999.

Boccaccini, Gabriele. 1991. *Middle Judaism: Jewish Thought 300 BCE to 200 CE*. Minneapolis, MN: Fortress.

Boccaccini, Gabriele. 1998. *Beyond the Essene Hypothesis: The Parting of the Ways between Qumran and Enochic Judaism*. Grand Rapids, MI: Eerdmans.

Bock, Darrell L., and Robert L. Webb, eds. 2010. *Key Events in the Life of the Historical Jesus: A Collaborative Exploration of Context and Coherence*. Grand Rapids, MI: Eerdmans.

Bockmuehl, Marcus, ed. 2001. *The Cambridge Companion to Jesus*. Cambridge: Cambridge University Press.

Bond, Helen K. 1998. *Pontius Pilate in History and Interpretation*. Cambridge: Cambridge University Press.

Bonnie, Rick, Raimo Hakola, and Ulla Tervahauta, eds. 2021. *The Synagogue in Ancient Palestine: Current Issues and Emerging Trends*. Göttingen: Vandenhoeck & Ruprecht.

Bons, Eberhard, and Patrick Pouchelle, eds. 2015. *The Psalms of Solomon: Language, History, Theology*. Atlanta: SBL.

Bourgel, Jonathan. 2016. "The Destruction of the Samaritan Temple by John Hyrcanus: A Reconsideration." *Journal of Biblical Literature* 135: 505–523.

Bowman, Alan K., Edward Champlin, and Andrew Lintott, eds. 1996. *The Cambridge Ancient History. Volume X: The Augustan Empire, 43 B.C.–A.D. 69.* 2nd ed. Cambridge: Cambridge University Press.

Bowman, Alan K., Peter Garnsey, and Dominic Rathbone, eds. 2000. *The Cambridge Ancient History. Volume XI: The High Empire, A.D. 70–192.* 2nd ed. Cambridge: Cambridge University Press.

Broshi, Magen. 1999. "The Archaeology of Palestine." Pp. 1–37 in Horbury, Davies, and Sturdy, eds. 1999.

Brown, Colin, with Craig A. Evans. 2022. *A History of the Quests for the Historical Jesus.* 2 vols. Grand Rapids, MI: Zondervan Academic.

Chancey, Mark A. 2005. *Greco-Roman Culture and the Galilee of Jesus.* Cambridge: Cambridge University Press.

Cohen, Shaye J. D. 1979. *Josephus in Galilee and Rome: His Vita and Development as a Historian.* Leiden: E. J. Brill.

Cohen, Shaye J. D. 1982. "Masada: Literary Tradition, Archaeological Remains, and the Credibility of Josephus." *Journal of Jewish Studies* 33: 385–405.

Cohen, Shaye J. D. 1987. *From the Maccabees to the Mishnah.* Philadelphia: Westminster.

Cohen, Shaye J. D. 1999. "The Temple and the Synagogue." Pp. 298–325 in Horbury, Davies, and Sturdy, eds. 1999.

Cohen, Shaye J. D. 2014. "The Ways That Parted: Jews, Christians, and Jewish-Christians, ca. 100–150 CE." Pp. 307–339 in Tomson and Schwartz 2014.

Collins, John J. 1993. *Daniel.* Hermeneia. Minneapolis, MN: Fortress.

Collins, John J. 1995. *The Scepter and the Star: Messianism in Light of the Dead Sea Scrolls.* Grand Rapids, MI: Eerdmans.

Collins, John J. 2010. *Beyond the Qumran Community: The Sectarian Movement of the Dead Sea Scrolls.* Grand Rapids, MI: Eerdmans.

Crook, J. A., Andrew Lintott, and Elizabeth Rawson, eds. 1994. *The Cambridge Ancient History. Volume IX: The Last Age of the Roman Republic, 146–43 B.C.* 2nd ed. Cambridge: Cambridge University Press.

Dąbrowa, Edward. 2010. *The Hasmoneans and Their State: A Study in History, Ideology, and the Institutions.* Krakow: Jagiellonian University Press.

Davies, W. D., and L. Finkelstein, eds. 1984. *The Cambridge History of Judaism.* Vol. 1, *The Persian Period.* Cambridge: Cambridge University Press.

Davies, W. D., and L. Finkelstein, eds. 1989. *The Cambridge History of Judaism.* Vol. 2, *The Hellenistic Period.* Cambridge: Cambridge University Press.

deSilva, D. A. 2012a. *The Jewish Teachers of Jesus, James, and Jude: What Earliest Christianity Learned from the Apocrypha and Pseudepigrapha.* Oxford: Oxford University Press.

deSilva, D. A. 2012b. *The Apocrypha.* Core Biblical Studies. Nashville, TN: Abingdon.

deSilva, D. A. 2015. *Day of Atonement. A Novel of the Maccabean Revolt.* Grand Rapids, MI: Kregel.

deSilva, D. A. 2018. *Introducing the Apocrypha: Message, Content, & Significance.* 2nd ed. Grand Rapids, MI: Baker Academic.

deSilva, D. A. 2022. *Honor, Patronage, Kinship, and Purity: Unlocking New Testament Culture.* 2nd ed. Downers Grove, IL: IVP Academic.

Doran, Robert. 1981. *Temple Propaganda: The Purpose and Character of 2 Maccabees.* CBQMS 12. Washington, DC: Catholic Biblical Association.

Doran, Robert. 1996. *The First Book of Maccabees: Introduction, Commentary, and Reflections. NIB* 4. Nashville, TN: Abingdon.

Doran, Robert. 2012. *2 Maccabees: A Critical Commentary*. Hermeneia. Philadelphia: Fortress.

Dušek, Jan. 2020. "The Importance of the Wadi Daliyeh Manuscripts for the History of Samaria and the Samaritans." *Religions* 11(2): 63. https://doi.org/10.3390/rel11020063

Eckhardt, Benedict. 2015. "The Psalms of Solomon as a Historical Source for the Late Hasmonean Period." Pp. 7–29 in Bons and Pouchelle 2015.

Edwards, Douglas R., and C. Thomas McCollough, eds. 1997. *Archaeology and the Galilee: Texts and Contexts in the Greco-Roman and Byzantine Periods*. Atlanta: Scholars Press.

Eshel, Hanan. 1996. "4QMMT and the History of the Hasmonean Period." Pp. 53–65 in *Reading 4QMMT: New Perspectives on Qumran Law and History*, edited by John Kampen and M. J. Bernstein. Atlanta: SBL.

Eshel, Hanan. 2008. *The Dead Sea Scrolls and the Hasmonean State*. Grand Rapids, MI: Eerdmans.

Fatkin, Danielle Steen. 2019. "Invention of a Bathing Tradition in Hasmonean Palestine." *Journal for the Study of Judaism* 50: 155–177.

Feldman, L. H. 1993. *Jew and Gentile in the Ancient World: Attitudes and Interactions from Alexander to Justinian*. Princeton, NJ: Princeton University Press.

Feldman, L. H., and M. Reinhold, eds. 1996. *Jewish Life and Thought among Greeks and Romans*. Minneapolis, MN: Fortress.

Fiensy, David. 2014a. "The Galilean Village." Pp. 177–207 in Fiensy and Strange, eds. 2014.

Fiensy, David. 2014b. "The Galilean House." Pp. 216–241 in Fiensy and Strange, eds. 2014.

Fiensy, David A., and James Riley Strange, eds. 2014. *Galilee in the Late Second Temple and Mishnaic Periods. Volume 1. Life, Culture, and Society*. Minneapolis, MN: Fortress.

Finkielsztejn, Gerald. 2021. "Contribution of the Rhodian Eponyms Amphora Stamps to the History of the Maccabees." Pp. 193–214 in Berlin and Kosmin, eds. 2021.

Fitzmyer, Joseph, and Daniel P. Harrington, eds. 1978. *A Manual of Palestinian Aramaic Texts*. Rome: Pontifical Biblical Institute.

Freyne, Sean. 1998. *Galilee from Alexander the Great to Hadrian*. Edinburgh: T. & T. Clark.

Furstenberg, Yair. 2021. "The Shared Image of Pharisaic Law in the Gospels and Rabbinic Tradition." Pp. 199–219 in Sievers and Levine, eds. 2021.

Gallagher, Edmon L. 2022. "Daniel and the Diadochi." *Journal of Biblical Literature* 141: 301–316.

Galor, Katharina, and Hanswulf Bloedhorn. 2013. *The Archaeology of Jerusalem: From the Origins to the Ottomans*. New Haven, CT: Yale University Press.

Garcia Martinez, Florentino, and Julio Trebolle Barrera. 1995. *The People of the Dead Sea Scrolls: Their Writings, Beliefs, and Practices*. Leiden: E. J. Brill.

Gardner, Gregg. 2007. "Jewish Leadership and Hellenistic Civic Benefaction in the Second Century B.C.E." *Journal of Biblical Literature* 126(2): 327–343.

Geiger, Joseph. 2002. "The Hasmoneans and Hellenistic Succession." *Journal of Jewish Studies* 53: 1–17.

Gera, Dov. 1998. *Judaea and Mediterranean Politics, 219 to 161 BCE.* Leiden: Brill.

Geva, Hillel. 1993. "Jerusalem, The Roman Period." In *New Encyclopedia of Archaeological Excavations in the Holy Land* 2, edited by E. Stern, 758–767. Jerusalem: Israel exploration Society/Carta.

Goldin, Judah. 1955. *The Fathers According to Rabbi Nathan.* New Haven, CT: Yale.

Goldingay. John E. 1989. *Daniel.* WBC 30. Waco, TX: Word Publishing.

Goldstein, J. A. 1976. *I Maccabees.* AB 41. Garden City, NY: Doubleday.

Goldstein, J. A. 1983. *II Maccabees.* AB 41A. Garden City, NY: Doubleday.

Goodman, Martin. 1987. *The Ruling Class of Judaea: The Origins of the Jewish Revolt AD 66–70.* Cambridge: Cambridge University Press.

Goodman, Martin. 1996. "Judaea." Pp. 737–781 in Bowman, Champlin, and Lintott 1996.

Goodman, Martin, ed. 1998. *Jews in a Greco-Roman World.* Oxford: Clarendon.

Goodman, Martin. 1999. "Galilean Judaism and Judean Judaism." Pp. 596–617 in Horbury, Davies, and Sturdy, eds. 1999.

Goodman, Martin. 2000. "Judea." Pp. 664–678 in Bowman, Garnsey, and Rathbone, eds. 2000.

Goodman, Martin. 2007. *Rome and Jerusalem: The Clash of Ancient Civilizations.* New York: Vintage.

Grabbe, Lester L. 1988. "Synagogues in Pre-70 Palestine: A Re-Assessment." *Journal of Theological Studies* 39: 401–410.

Grabbe, Lester L. 1991. "Maccabean Chronology: 167–164 or 168–165 BCE." *Journal of Biblical Literature* 110: 59–74.

Grabbe, Lester L. 1992. *Judaism from Cyrus to Hadrian.* Vol. 1, *The Persian and Greek Periods,* 1–312. Vol. 2, *The Roman Period,* 313–722. Minneapolis, MN: Fortress.

Grabbe, Lester L. 2008. *A History of the Jews and Judaism in the Second Temple Period. Volume 2: The Coming of the Greeks: The Early Hellenistic Period (335–175 BCE).* London: T. & T. Clark.

Grabbe, Lester L. 2010. *An Introduction to Second Temple Judaism: History and Religion of the Jews in the Time of Nehemiah, the Maccabees, Hillel, and Jesus.* London: T. & T. Clark.

Grabbe, Lester L. 2020. *A History of the Jews and Judaism in the Second Temple Period. Volume 3: The Maccabean Revolt, Hasmonean Rule, and Herod the Great (175–4 BCE).* London: T. & T. Clark.

Grabbe, Lester L. 2021. *A History of the Jews and Judaism in the Second Temple Period. Volume 4: The Jews Under the Shadow of Rome (4 BCE–150 CE).* London: T. & T. Clark.

Green, Peter. 1990. *Alexander to Actium: The Hellenistic Age.* London: Thames & Hudson.

Green, William Scott. 2007. "What Do We Really Know about the Pharisees, and How Do We Know It?" Pp. 409–423 in Neusner and Chilton, eds. 2007.

Gruen, Erich S. 2018. *Constructs of Identity in Hellenistic Judaism.* Berlin: Walter de Gruyter.

Habicht, Christian. 1976. "Royal Documents in II Maccabees." *Harvard Studies in Classical Philology* 80: 1–18.

Habicht, Christian. 1989. "The Seleucids and Their Rivals." Pp. 324–387 in Astin et al. 1989.

Halpern-Zylberstein, Marie-Christine. 1989. "The Archaeology of Hellenistic Palestine." Pp. 1–34 in Davies and Finkelstein, eds. 1989.

Hamel, Gildas. 2010. "Poverty and Charity." Pp. 308–324 in Hezser, ed. 2010.

Harrington, Daniel J. 1988. *The Maccabean Revolt: Anatomy of a Biblical Revolution*. Wilmington, DE: Glazier. Reprint ed., 2009. Eugene, OR: Wipf & Stock.

Heinen, Heinz. 1984. "The Syrian-Egyptian Wars and the New Kingdoms of Asia Minor." Pp. 412–445 in Walbank et al. 1984.

Hengel, Martin. 1974. *Judaism and Hellenism*. 2 vols. Philadelphia: Fortress.

Hengel, Martin. 1980. *Jews, Greeks, and Barbarians*. Philadelphia: Fortress.

Hengel, Martin. 1989a. *The Zealots: Investigations into the Jewish Freedom Movement in the Period from Herod I until 70 A.D.* Edinburgh: T. & T. Clark.

Hengel, Martin. 1989b. *The "Hellenization" of Judaea in the First Century after Christ*. Translated by John Bowden. Philadelphia: Trinity Press International.

Hengel, Martin. 1989c. "The Interpenetration of Judaism and Hellenism in the Pre-Maccabean Period." Pp. 167–228 in Davies and Finkelstein, eds. 1989.

Hezser, Catherine, ed. 2010. *The Oxford Handbook of Jewish Daily Life in Roman Palestine*. New York: Oxford University Press.

Horbury, William. 1999. "Women in the Synagogue." Pp. 358–401 in Horbury, Davies, and Sturdy, eds. 1999.

Horbury, William. 2014. *Jewish War Under Trajan and Hadrian*. Cambridge: Cambridge University Press.

Horbury, William, W. D. Davies, and J. Sturdy, eds. 1999. *The Cambridge History of Judaism*. Vol. 3, *The Early Roman Period*. Cambridge: Cambridge University Press.

Horsley, Richard A. 1993. *Jesus and the Spiral of Violence: Popular Jewish Resistance in Roman Palestine*. Minneapolis, MN: Fortress Press.

Horsley, Richard A. 1996. *Archaeology, History, and Society in Galilee: The Social Context of Jesus and the Rabbis*. Philadelphia: Trinity Press International.

Horsley, Richard A. 2002. "Power Vacuum and Power Struggle in 66–7 C.E." Pp. 87–109 in Berlin and Overman 2002.

Ilan, Tal. 1996. *Jewish Women in Greco-Roman Palestine*. Peabody, MA: Hendrickson.

Ilan, Tal. 2010. "Gender Issues and Daily Life." Pp. 48–70 in Hezser, ed. 2010.

Isser, Stanley. 1999. "The Samaritans and Their Sects." Pp. 569–595 in Horbury, Davies, and Sturdy, eds. 1999.

Jensen, Morten Hørning. 2006. *Herod Antipas in Galilee*. Tübingen: Mohr Siebeck.

Jobes, Karen, and Moises Silva. 2015. *Invitation to the Septuagint*. Rev. ed. Grand Rapids, MI: Baker Academic.

Kampen, John. 1988. *The Hasideans and the Origin of Pharisaism: A Study in 1 and 2 Maccabees*. SBLSCS 24. Atlanta: Scholars.

Kasher, Aryeh. 1988. *Jews, Idumeans, and Ancient Arabs*. Tübingen: Mohr/Siebeck.

Keddie, G. Anthony. 2018. "*Iudaea Capta* vs. Mother Zion: The Flavian Discourse on Judaeans and Its Delegitimation in 4 Ezra." *Journal for the Study of Judaism* 49: 498–550.

Killebrew, Anne. 2010. "Village and Countryside." Pp. 189–209 in Hezser, ed. 2010.

Klawans, Jonathan. 2012. *Josephus and the Theologies of Ancient Judaism.* Oxford: Oxford University Press.

Kraemer, David. 2010. "Food, Eating, and Meals." Pp. 403–419 in Hezser, ed. 2010.

Lapp, Paul, and Nancy Lapp. 1974. *Discoveries in the Wadi ed-Daliyeh.* Cambridge: ASOR.

Leibner, Uzi. 2021. "Galilee in the Second Century BCE." Pp. 123–144 in Berlin and Kosmin 2021.

Leoni, Tommaso. 2007. "'Against Caesar's Wishes': Flavius Josephus as a Source for the Burning of the Temple." *Journal of Jewish Studies* 58: 39–51.

Levine, Lee I. 2002. *Jerusalem: Portrait of the City in the Second Temple Period (538 BCE–70 CE).* Philadelphia: Jewish Publication Society.

Levine, Lee I. 2005. *The Ancient Synagogue: The First Thousand Years.* New Haven, CT: Yale University Press.

Lichtenberger, Hermann. 2007. "History-Writing and History-Telling in First and Second Maccabees." In *Memory in the Bible and Antiquity*, edited by S. C. Barton, L. T. Stuckenbruck, and B. G. Wold, 95–110. WUNT 212. Tubingen: Mohr Siebeck.

Lim, Timothy, and John J. Collins, eds. 2010. *The Oxford Handbook of the Dead Sea Scrolls.* New York: Oxford University Press.

Ma, John. 2012. "Relire les institutions des Séleucides de Bikerman." Pp. 59–84 in *Rome, a City and Its Empire in Perspective: The Impact of the Roman World through Fergus Millar's Research*, edited by Stéphane Benoist. Leiden: Brill.

Magen, Yitzhak. 2008. *Mount Gerizim Excavations, vol. 2: A Temple City.* Jerusalem: Israel Antiquities Authority.

Magen, Yitzhak. 2009. "The Dating of the First Phase of the Samaritan Temple on Mount Gerizim." Pp. 157–211 in *Judah and the Judeans in the Fourth Century BCE*, edited by Oded Lipschitz, Gary Knoppers, and Rainer Albertz. Winona Lake, IN: Eisenbrauns.

Magie, David. 1950. *Roman Rule in Asia Minor.* 2 vols. Princeton, NJ: Princeton University Press.

Magness, Jodi. 2002. *The Archaeology of Qumran and the Dead Sea Scrolls.* Grand Rapids, MI: Eerdmans.

Magness, Jodi. 2008. "The Arch of Titus at Rome and the Fate of the God of Israel." *Journal of Jewish Studies* 59: 201–217.

Magness, Jodi. 2012. *The Archaeology of the Holy Land: From the Destruction of Solomon's Temple to the Muslim Conquest.* Cambridge: Cambridge University Press.

Magness, Jodi. 2019. *Masada: From Jewish Revolt to Modern Myth.* Princeton, NJ: Princeton University Press.

Marshak, Adam Kolman. 2015. *The Many Faces of Herod the Great.* Grand Rapids, MI: Eerdmans.

Mason, Steve. 2009. *Josephus, Judea, and Christian Origins.* Peabody, MA: Hendrickson.

Mason, Steve. 2014. "Why Did Judaeans Go to War with Rome in 66–67 CE? Realist-Regional Perspectives." Pp. 126–206 Tomson and Schwartz 2014.

Mason, Steve. 2016. *A History of the Jewish War: A.D. 66–74.* Cambridge: Cambridge University Press.

Meier, John P. 1994. *A Marginal Jew. Volume 2: Mentor, Message and Miracles*. New York: Doubleday.

Millar, Fergus. 1978. "The Background to the Maccabean Revolution: Reflections on Martin Hengel's 'Judaism and Hellenism.'" *Journal of Jewish Studies* 29: 1–21.

Momigliano, Arnaldo. 1979. "Flavius Josephus and Alexander's Visit to Jerusalem." *Athenaeum* 57: 442–448.

Mor, Menahem. 2016. *The Second Jewish Revolt: The Bar Kokhba War 132–136 CE*. Leiden: Brill.

Mørkholm, Otto. 1966. *Antiochus IV of Syria*. Copenhagen: Gyldendal Press.

Mørkholm, Otto. 1989. "Antiochus IV." Pp. 278–291 in Davies and Finkelstein 1989.

Murphy-O'Connor, Jerome. 1994. "The Location of the Capitol in Aelia Capitolina." *Revue Biblique* 101: 407–415.

Murphy-O'Connor, Jerome. 2008. *The Holy Land: An Oxford Archaeological Guide*. 5th ed. New York: Oxford University Press.

Netzer, Ehud. 2018. *The Palaces of the Hasmoneans and Herod the Great*. Reprinted and expanded edition. Jerusalem: Israel Exploration Society.

Netzer, Ehud. 2008. *The Architecture of Herod, the Great Builder*. Grand Rapids, MI: Baker Academic.

Neusner, Jacob. 2007. "The Rabbinic Traditions about the Pharisees before 70 CE: An Overview." Pp. 297–311 in Neusner and Chilton, eds. 2007.

Neusner, Jacob. 1973. *From Politics to Piety: The Emergence of Pharisaic Judaism*. Englewood Cliffs, NJ: Prentice-Hall.

Neusner, Jacob. 1971. *The Rabbinic Traditions about the Pharisees before 70*. 3 vols. Leiden: Brill.

Neusner, Jacob, and Bruce D. Chilton, eds. 2007. *In Quest of the Historical Pharisees*. Waco, TX: Baylor University Press.

Newsom, Carol. 2014. *Daniel: A Commentary*. Louisville, KY: Westminster John Knox Press.

Nickelsburg, George W.E. 2001. *1 Enoch 1: A Commentary on the Book of 1 Enoch, Chapter 1–36; 81–108*. Minneapolis, MN: Fortress.

Novenson, Matthew V. 2017. *The Grammar of Messianism: An Ancient Jewish Political Idiom and Its Users*. Oxford: Oxford University Press.

Oakman, Douglas. 2014. "Was the Galilean Economy Oppressive or Prosperous?" Pp. 346–356 in Fiensy and Strange, eds. 2014.

Perdue, Leo, and Warren Carter. 2015. *Israel and Empire: A Postcolonial History of Israel and Early Judaism*. London: Bloomsbury T. & T. Clark.

Portier-Young, A. E. 2011. *Apocalypse against Empire: Theologies of Resistance in Early Judaism*. Grand Rapids, MI: Eerdmans.

Powell, Mark A. 2013. *Jesus as a Figure in History*. 2nd ed. Louisville, KY: Westminster John Knox Press.

Purvis, James D. 1989. "The Samaritans." Pp. 591–613 in Davies and Finkelstein, eds. 1989.

Qimron, Elisha, and John Strugnell. 1994. *Qumran Cave 4.V: Miqsat Ma'ase ha-Torah*. Discoveries in the Judean Desert 10. Oxford: Clarendon.

Rajak, Tessa. 1994. "The Jews Under Hasmonean Rule." Pp. 274–309 in Crook, Lintott, and Rawson 1994.

Rajak, Tessa. 2002. *Josephus: The Historian and His Society*. London: Duckworth.

Reed, Jonathan L. 2000. *Archaeology and the Galilean Jesus: A Re-Examination of the Evidence*. Harrisburg, PA: Trinity.

Regev, Eyal. 2017. "The Hellenization of the Hasmoneans Revisited: The Archaeological Evidence." *Advances in Anthropology* 7: 175–196.

Regev, Eyal. 2013. *The Hasmoneans: Ideology, Archaeology, Identity.* Journal of Ancient Judaism Supplements 10. Göttingen: Vandenhoeck & Ruprecht.

Reif, Stefan C. 1999. "The Early Liturgy of the Synagogue." Pp. 326–357 in Horbury, Davies, and Sturdy, eds. 1999.

Richardson, Peter. 1996. *Herod: King of the Jews and Friend of the Romans.* Columbia: University of South Carolina Press.

Safrai, Zeev. 2010. "Agriculture and Farming." Pp. 246–263 in Hezser, ed. 2010.

Saldarini, Anthony J. 2001. *Pharisees, Scribes and Sadducees in Palestinian Society.* Grand Rapids, MI: Eerdmans.

Sanders, E. P. 1992. *Judaism: Practice and Belief 63 BCE–66 CE.* Philadelphia: Trinity Press International.

Sanders, E. P. and W. D. Davies. 1999. "Jesus: From the Jewish Point of View," P. 618–677 in Horbury, Davies, and Sturdy, eds. 1999.

Sartre, Maurice. 2000. "Syria and Arabia." Pp. 635–663 in Bowman, Garnsey, and Rathbone, eds. 2000.

Schäfer, Peter. 1997. *Judeophobia: Attitudes towards the Jews in the Ancient World.* Cambridge, MA: Harvard University Press.

Schäfer, Peter. 2003. *The History of the Jews in the Greco-Roman World.* Rev. ed. London: Routledge.

Schaper, Joachim. 1999. "The Pharisees." Pp. 402–427 in Horbury, Davies, and Sturdy, eds. 1999.

Schiffman, Lawrence H. 1994. *Reclaiming the Dead Sea Scrolls.* New York: Doubleday.

Schiffman, Lawrence H. 2010. *Qumran and Jerusalem: Studies in the Dead Sea Scrolls and the History of Judaism.* Grand Rapids, MI: Eerdmans.

Schröter, Jens, and Christine Jacobi, eds. 2022. *The Jesus Handbook.* Grand Rapids, MI: Eerdmans.

Schwartz, Daniel R. 1990. *Agrippa I: The Last King of Judea.* Tübingen: J. C. B. Mohr.

Schwartz, Daniel R. 2008. *2 Maccabees.* CEJL. Berlin: de Gruyter.

Schwartz, Joshua J. 2014. "Yavne Revisited: Jewish 'Survival' in the Wake of the War of Destruction." Pp. 238–248 in Tomson and Schwartz 2014.

Sharon, Nadav. 2017. *Judea Under Roman Domination: The First Generation of Statelessness and Its Legacy.* Atlanta: Society of Biblical Literature.

Sievers, Joseph. 1990. *The Hasmoneans and Their Supporters from Mattathias to the Death of John Hyrcanus I.* SFSHJ 6. Atlanta: Scholars.

Sievers, Joseph, and Amy-Jill Levine, eds. 2021. *The Pharisees.* Grand Rapids, MI: Eerdmans.

Smallwood, E. Mary. 1981. *The Jews under Roman Rule: From Pompey to Diocletian.* Leiden: Brill.

Smith, Morton. 1999. "The Troublemakers." Pp. 501–568 in Horbury, Davies, and Sturdy, eds. 1999.

Stemberger, Günter. 1999. "The Sadducees—Their History and Doctrines." Pp. 428–443 in Horbury, Davies, and Sturdy, eds. 1999.

Stern, Menahem. 1976a. "The Period of the Second Temple." In *A History of the Jewish People,* edited by H. H. Ben-Sasson, 185–303. Cambridge, MA: Harvard University Press.

Stern, Menahem, ed. 1976b. *Greek and Latin Authors on Jews and Judaism. Volume I: From Herodotus to Plutarch.* Jerusalem: Israel Academy of Humanities and Sciences.

Stern, Menahem, ed. 1980. *Greek and Latin Authors on Jews and Judaism. Volume II: From Tacitus to Simplicius.* Jerusalem: Israel Academy of Humanities and Sciences.

Stone, Michael E., ed. 1984. *Jewish Writings of the Second Temple Period.* Assen: Van Gorcum.

Stone, Michael E. 1990. *Fourth Ezra.* Hermeneia. Minneapolis, MN: Fortress.

Strange, James. 2007. "Archaeology and the Pharisees." Pp. 237–251 in Neusner and Chilton, eds. 2007.

Syon, Danny. 2021. "The Hasmonean Settlement in Galilee: A Numismatic Perspective." Pp. 177–192 in Berlin and Kosmin, eds. 2021.

Syon, Danny. 2002. "Gamla: City of Refuge." Pp. 134–153 in Berlin and Overman 2002.

Tcherikover, Viktor. 1959. *Hellenistic Civilization and the Jews.* Philadelphia: Jewish Publication Society of America. Reprint ed., 1999. Peabody, MA: Hendrickson.

Theissen, Gerd, and Annette Merz. 1998. *The Historical Jesus: A Comprehensive Guide.* Minneapolis, MN: Fortress.

Tilly, Matthias. 2015. *1 Makkabäer.* HThKAT. Freiburg: Herders.

Toher, Mark. 2016. *Nicolaus of Damascus: The Life of Augustus and the Autobiography.* Cambridge: Cambridge University Press.

Tomson, Peter J., and Joshua J. Schwartz, eds. 2014. *Jews and Christians in the First and Second Centuries: How to Write Their History.* Leiden: Brill.

VanderKam, James C. 1994. *The Dead Sea Scrolls Today.* Grand Rapids, MI: Eerdmans.

VanderKam, James C. 2004. *From Joshua to Caiaphas: High Priests after the Exile.* Minneapolis, MN: Fortress.

Vermès, Geza. 2004. *The Complete Dead Sea Scrolls in English.* Rev. ed. New York: Penguin.

Walbank, F. W., A. E. Astin, M. W. Frederiksen, and R. M. Ogilvie, eds. 1984. *The Cambridge Ancient History. Volume VII, Part I: The Hellenistic World.* 2nd ed. Cambridge: Cambridge University Press.

Weksler-Bdolah, Shlomit. 2020. *Aelia Capitolina—Jerusalem in the Roman Period.* Leiden: Brill.

Williams, Margaret. 1999. "The Contribution of Jewish Inscriptions to the Study of Judaism." Pp. 75–93 in Horbury, Davies, and Sturdy, eds. 1999.

Witherington, Ben, III. 1997. *The Jesus Quest: The Third Search for the Jew of Nazareth.* Rev. ed. Downers Grove, IL: IVP.

Yadin, Yigael. 1971. *Bar-Kokhba: The Rediscovery of the Legendary Hero of the Second Jewish Revolt against Rome.* New York: Random House.

Zeitlin, Solomon. 1962. *The Rise and Fall of the Judaean State: A Political, Social, and Religious History of the Second Commonwealth.* Philadelphia: Jewish Publication Society.

Zilberstein, Ayala. 2021. "Hellenistic Military Architecture from the Giv'ati Parking Lot Excavations, Jerusalem." Pp. 37–52 in Berlin and Kosmin, eds. 2021.

Index of Ancient Texts

For the benefit of digital users, indexed terms that span two pages (e.g., 52–53) may, on occasion, appear on only one of those pages.

Figures are indicated by an italic *f* following the paragraph number.

Subject Index

For the benefit of digital users, indexed terms that span two pages (e.g., 52–53) may, on occasion, appear on only one of those pages.